DAMN THE DIAGNOSIS

How I survived cancer

JOEL NATHAN

DAMN THE DIAGNOSIS
Copyright © 2014 Joel Nathan
ISBN-13: 978-0-646-92341-3
ISBN-10: 0-646-9234-12

All Rights Reserved. Without limiting the rights under copyright reserved above, no part of this book may be reproduced, stored in or introduced into a retrieval system, or transmitted in any form or by any means (including electronic or mechanical, photocopying, recording or by any information storage and retrieval system), without prior permission in writing from the author.

DEDICATION

This book is dedicated with love to
my wife, René, for her unconditional love, support
and steadfast belief in me
my mother and my father,
my much-loved sons and treasured grandchildren,
the gifted doctors who saved my life - again and again,
and the humanist and brilliant doctor,
Dr John Sullivan.

PREFACE

Joel Nathan was born in Johannesburg, South Africa. Disgusted by the Apartheid system, he emigrated with his family to London and later to Australia where he now lives.

ACKNOWLEDGEMENTS

This book could not have been written without the help of some very special people: in particular, Dr John Sullivan, who was the most compassionate and knowledgeable doctor anyone could ever wish to know, Dr Jeanne Daly for her wise and critical suggestions in maintaining the consistency of my narrative, to Eve Camakaris who reminded me that prudent culling can make what remains more compelling, to Mark Gazzola without whose forensic engineering and IT nous, the pen-ultimate MSS of this updated version would have been lost in cyberspace, and to my partner in life and wife René whose forensic editing and demand for perfection I believe brought out the best in my narrative. Underneath it all, this book could never have been written without the guiding spirits of John Ndmande and Francois de Guigne.

The names of some of the people in this book have been changed to protect their identities.

FOREWORD

I first met Joel Nathan in December 1983, when he was devastated by the diagnosis of cancer in the form of Hairy Cell Leukemia. Initial medical advice he received was to have his spleen removed and then to undergo cortisone treatment but this only increased his anxiety and he had decided against surgery. His reasons for rejecting this advice were unclear to me at the time but seemed to come from a strong, inner feeling that, for him, this was not the course to take.

As an advertising executive, Joel's training and profession lead him to believe that all problems could be brainstormed and eventually solved but for this problem there was no obvious solution.

My role when I first met Joel was to offer reassurance and to suggest that it was possible to survive within the limits he had set, at least for a time, and that there was no need to make hasty decisions.

Joel's character was defined by an over-riding optimism and interest in people and things. These eclectic approaches, and his determination to be in control, lead him to explore a variety of alternative medical treatments in series and parallel. By persistence and via a circuitous route, which he documents in detail and with some humor, he became the right patient at the right time to be given a new and partly experimental drug, interferon. Treatment with the new drug proved to be effective for Joel's disease although the contribution of other treatments is acknowledged. The many and varied effects that a diagnosis of malignancy can have on a person's life, family and friends, are well documented in this honest and moving story which should provide comfort and hope to others facing similar situations.

    John R. Sullivan   MD, MRCP (UK), FRACP

PROLOGUE

Humpty Dumpty sat on a wall,
Humpty Dumpty had a big fall;
All the King's horses
And all the King's men
Couldn't put Humpty together again.

(Anon.)

Humpty did!

(Joel Nathan)

'If you ignore the dragon, it will eat you.
If you try to confront the dragon it will overpower you.
If you ride the dragon you will take advantage of its
might and power.'

(Chinese Proverb)

BACKGROUND

We are such stuff
As dreams are made on, and our little life
Is rounded with a sleep.

(The Tempest. William Shakespeare)

Since my first book, *Time of my Life* (Penguin Books, 1992), was first published, many people wanted to know what happened to me afterwards. Did he die or did he survive? I hope this sequel answers their questions.

In this book I describe how I faced and overcame even greater hurdles since then, and how every subsequent act of survival became a deferral of death.

I have tried to write this book in a way that retains the immediacy of *Time of my Life* with the hindsight of twenty-two years. It presented a challenge I hope I have met by not distracting you from appreciating what I went through originally, what I thought and understood at the time and therefore why I did what I did.

Over the years, some people believed that in my telling of my experiences with alternative and non-medical treatments, I advocate their use. Nothing could be further from the truth. I desperately followed their promises and in doing so came to fully understand the folly of false hope.

My survival is the result of scientific discoveries and medical treatments combined with the experiences and lessons of my childhood growing up in South Africa informing my perseverance and patience, taking control of my choices, and my abiding belief that I would survive. Only my discovery of interferon and 2-CDA and the knack of making my own luck saved my life from leukemia.

CHAPTER ONE

I first came to understand the meaning of my life when I was told I was going to die.

I was at work when I received a phone call from my doctor's receptionist.

"Dr Ironbark would like to see you this afternoon."

After months of fruitless tests to find out why my blood counts kept falling and even though I suspected the worst, I deferred my appointment to the following day. Still, I was unprepared for what he had to say.

"You have leukemia."

Suddenly, my ears began to ring. I felt a cold numbness slide over my body and momentarily shut down all my senses. I was vaguely aware of the sound of my breathing and the thudding of my heart. The sound of the traffic outside the window disappeared. I saw the doctor's mouth moving but heard nothing. For a moment my world stopped. Then I heard, as a distant echo in my head, the words I had last heard when I was a child growing up in South Africa.

"Jwa (Joel), to be clever is to be still," John Ndmande used to say, drawing on his long-stemmed, hardwood pipe.

I took a deep breath and asked, "Is there a cure?"

"No. There is no cure."

How I handled that news and what I did next is linked to events that occurred long ago, events that had a bearing directly and indirectly on what happened to me following that afternoon in November, 1983.

My parents employed John as a general factotum in our

house in Highlands North, a new middle-class suburb with as yet unpaved streets in Johannesburg. With my father away at war and my mother at work, his kind, wrinkled face and tobacco-yellowed teeth were my source of comfort and wisdom. His lessons in survival played a large part in shaping my independent and fighting spirit.

He knew little English, so he taught me Zulu. For hours on end I would listen wide-eyed to his chilling tales of Shaka, King of the Zulus and whose impis (warriors) armed only with their rawhide shields and assegais (spears), challenged waves of British redcoats and later, Boers, across the rolling hills and winding rivers of Natal. I imagined I was an impi facing innumerable foes. With short, sharp stabs of the homemade assegai and small rawhide shield he had given me, and accompanied by repeated shouts of *"Bulala!"* (Kill!) to bolster my courage, I always emerged victorious. Naturally.

I learned other things from John. A Zulu, he told me, relies on his wits and ingenuity to survive. When he is out hunting, and armed only with his assegai and his shield, a hunter must be alert to every detail and watch out for his back.

"Always," John said, waving a forefinger in the air, "make sure the wind is blowing towards you so the simba (lion) cannot smell you. You must be prepared." Just in case, I made sure I always carried my toy Colt .45 and my trusty catapult with me. Armed to the teeth, I created endless war games whenever John deserted me to cook the meals or mow the lawn or hide behind the smokescreen of his pipe.

My dog, Bingo, was my fellow impi. Part-Doberman, part-terrier, I could always rely on him to take care of those who sneaked up behind me under cover of our rhododendron bushes. John taught me to try not to leave anything to chance.

My survival skills were aroused much earlier, though. When I was born in May 1940, at the Queen Victoria Maternity Hospital in Johannesburg, I weighed 2.7 kilos. As I was often reminded, my mother had been watching the almost three-hour long movie *Gone with the Wind* when her contractions began. She was determined to watch to the end, but to her chagrin my arrival prevented her from seeing the final scenes. A few weeks later, my mother saw that I couldn't keep her milk down. I was admitted to the Sunday Times ward at the Transvaal Memorial Hospital for Children with pyloric stenosis - a constriction of the pylorus that prevents food from passing from the stomach into the intestine. For a while, I was given fluids intravenously through my big toe. When my weight fell to 1.3 kilos, and although at the time a pyloromyotomy was considered a life-threatening operation, I was operated upon. Successfully.

A telegram was sent to my father. 'Come home urgently.'

He was in the air force, stationed at No. 52 Coastal Bomber Command, Mtubatuba, in the Transkei.

In response to the call, he persuaded the pilot of a Ventura bomber to make a detour of over a thousand kilometers for my sake. Entering the hospital ward, he fainted at the sight of his only child attached to an overhanging jungle of bottles and tubes.

"Don't worry," the surgeon-in-charge and well-known cricketer, Dr Basil Melle, told my father when he had recovered. "With a chest that big, he'll pull through." My father fainted again.

I do not remember these dramatic events, but they were related to me so many times, I can hardly forget my birth story. It was an irony of fate that I found out, much later, that

Dr Melle was a particular favorite of Sir William Osler regarded as the father of modern medicine and much admired by Dr John Sullivan who became my ally in my later battles for survival.

Whereas my father travelled so far to visit me, my mother saw her role quite differently: "The sacrifices I made for you," was how she summed up taking her milk to the hospital three times a week.

What does stand out in my memory is waiting for my father to come home on furlough during the war. Those Santa Claus visits by him were the highlight of my childhood. He would return for a weekend every few months, and in anticipation I would wait at our gate for him to walk up the road from the bus stop, with his brilliant white duffel bag slung over his shoulder. As soon as I saw that unmistakable silhouette – he was built like a Sherman tank – I'd race down the road to be swept into his arms. How we hugged each other! It wasn't his sparkling tunic buttons or his dazzling Sam Browne belt and toecaps, but rather the contents of that duffel bag that fascinated me most. Dad was a sergeant-major in charge of catering at a time when food was in short supply, so there was always butter, meat, cheese, sugar and, best of all, candy and bubble gum for me.

My survival skills were further honed when I was three, and started kindergarten. For a while, John walked me there every morning and brought me back at lunchtime. On the way, he showed me how to cross roads safely and to avoid barking dogs. I learned quickly. After a few days, I insisted on going on my own. My mother was hesitant as the school was several blocks away. John persuaded her I was quite capable of looking after myself. Admittedly, there wasn't much traffic in our neighborhood, but I had taken the first steps on the path to self-reliance – and self-preservation. Years later I found out that he had followed me out of sight for a few days to make sure I was safe.

John also taught me to eat like a Zulu. Their staple food is called *uphuthu*, stiff, well-cooked maize meal porridge. John would place a bowl of this between us in the back yard next to the coal-fire brazier he lit when the evenings became cool.

"Hoza lapa, Jwa!" 'Come here, Joel', he would call. He showed me how to spear the hot, pulpy white mixture with my fingertips, my thumb well out of the way. Then, dipping my loaded fingers into the accompanying thin meat stew he had prepared separately, I would scoop the mix into my mouth. After I'd burnt my tongue a few times, I realized that taking less and from the edge was safer. This meant eating more slowly and, as John was the faster eater, he finished his meal first. This didn't matter though. As he waited patiently for me to finish, he would fill the time by feeding my wide-eyed imagination with stories about his life growing up in the village of Weenen in the heartland of Natal now known as KwaZulu-Natal.

As I grew older, he taught me Zulu stick fighting in the manner he had been taught as a boy to build courage and skills for self-defense and war. To help me master the art, he shortened an old broom handle for me and invited me to attack him as he defended himself with his full-length one. He taught me how to parry and thrust. Occasionally, I got through his guard (did he let me?). I had added to my arsenal of weapons to fight the British.

How I longed to be a real Zulu!

When I was four, a fellow pupil at kindergarten snatched away my lunchbox and refused to give it back. I picked up a hoe with which we had been gardening, hit him on the head and retrieved the box. As young as I was, I knew I was in trouble. I ran home as fast as I could and hid in the compost heap at the bottom of our garden. Not long afterwards I was declared 'missing' and the search for me began. Hours later, and despite people calling out my name, the setting sun and hunger compelled me to surrender. I had learned my lesson that every action has a consequence. At least that boy never tried to take away my lunch box again.

In the same year, the youngest of my half-brothers, Syd, who was sixteen years older than I, saved my life.

He and his fiancé, Maisie, had joined my parents on vacation in Scottborough, a small resort town on the Natal south coast. I was building sand castles when I saw my brother and his fiancé walking on the beach some distance away. I decided to run to him. With my eyes focused on them, I did not see the little river that flows into the sea, and fell in. All of a sudden I was gulping water as I tried frantically to recover and surface. I was drowning. Then I was on the beach with him holding me in his arms.

He said that he had heard me calling his name, turned towards me, saw me disappear from view, and raced to rescue me. He had been a champion sprinter and on that day easily beat his best time. As young as I was, I knew I had been lucky.

When I was seven, Syd married and left our home. Over the years, he always showed me great affection and continued to call me "My little bro' " until he died, suddenly, of septicemia in November 2006 a week before I was scheduled to fly to South Africa to visit with him.

He was a tenacious and highly competitive sportsman. Apart from his prowess on the track, he played cricket for his State, was a scratch golfer, and veteran lawn bowls champion.

I was never as skilled as he, but he passed on to me some of his competitiveness as well as a lifelong passion for sport. When I was fourteen, he gave me a revealing, eye-opening book on the facts of life that provided me with the theory I was able to put into practice a year later.

By the age of six, the Zulus competed with my comic book heroes, Tarzan, Superman, Captain Marvel, Green Lantern and Hawkman. Depending on who I was on the day, I would swing fearlessly from branch to branch on the tallest trees in our garden, or leap from the top of a wardrobe onto my bed with a towel knotted around my neck. If Superman could fly, so could I! But whereas Captain Marvel could say "Shazam!" and save the world, his incantation failed to prevent my mother from burning my comics.

"Read proper books," she said, as, through my tears, I watched the sources of my invincibility and avenues of escape going up in smoke. Fortunately, John's wisdom was fireproof. I stayed downwind as he had taught me. To escape my mother's ire and the constant taunting of the second eldest of my three half-brothers who patterned his behavior after her, I let them see me read 'proper' books such as Just William, The Hardy Boys and Biggles. I hid my comics and their Annuals, Rover, Hotspur, Beano, Wizard, Dandy, Lion and Champion, under my bed. My mother also banned me from chewing gum, so I hid my store of Topps, Dubble Bubble and Bazooka bubble gum on top of my wardrobe.

Like most children, I was afraid of the shadowy Bogeyman whose imminent appearance was invoked by my half-brothers for their amusement and by my mother for control over me.

"The Bogeyman will get you," my mother used to say whenever I failed to do what she wanted. To counter her threats and to ensure he couldn't sneak through my bedroom window at night, I kept a torch and catapult under my pillow and made sure my dog always slept beside my bed.

My mother's most powerful weapon was her threat to send me to boarding school. I had heard terrifying stories from my half-brothers of mistreatment at the hands of their teachers. Whether these were true or not, the prospect of being separated from John and Bingo scared me into submission. I cannot imagine what crimes I must have committed to invoke her wrath. Whenever she reached a certain pitch of rage, she reached for the telephone.

"If you don't do as I say, I'm going to get them to come and take you away."

"Please don't!" I would scream.

As young as I was, I saw that our relationship was based on a constant battle between her need for control and my desire to maintain my independence. What I could not have appreciated then was that had she been born a generation or two later, she might have had more opportunities to fulfill her intellectual and emotional needs. Instead, I became the lightning rod for her frustrations and unrequited dreams. The feminist movement arrived too late for her - and for me.

She was a voracious reader, and knew the works of Shakespeare, Walt Whitman and Heinrich Heine so well she would quote them to fit any and every situation. She knew every popular aria and, with her expansive soprano voice, filled the house with song whenever she cooked. Not surprisingly, she was a lousy cook, but I learned to love music.

My mother had three sons from a previous marriage, all very much older than I. In 1929, at the height of the Great Depression, when she was thirty-two, she bravely took her three young children and left her husband. From all accounts, he had been cruel, abusive and violent, and used to drag her around the house by her hair. Forced to earn a living, she became a seamstress and put her boys into the Marist Brothers' boarding school. Eventually, she saved enough money to buy a house large enough to rent out rooms to pay the mortgage. My father was one of her first boarders. They pursued a clandestine love affair through the 1930s. He married my mother in 1937 three weeks after he obtained a divorce from his first wife. I was born three years later. She was forty-three. He was thirty-eight.

In contrast to her first husband, my father was easy-going, gentle and kind. She also married him for his ability to support her and her children. Always the optimist and the extrovert, my father was a wonderful storyteller with a seemingly endless treasure trove of real and imagined adventures. Over time, she begrudged these qualities as weaknesses and came to resent him and his unconditional relationship with me.

For her, I was an unwanted child.

From as far back as I can remember, she would tell me she had wanted a daughter. She had even chosen a girl's name for me.

"I wanted a daughter for my old age," she used to say to me at every opportunity.

I can now appreciate why, in so many ways, my presence was a constant reminder of her regret and why she projected all her anger and frustration onto me. I was another son, not a daughter. I was born when she was old enough to be my grandmother not my mother. I had almost died at birth. She had a previously failed marriage, had not fulfilled her literary and musical dreams and ambitions and had been compelled to work, as she put it, her "fingers to the bone." I also had educational advantages neither she nor her others sons had enjoyed.

Freedom was my battle cry as I sought to escape from her re-directed anger and irresolvable internal conflicts.

"I will be obeyed!" she shouted as she smacked me whenever her rage erupted.

"My word is Law," as she smacked me again and again.

Now that I understand her drivers, I am able to forgive her. However, I cannot forget. The scars are too deeply embedded to ignore. Through the ways I learned to respond to her behavior, so I developed resilience. Through the ways I sought to escape her fury, so I developed a fighting spirit. She tried to break my will and bend it to hers. The harder she tried, the harder I resisted. I chose to withdraw and so was able to keep my spirit and my soul intact.

It was as well I did. Her middle son was an industrial chemist. A latter-day Mr Gradgrind, his focus was on the sciences with a total disdain for anything not based on cold, hard facts. He was her favorite son - a fact attested to by his brothers – so she favored his advice over my father's, and gave him free rein to treat me as he wished.

"You have a vivid imagination! Pay more attention to the facts," they would yell. To reinforce her point, he repeated what she said. And just as she smacked me, so did he, often and harder than she had. The pecking order became a slapping order.

I was lucky, she would tell me by way of a threat, that she did not punish me as she had been punished. When she was a child at school in Germany, she would say, naughty children had to stand in a corner of the classroom holding a brick above their heads until the teacher thought they had been punished enough. Of course, if they dropped the brick on their head they deserved it. Instead, my mother sent me to bed without dinner whenever I was 'disobedient' - the word she used when she refused to believe anything I said or if I turned down eating her over-cooked cabbage. I am not sure whether the surgery to correct the stenosis of my pylorus had been very effective or whether it was my mother's cooking, but until I was ten, I was unable to keep down my dinners.

If I complained to my father about the way my mother treated me, she would say, "Joel is making it up. You know he has a fertile imagination."

"For the sake of peace," he would say, "Say sorry to your mother."

I refused. I was furious at the way he never stood up for me. Sometimes, to assuage his guilt, he would bring me something to eat in bed while she was reading in the lounge-room. Most times, however, I would sneak into the kitchen late at night and make something to eat, a habit that has lasted all my life.

There seemed no end to her anger. Any hope I may have had that she would treat me fairly was finally extinguished when I was nine.

I came home from school and Bingo was gone!

"I gave him away. It's unfair to keep a dog in an apartment," she said.

The suddenness of her action, her failure to discuss the matter with me beforehand, and the loss of my true companion, all combined to have the most telling effect on me. I believe that from that moment, I stopped trusting my mother and all authority figures that asserted they knew what was best for me. Later, this attitude would influence the way I responded to domineering teachers and paternalistic doctors.

Whereas my mother tried to bully me into submission, my

father understood I responded to love and kindness. He was always gentle, rarely raised his voice, and except once when spurred on by my mother, never laid a finger on me.

Perhaps because I came so close to death as a baby, my mother was convinced I needed toughening up if I was to endure. Citing her 'character-building' childhood experiences at school in Germany, from about the age of five, she subjected me to a similarly rigorous discipline. This involved taking cold showers, even in winter, and daily calisthenics. I had to endure long walks along the beach and swims in the surf at dawn whenever we went on holiday to the coast. When I was six, my eldest half-brother gave me a set of chest expanders as a birthday present. I then broke my nose with it as it was designed for boys at least ten years older. These rigors became second nature, and until I was diagnosed with leukemia, keeping fit and playing sport occupied a significant part of my life. According to my doctors, I owe a large part of my survival to my long-time physical fitness.

I first learned about death when I was four.

On a cold, grey, afternoon, Geoffrey who lived next-door came to play and told me his mother had died and gone "far away". I didn't understand what he meant, so when my mother returned from work, I asked her to explain.

"She's gone to heaven."

"Where's heaven?"

"Far, far, away."

"Will she come back," I asked, naïvely.

I learned that loss is the face of death a year later. My grandmother died aged eighty-six. She had lived with us in her later years, and every morning would sit with me at the breakfast table. Her pale, blue eyes fascinated me. She spoke little English, but I was much comforted when she hugged me against her soft cheeks. I later found out that although she indulged her grandchildren she had ruled her family of seven on a strict religious basis. Now her chair was empty. She was gone. To heaven, I supposed. For a long time, I pictured heaven as being somewhere out in space, too far from which to return. I am reminded of her absence today when I gaze on her picture in my study.

When I was six or seven, reality overtook my mother's explanation. Walking to the shops to buy bubble gum, I heard a loud thump. I looked up to see a horse that had been pulling a dairy cart had been struck by a car and was lying face down between the traces. As I watched, I saw a pool of crimson blood begin to spread in a lake across the road. I drew closer and remember being shocked that none of the gathering crowd was doing anything to help the horse, which was pawing faintly at the road. He was harnessed when the car struck him, so he could not have avoided his fate. In that moment I knew how completely helpless he must have felt. No one to help him. No one to save him. He was dying in front of me, away from his kind, alone. For the first time in my short life, I felt the terrifying possibility of my own vulnerability. My sense of irretrievable loss and the inevitability of death were surely imprinted on me that afternoon so long ago. From that moment I lived with a nightmare fear of death until I was told there was no cure for my cancer. My first diagnosis revealed the depth of my angst and what I was prepared to do in an attempt to overcome it.

CHAPTER TWO

I learned to ride a bicycle when I was six by doggedly riding it again and again into our neighbor's, Mrs Poxen's, red rose bushes until I mastered the skill of turning the handlebar. A few years later, I gained my first taste of independence and chance to escape from my mother temporarily when my eldest brother presented me with my own Raleigh bicycle as a birthday present All the distant places I longed to visit were now within reach: the Mud Deep Dam where my friends and I trolled for freshwater cray; the towering gold mine dumps we tried to cycle down but mostly tumbled down. When I was a little older, I rode further afield to hang on to the flying fox at Henley-on-Klip and swim across the broad Vaal River. We had not yet heard about the danger of bilharzia.

We had moved to a brand-new house in a small country town, Krugersdorp, and to my joy found that my father also had a bicycle he used instead of his car, a Studebaker, when the weather was fine to ride to and from his general store. One day he invited me to come with him to his office where I found the most wondrous toy: a black, silver-keyed Underwood typewriter. I was transfixed by the magic of creating and manipulating words. I dreamed of being a writer and owning my very own typewriter. The added joy was being with Dad. It was the first time in my life I could be as close to him as often as I wanted.

I was eight when my world was turned upside down by another event that was to have a profound effect on my life.

It was illegal in South Africa at the time to drink or brew

skokiaan - an African beer the government had banned and which incurred a very high fine or even jail for the culprit if caught. Selling yeast to black Africans in order to make the beer was considered an equally 'heinous crime'. My father, with his compassion for the harsh conditions under which they lived, had no reservations in selling it to them. As a result, he was targeted in a 'sting' operation. The officials involved blackmailed then threatened him with bankruptcy for his 'crime' unless they were suitably compensated to keep the matter quiet. Dad refused and so was compelled to sell his general goods and canteen business to buy his way out of going to jail. As soon as they were paid, those corrupt officials withdrew my father's license to trade in an urban area and so he was forced to find work in remote and rural areas. Our financial situation was dire. My mother was compelled to sell our house and move back to Johannesburg into an apartment in the Jacaranda-lined streets of the suburb, Parktown. The blow of this relocation was softened by the comforting presence of John and, until she gave him away, my beloved dog. For the following few years my father was seldom at home and I only saw him on occasional weekends.

When I was nine, my mother 'retired' John from our employment to reduce expenses and took in a retired British army private, Victor Lyons, as a lodger to make up the shortfall from my father's lowered earnings. Without the protection of John, my father and, by now, my dog and my ally, Bingo, he sexually abused me for several months. He preyed on my vulnerability.

"I know you'll never tell your mother", he used to chide me. "She never believes anything you tell her anyway."

When I threatened to tell my father, he bribed with me presents adding, "If your mother won't believe you, nor will your father. He's not here, anyway."

He always seemed to be around. When I came home from school. When my mother went shopping. When my parents went out to the movies or to visit friends.

I felt so alone and helpless. It was a most terrifying and lonely period. I tried to escape by spending as much time as I could with my friends, often returning home late for dinner. There were moments when I wished I were dead.

Whenever I asked my mother why he lived with us, she used to say, "You keep asking me the same question. I don't understand. He's so nice to you."

How could I tell her what her idea of 'nice' meant when, as always, she accused me of having 'a fertile imagination'? I was desperate for someone to stand up for me, but I was too small and intimidated to make myself heard. I knew no one would believe me. I was terrified. I retreated into the safety of my imagination and the wonderland of mythical figures that peopled it. I needed allies in the real world but there were none. Instead, I found them in the novel *The Three Musketeers*. I became d'Artagnan. I made a sword out of a long stick with a can tied over the end as the hand guard. I found a feather and taped it to the side of my head. I persuaded three of my friends to become Athos, Porthos, and Aramis. I made their catch-cry ours. In 'One for all, and all for one!' I drew courage from our alliance and imagined I was protected from my predator. We fought pitched battles behind the shrubbery, fought duels on the lawn in our garden. They never knew the real enemy I was fighting. The foe I really wanted dead.

On Saturday mornings, I met other boys of my age in the foyer of the Plaza movie theatre where we swapped comics. Our transactions complete, we would buy Cracker Jack and Pepsi-Cola, and watch the adventures of Rocket Man,

Superman, Hopalong Cassidy, Roy Rogers and the Durango Kid. Afterwards, we would re-enact the film we had seen. This usually involved one of us hiding in a tree and then dropping down from the branch onto "the baddy". It's amazing how we weren't seriously injured!

"Bang! Bang! You're dead!"

"No, I'm not!"

"Yes, you are."

My enemy was very real. I wanted him very, very dead. I longed to be older and bigger with the courage of a Zulu warrior to kill this British redcoat.

At dinnertime one evening, my eldest brother and he had a loud and heated argument. Victor boasted how he had fought for 'King and Country'. My brother, at age twenty-two had been wounded at the battle of El Alamein.

"I was wounded for your King," my brother shouted. "What did you do?"

Suddenly the conversation changed. My brother accused Victor of being a sexual pervert. My mother and my brother argued. She said that he was a kind man with good manners. He said that she was blind to what everyone else could see he was doing to me. They sent me out of the room. From behind a closed door, I heard him threaten to kill Victor unless he left our house, at once. Given my brother's fiery and notorious temper and superb boxing skills – in a sparring session he had knocked out Johnny Ralph, at one time South Africa's heavyweight champion - I am sure he knew this was not a vain threat. At last, someone had stood up for me. At last, my prayers had been answered. I remember the incredible feeling of relief that swept over me. The nightmare of the past few months was over. Under the glowering gaze of my brother, he packed his suitcase and left that very evening. From that moment on, no one talked about what had happened. To this day, I have no idea what my mother thought. I felt lucky to have someone stand up for me, and in later years realized how much I owed my eldest half-brother. Realizing there were some battles in which I needed a strong ally was a defining moment: there were some battles I could not win on my own. I believe my mettle was annealed by the hammering of these events. I no longer had to tremble at the scent of his approaching mask of eau de cologne and unctuous pomade. Even though I did not know the word 'pedophilia' at the time, I knew that what he had done to me was evil and brutal. I wished my brother had killed him. To this day, I believe pedophiles deserve even harsher sentencing than is meted out for pre-meditated murder.

When I was eight, I sat with my parents at the kitchen table one evening as we listened to the news on the radio for the results of the general election. Three years after the end of WWII, those who had supported Hitler and been interned for the duration of the war were voted into government by a narrow majority. The National Party was now in power in South Africa and with a mandate to begin their policy of Apartheid.

A year later, I first saw their rules translated into practice. I was walking home from school when a khaki-colored police van pull up alongside a black African man walking on the opposite side of the road. Two heavily built and armed policemen stepped out and confronted him. I could not hear what they were saying, but suddenly they picked him up and threw him into the back of their van. To this day, I can still hear the thud as his body landed and the sound that reverberated across the road.

"Don't ever say a word about this to anyone," my mother

said after I told her what I had seen. "These people are evil. Just like Hitler."

"Why don't we leave this country?" I asked.

"Where would we go at my age? We came to this country to make a new life. We have to make the best of it."

Over the years many South Africans justified their lack of protest for similar reasons.

I was shaken. I felt powerless. I was angry. I decided that when I was older, I would leave the country, which I eventually did, and with no regrets.

Schooldays were not the best days of my life. We had moved house too often for me to feel secure though one or two friendships survived these traumatizing relocations. My mother's threats of sending me to boarding school were almost realized when I started high school. At the behest of her middle son she did the next best thing and sent to me to a high school on the other side of the city.

Whereas my friends from Yeoville Boys' junior school could walk or cycle to a high school close to where we lived, I was compelled to ride two double-decker trams to the other side of town. On most schooldays, I was out of the house before seven o'clock every morning until six o'clock in the evening.

"Jeppe is the best high school you could possibly attend," said my mother reinforced by her middle son. "All the best sportsmen go there."

I didn't want to be the best sportsman. I wanted to go to one or other of the two schools closest to where we lived and to which all my friends from junior school had gone. In the end, only a few of my classmates became my friends. I don't think it ever occurred to my mother how her ill-informed decision affected me. My years at that school were some of the unhappiest and dislocated of my life.

The pursuit of girls gave me an opportunity to find affection, build up my self-esteem and help me loosen the stranglehold of my mother. I first kissed a girl and lost my heart to her when I was thirteen. When I was fifteen, I lost my virginity to an older girl. In the softness of girls I sought the gentleness I craved from my mother and so, whenever an opportunity presented itself, I sought their company. Although I attended all my classes, my thoughts were usually elsewhere. I was a normal teenager with normal urges. It was the Fifties, a great time to be young and having fun. Saturday nights were party nights. Bill Hayley, Ray Conniff, Buddy Holly and Elvis Presley changed the rhythm of my life and provided the soundtrack for my blue suede shoes, yellow socks, pink shirts, and charcoal grey slacks. James Dean showed me how to comb my hair and Marlon Brando how to be cool. My heroes were no longer to be found in comic books.

At the time, I was a panel member of a famous radio program broadcast around the country, *The Quiz Kids*.

When I was fourteen, my mother saw an advertisement in a local newspaper seeking to interview likely participants aged 13 - 16 who had extensive general knowledge. After a series of interviews after school, I was thrilled to be accepted as a panel member for the following two years. Hosted by Henry Howell who later became head of the radio station at Broadcast House, recording sessions provided me with a rare opportunity to be with kids with like interests. Each show started with a chorus of us saying 'Good evening Mr Howell' and then, as he asked us questions, we tried to show each other and the listeners just how smart we were. We spurred each other on. We shared books and ideas. We were all enriched by the experience, and by the £1.00 a program the radio station paid us - a handsome sum of pocket money at the time.

My English teacher, Mr Beckwith, decided that because I was a Quiz Kid he would call me "Mr Know-All" and so raised my pass mark to 95%. The pass-mark for the rest of the class was 40%. Whenever I failed to achieve this mark, he sent me to the Vice-Principal, Mr Schoon, for a caning, an accepted practice at the time. If, as I tried on one or two occasions to tell him how unfair this was and ask why I had been singled out, all he would say was, "Silence! Bend over!" Then he would hit me, again.

I was punished this way for years. One day, as I was coming out of the shower, my father saw the welts on my buttocks. I could not avoid telling him. He was furious. He visited the headmaster and, as I later found out, threatened the Principal, Mr Grant, with bodily harm if any one of the teachers or the Vice-Principal ever laid a finger on me again. The unintended consequence of his action was that from that day on, none of my teachers paid any attention to me, refused to answer my questions in class or to mark my essays or any of my homework. I was also barred from attending our final year formal school dance. I was now an outsider.

Two teachers, however, ignored their peers. One was Mr Bainbridge, my history teacher. Through his asides into the back stories that did not appear in our government's education department's censored history books, he breathed life into the subject for me and taught us why we need to remember past events to ensure we don't repeat the errors. "History is the bridge to the future," was his catchphrase. I loved his passion. I excelled in his subject.

The other was Francois de Guigne, who started out as my

mathematics teacher but ended up teaching me so much more.

He was Comte de Guigne. His title and coat of arms were awarded for one of his ancestor's gallantry at the battle of Crécy. He was educated at the Sorbonne and volunteered for action during World War I when he was gassed at the Battle of Verdun. In a bold move to save his life, his doctors shipped him off to the dry, rarefied atmosphere of the Highveld in South Africa. There, 6000ft above sea level, he recovered, completed further degrees in Science and Latin, and became headmaster of the Twist Street Junior School before joining the staff at Jeppe Boys High on a "temporary basis" that lasted fifteen years.

A polymath and a polyglot, he described how, in the late 1930s, he had undertaken a secret mission to Europe on behalf of his friend, later President of France, Charles De Gaulle, with whom he had served and been wounded at the battle of Verdun in 1916. He was later awarded the Croix de Guerre for his activities. He was a lifelong member of the Virgil club where, on the anniversary of Virgil's death he, together with his friend, Dr Haarhoff, and others, read their own Latin compositions to each other. I feel privileged to have been his student.

He was my English and Mathematics teacher when I started high school. When I was thirteen, he singled me out to set an example of the consequences of talking in class, and ordered me to the headmaster's office. I had heard terrifying stories from other boys of being caned, so I waited outside the classroom door until the lesson was over. He came out, and when he saw me, asked me if I had been to see the headmaster.

I told him I had not because I was scared.

"I like you, Nathan," he said. "You told me the truth. Just make sure I don't catch you talking in my class again."

What I did not know was that I reminded him of his only son, Angelo, whom he named after Michelangelo. He considered his son to be so remarkably intelligent that no school was worthy of his attendance, and so he taught him at home. He clearly knew his son well, because he matriculated at sixteen with distinction in every subject. Angelo was seventeen when, while experimenting with photographing explosions under water, he misjudged the power of the explosive he had made, and was killed. The shock of his death left permanent lines of sadness on de Guigne's face.

Students, as a matter of principle, are never provided with the results of their IQ tests. Angered by the actions of the other teachers, de Guigne drew me aside one day and said, "Joel, your I.Q. is over 138. You don't deserve to be treated this way. Between us, let's show them what fools they are." With this, he took it upon himself to ensure that I excelled in those subjects the other teachers had refused to teach me, and so offered me free tuition on Saturday mornings.

He was also aware that, in order to get to school, I had to travel across town. His house at 23, Urania Street, Observatory, was a short twenty-minute walk from mine, so he suggested that it would save me a considerable amount of time if I rode with him in his car on those days when I did not have to play sport. In addition to my time with him on Saturdays, I became his spellbound passenger as he spoke about his son, his family history, years in the army, or other topic that took his fancy on the day. It was heady stuff for a teenager. I reveled in his candor and willingness to teach me what he knew. Talk of death was never far away. He was born a Catholic but was a pantheist at heart. He saw God's handiwork in everything. He was sustained through the terrible, unremitting agony of the loss of his son by his outpourings in poetry, painting, music composition and gardening. Teaching kept him in constant contact with younger people, and with me in particular.

For years, I visited with him and his wife, Peggy, at their home that became my sanctuary. She would serve us tea and homemade shortbread biscuits on distinctive Wedgewood china in his study. He tutored me in History and especially Latin, a subject he viewed as important as mathematics. For a further hour or so after each lesson, he taught me other things. He explained the origin and technique of every one of his paintings that covered the walls of his house, and played sonatas by Bach for me – "the only mathematically correct composer" - on his violin and on his piano. He showed me how he grafted fruit trees and vines, and how to use a fret saw to make ornate woodcarvings. He encouraged me to write poetry and imbued me with the tension and precision of the iambic pentameter and the sonnet form. He quoted, whenever he thought it relevant, the poems of Wordsworth, Shelley, Ovid, Horace, and the one he admired most, Swinburne. In the meanwhile, I began writing my own poetry and found that it enabled me to channel my existential angst into something pliable that I could control. To this day, I am reminded of de Guigne's profound influence on my life whenever I listen to classical music, when I look upon his moody painting of the Schwarzwald on my study wall, reflect on my own life journey, and when I read his poetry and feel the haunting rhythm of the words:

> *'Dark the way that our feet must follow,*
> *O dark the way, and the end is unknown:*
> *For who shall say he has seen the goal?*

> *None comes back, neither loved, nor lover,*
> *Falls the doom upon hovel or throne,*
> *And lowering shadows enshrine the whole.'*

Irreplaceable as his son was, he saw in me an opportunity to continue his son's education and to shower me with some of the love and affection he had felt for him. He had met both my parents, spent hours swapping yarns with my father of their WWI exploits, his on the Western Front, my father on the Eastern. He conversed with my mother in German, and as he became familiar with her character, tried with some degree of success to ameliorate my strained relationship with her. He favored me with his wisdom. Where my imagination had once been my escape from reality, he showed me its limitless freedom. He taught me to trust my instinct, to be the captain of my soul, to appreciate that a life without purpose is meaningless.

> *There is no wind blown*
> *Over the earth at hazard; no weed grown*
> *But hath some purpose somewhere to fulfil.'*

He explained to me that nothing is impossible if you want it badly enough. I learned about possibility thinking from him long before I heard, met and was embraced by Dr Robert Schuller, an American televangelist when he visited Australia. From them, I was reminded that will power and the self-confidence it inspires is a defining principle by which we can become the measure of who we are. De Guigne helped me to fulfill my potential by valuing me for who I was. In some of the darker moments of my life his lessons cast a ray of light for me to see more clearly where I have the power to influence events.

As busy as I was with *Quiz Kids* shows, homework, and de Guigne's lessons, I strove to maintain and build up my physical strength by swimming, playing water polo, athletics, and weightlifting. During my final years at high school and after I entered university, George Mavros added to my growing self-confidence by teaching me a variety of martial arts.

George owned a gymnasium in the city. We called him the Pocket Hercules. He stood 1.5 meters tall with seemingly equally broad and highly muscled shoulders. He was the sole instructor, and, despite running classes all day, never seem to tire. In tandem with his wife, he ran exercise and fitness courses for men and for women. He was also an expert masseur.

George was as strong as he was agile. He had been a commando instructor during World War II and believed that fitness and strength were as important as technique. To teach us strength and balance, we performed the 'crucifix' on the rings and climbed ropes until our shoulders burned. To build our stamina, we went through timed and variable exercise routines, the forerunner of modern circuit training. Boxing, wrestling, judo and karate were all part of the varied, rigorous and exhausting regimen. His reward was simple and much appreciated: at the end of each class, he would single someone out for a free massage! There was no better cure for our aching muscles, so we fought like mad for the privilege. Years later, I was saddened to learn that George had died of a heart attack lying in his deck chair on a beach in Cape Town while on holiday with his wife. He had seemed invincible. As the horse had been struck down when I was a child, so George could not avoid his fate. I was chilled to the bone at the news and the memories it brought back. I was forcibly reminded that no matter how well prepared or how strong we are, death is ever imminent, its blackness overwhelming.

When I was fifteen, my father had his first heart attack.

"What will happen to me," wailed my mother outside the Emergency Room.

I recoiled at what seemed to me, at the time, to be a selfish response. It wasn't until much later that I became aware just how vulnerable she must have felt.

My father, on the other hand, took life as it came. He had been wounded on three separate occasions during World War 1, and bore the marks to show for them. A scar on each side of his left wrist revealed where a bullet had gone straight through, an elongated depression along the right side of his head showed where a bullet had creased his skull, and another scar on his thigh where yet another bullet had lain embedded for weeks. He had refused field surgery even though he was warned gangrene was inevitable. He had also been trapped behind enemy lines and survived on raw potatoes for three weeks before being rescued by some local nuns who nursed him back to health and he was able to re-join his combat unit. The way in which he talked about the war and the sheer adventure of it with battle scars to show, it was clear to everyone that the rest of his life would never excite him as much. I believe that his easy-going and fearless nature was a result of his many close encounters with death. His relaxed attitude to life conflicted with my mother's stern, disciplined and fear-filled views. They were ill suited to each other. And they were also constantly at odds as to how I should be raised.

Dad recovered from his heart attack, but the tension between my mother and me increased and I was drawn unwittingly into the conflict between my parents. After a subsequent heart attack, he retired from full-time work and, for the first time, had to deal with my mother's bitterness on a daily basis. Finally, he understood how his absences from home had resulted in my becoming the focus of her redirected anger and frustration with her life.

Before my twentieth birthday, I left home to study philosophy at Natal University 600 kilometers away. The years away from my mother's constant tirades were among my happiest. Without my presence, and my father staying out of her line of fire as much as he could, she internalized her bitterness with life and berated everyone for failing to give her the respect she demanded. The force of this was revealed to me when my father called me late one night to say that my mother was dying and that I should come home by overnight train.

"I'm here because of you," she said, as soon I walked into the hospital ward.

What she didn't say and what I didn't understand then, was that her marriage had become empty and purposeless. In my naivety, I turned around and walked out of the ward, left town and went back to university. She, however, recovered from her unexplained illness. In the vain belief that I might be able to help them reconcile their differences, two years later at my father's request I returned to live with them. I moved out after a few months when I realized that they had passed the point of no return and that I could not dispel her grief or anger.

While I was at university, I developed a close relationship with my clinical psychology supervisor, Professor Michael Smith. Over the years, he had observed my mother on many occasions, and seeing her changing moods, kindly offered to treat her privately and free of charge.

I knew I would need the support of all three of my half-brothers to persuade her to meet with him, so I called a meeting with them. Not surprisingly, my middle brother dissented. He said that there was nothing wrong with her and that I was solely to blame for all her problems. My eldest brother remained silent, while the youngest brother said he did not know enough and so could not support my initiative. I was outvoted. Eight years later, my parents divorced, two months after my father's third heart attack.

"You now have your wish," she said. "You can have your father all to yourself."

Dad came to live with my young family and me for what my wife and I thought would be a brief period of rest, recovery and readjustment. He lived with me until he died, 18 years later.

Shortly after my parents' divorce, my mother wrote me out of her life in a letter stating that she never wished to see me again; that as far as she was concerned I was dead. I never saw her again. Years later I was told that her condition had become progressively worse. She lived, variously, with her three sons until, as I found out subsequently, they were unable to manage what seemed to be delusional episodes arising from her increasing senility. They placed her in an aged-care home where she died at eighty-three. By then, I had already left the country of my birth taking my family, including my father, to live in London. Apartheid was not yet dead, but its pyre had just been lit and its ashes were ready to darken the skies.

CHAPTER THREE

If it is true that change shapes resilience and that adapting to many changes breeds fortitude, then the personal, political and economic events I faced before and after I emigrated from South Africa to England, then again to Australia, certainly prepared me for the challenges ahead.

From the 1980s through 1990s, South Africa was engaged in a protracted and bloody liberation war along its borders with Portuguese-controlled Angola, and South West Africa, now known as Namibia. One independence movement was supported by Cuban troops, the other by USA-backed troops from South Africa and Zaire.

South Africa could draw on a continuous supply of soldiers as the Apartheid government in 1967 had introduced compulsory military conscription for white South African males over the age of sixteen or when they left school, whichever was the later. I vividly recall the thrill and the relief I felt when I received a notice advising me that the army did not want me. As I soon found out, all my Jewish friends had received similar notices. With so many Jewish people advocating against the Apartheid regime, one can only speculate that the government may have feared having a fifth column in their army. Years later, when I was married, my wife and I were keenly aware that when they finished school any of our children could be called up to fight on behalf of a government whose racial policies we abhorred. Against this background, 1960 turned out to be a turning point for South Africa through an event that shocked the world.

In order to promote its Apartheid policy, the National

Party government had introduced passbooks which black African men were required to carry if they wished to move from place to place. This draconian law was designed to enforce segregation and harass the many opponents of the law. To protest against a new law the government had introduced that required black African women to carry passbooks as well, in March 1960 a group of several thousand people, later growing to over 19,000, converged on the Sharpeville police station in Transvaal, now known as Gauteng. No one is sure what finally provoked them, but the police opened fire on the crowd killing 69 and injuring a further 180. The uproar that followed was global. Undaunted, the government banned all political opposition and, later, sentenced many leaders, including, Nelson Mandela, to imprisonment.

It was a terrifying time. The police intimidated anyone who protested. Everyone knew someone who had 'fallen off the 10th floor' or 'starved to death' at the infamous John Vorster Square police headquarters in Johannesburg. Student unions were singled out. Natal University, with its large non-white campus, was a special focus of theirs. We took part in student union protests, and as careful as we were not to attract too much attention, the police were on to our every move. I was shocked one day to learn that David Stern, a close friend who attended the same university had 'disappeared.' I later heard the police had arrested him. I never saw him again.

To stay downwind, I focused on my studies. In my spare time, I wrote essays, plays and poetry and many of these were printed in a local magazine and later in a daily newspaper. One day, while attending lectures, Arthur, a fellow student approached me, saying he had enjoyed reading some of my poems and short stories. Much older than I, he was married with a young child and attended lectures as a part-time student while he worked as an account executive at Lintas, a well-known international advertising agency. We became friends and he often invited me for dinner of a Friday evening to compensate for the meals I cooked for myself as a student living on my own.

"Have you ever thought of writing for a living?" he asked.

"Yes. When I publish my Great American novel."

Arthur said he thought I might be creative enough to become a copywriter. He asked me to select, at random, several newspaper advertisements and to rework them in words and visuals as I saw fit. I spent a weekend doing this and gave them to him a week later.

He called me after a few days and said that the creative director of the agency had seen my scribbles and wished to see me. Soon afterwards, I met John Herring who offered me a job as a junior copywriter starting forthwith. I pointed out to him that I had a thesis to complete for my degree.

"Can you complete it in your spare time?"

"I will need to get permission from the dean of faculty," I replied.

"So, find out and let me know as soon as possible."

I called my parents to let them know what I had decided to do. My mother was scornful of my decision saying, "Are you a philosopher or a psychologist? Make up your mind. How can you earn a living in advertising?" I tried, in vain, to explain how I now had a unique opportunity to follow my passion to write - and to be paid to do so. With no room for further discussion, two weeks later I started my career in advertising. A few months later I handed in my thesis and completed my degree.

I was hooked from the moment I sat down in front of my typewriter with my first assignment: the launch of a new flavor of Wall's ice cream. For several months I worked with other high-spirited and highly talented people. I soon realized that advertising was more than putting word and picture together but a hard, competitive industry focused on persuading people to buy our clients' products or services.

Some of the products we advertised were aimed at the indigenous market and to help us better understand it, the company was a pioneer in employing a black African man. Horace Mpanza had graduated in economics from the University of Fort Hare that offered a Western-style, academically excellent education exclusively for black Africans. Horace was the first tertiary-educated black man I met who was not a servant. He had attended Harvard Business School and became an icon in black South African advertising until he retired in 2003. With passbook laws in place, our meetings were confined to the office during lunch breaks and after work before we headed home. He spoke freely with me about politics and economics from his personal and academic experiences. For the first time, I learned what it was like to be an educated black African living under a regime that considered people like him to be intellectually inferior.

My introduction to advertising and my meetings with Horace were relatively short-lived. I received a frantic call from my father urging me to come home as my mother was in hospital again. Torn between what I felt was my filial duty and appreciation that this period away from home had been among my happiest, I reluctantly resigned from my job and returned to Johannesburg to stay with my parents.

I tried to find employment with an advertising agency but

was told by each company I called on that as good as my small portfolio of work was, I had too little experience for the positions that were vacant. As the weeks went by and I toyed with the idea of returning to university to complete a doctorate, one of my friends who was a teacher asked me whether I would consider teaching English to high school students. He told me that the Senior English teacher at King David High, a private fee-based day school, had retired and they were eager to replace her. Would I consider an interview with the school principal and, if so, he would arrange this as soon as possible?

I agreed. On a Thursday afternoon a week later, I met Norman Sandler. Seated behind his large desk, I saw a friendly, tanned face with combed-back jet-black hair and penetrating, enquiring eyes peering at me through black-framed glasses. I was a little anxious. He was considered a stern doyen of teaching who demanded and expected the highest standard of erudition from his staff. Through his leadership, the school achieved many of the top scores in the country.

"I remember you as a Quiz Kid," he started saying. "But right now I have big shoes to fill and your friend thinks you're 'it'."

Still off guard from his comment, I spluttered my way through a discussion on Latin, the wonders of grammar and syntax, Shakespeare, poetry in general and Dylan Thomas in particular. Just when I thought I was about to be told, politely, that our discussion had been 'interesting', he said, "I'd like you to start on Monday. Here are the set books for Forms 4 and 5, and here is your timetable."

I was flabbergasted. I had never considering a career in teaching but decided that I would accept his offer and bide my time until I could get back to advertising. In three days I brought myself up to speed and on the following Monday taught my first class. I was surprised at how natural it felt and how easy it was to teach classrooms full of eager and questioning minds. I am sure I learned more from teaching than I ever did from being taught. As with the other male staff members, my duties included coaching cricket teams and umpiring cricket and rugby matches. The average age of the staff was around 28 and so our similar ages and interests combined to forge a bond between us both academically and socially. I have no doubt that had the pay been better, in spite of marking often hard to read essays until midnight on most nights, I would never have left teaching. The fact that Norman was the second best person I ever worked for made it even harder to leave when I did.

I was twenty-four when I met Janet. She was eighteen and had just left school. She was most attractive. I was smitten. D. H. Lawrence's *Sons and Lovers* was her set book at university. I knew the book well, so to gain her attention I offered to teach her. Unbeknown to me, she had expressed her lack of understanding of the book to gain my attention. Three weeks later, I proposed. After a six-month engagement we were married in 1965. She was nineteen, a not unusual age for girls to marry at the time. Some eighteen months' later, expecting our first child and with increased expenses looming, I tried even harder, and succeeded, in getting back into advertising, starting at Lindsay Smithers, now known as Draftfcb.

I worked long hours and was eventually rewarded for my efforts. A television commercial I wrote for a well-known brand of vodka was awarded a Golden Lion at the Venice Film Festival in the Advertising Awards category and prompted an almost immediate promotion. A year later, I was offered the position of Senior Copywriter at JWT, a world-famous advertising agency. In an irony of fate, John Herring whom I had first worked for in advertising at Lintas joined JWT as a copywriter. He resigned shortly afterwards when he found it hard to accept that I had a more senior position to his. In 1969 and the year after our second son was born, I was employed by Grant Advertising (now known as McCann) as Chief Copywriter. One year later, I was appointed Creative Director. Then, and later, the time I spent in advertising was, for the most part, best summed up by the words of a well-known advertising man of the day, Jerry Della Femina, who wrote, 'Advertising is the most fun you can have with your clothes on.' I thought 'and with your clothes off.'

The chairman of Grant was David Hart, a short trim man with grey, toothbrush moustache and clipped grey hair. His firmly erect posture and swagger spoke of his background in the British army. Although many of the staff and people at large spoke of his peremptory manner and often-unpredictable actions (he once fired someone for going to a local store during office hours to buy cigarettes), he was the best person I ever worked for. He rewarded me handsomely for my work, praised me without reserve when we landed a new account or when the company's profits increased. I often went to his home where, sitting beside his pool with his son splashing in the water and his wife entertaining guests in the sitting room, we talked at length about our private lives and shared some of the more difficult personal issues we each faced.

When I wasn't at work, I tried to spend as much time as I could with my sons. To keep up my exercise program, I practised karate, played squash and cricket and, when opportunity permitted, played golf on weekends with friends and sometimes during the week with clients.

In 1971 our youngest son was born. My father remained with us as grandfather-in-residence and, as it turned out, a surrogate parent to him. In the same way that John Ndmande had become my father in absentia when Dad was at war, so he brought his wisdom to the children when I was away at work. Over the years, he also became a proxy father to Janet, whose own father was an infrequent visitor to our home. My success as a creative director drew the attention of a start-up advertising agency. With a mortgage to pay, Janet still at university, and with ever-increasing expenses, I found their generous offer highly attractive. With some misgivings over leaving McCann and the friends I had made - and much to David Hart's distress - I accepted.

It was a fateful move. Over the next few months, each campaign I directed was a success. We added a new client every few weeks. The business grew and grew. Then one Saturday evening, standing on our veranda waiting for dinner guests to arrive, I saw a figure walking up my driveway. I recognized the chairman's general factotum. He handed me an envelope and when I asked him what it contained, he turned around without a word and walked away. I opened it and saw a check for what amounted to six months' salary. The accompanying letter from the chairman stated that as the company and I were incompatible it was best they terminate our agreement. They had employed me to help them win new business and as soon as we did, had no further use for me. I was livid. Their offer to me had been spurious. There was no time to vent my anger as our guests had started to arrive. The rest of the evening was a blur. When everyone had left, I told Janet what had happened. She was shocked and irate.

"After all you did for them! It's a disgrace", she yelled.

We discussed my options; it became clear to me that with extra money in the bank, I could afford to take my time looking for another position. I telephoned David Hart the following day and told him what had happened. He was as furious as I, and all the more so, as he explained, because he had only managed to find a replacement for me some three days' previously.

"If only you had received that letter a week ago, I would have given you your old job back in a flash. Don't worry," he said. "I'll make sure everyone in town knows what they did to you."

A few days later, I received a telephone call from an acquaintance asking me if I would be interested in a directorship and shareholding in a small company in which he was a partner. The founder of the company, Tom Downing, was planning to retire and to sell out. It was a remarkable opportunity, all the more so as I would now wear two hats: one as a creative director and one as an accounts manager. A year later, Tom retired and we gained full control of the company. With no chairman or managing director, we operated as a team with equal responsibilities and authorities. It was unusual. It was friendly and cooperative. It was also successful. On reflection, it was not surprising that we were approached to merge with a much larger company. A year later, David Jones and I joined the board of Barker McCormack, with lesser roles assigned to those who were not offered directorships but whose positions were retained. Sadly, one of the few people I had formed a close relationship over the years – first at McCann and then Downing - was André Cronje who was not invited to join. For years, I was filled with regret at how naïve and mercenary David and I had been in not insisting that he should be offered a directorship in the merged company. For years I sought him out to apologize and after some considerable time learned, too late, he had died in 2009.

While my business life was flourishing, political problems were becoming increasingly intrusive. When I was a child, I witnessed the brutality of the police towards a black African man and vowed I would eventually leave South Africa. The event that finally shocked me into action occurred on 16 June 1976 when several thousand high school students protested against a government decree that Afrikaans must be taught on a 50-50 basis with English. The police opened fire on them. Officials claimed that only 23 were killed although estimates put the figure as high as 700. Further protests led to more deaths around the country. A few weeks later I came face to face with what was fast-becoming a black versus white confrontation. I was in a meeting with one of our clients when his secretary burst into the office to say that hundreds of black African men were marching down the road. We raced outside and saw a phalanx of people wielding sticks bearing down on us, and smashing shop windows and cars as they advanced. We raced indoors shutting the security doors behind us. It was time to leave the country of my birth and to which I felt no attachment. Despite Janet's tearful pleas and her reluctance to leave family, friends and pets behind, in 1978 we left for London.

Having been a director and partner in one of the largest advertising agencies in South Africa, I came to England with high hopes and with the expectation my skills would be welcomed with open arms. I was naïve. I had no mentor to advise me that the wise choice would have been to start out lower down the corporate ladder and work my way back to the top, which should have been easy and rapid. Nobody set me right and so I found myself working at a level well below my capability. The cold and uncompromising English weather became a metaphor for my personal dilemma. There seemed no way out. The catalyst in the end was parents' night at my eldest son's school, Park High in Stanmore.

In South Africa, Greg had almost always been top of his class. Now he was rock bottom. Feigning ignorance of Latin I had studied at university, I questioned his teacher how she taught grammar.

"We don't teach grammar," she said.

"Why not?" I was perplexed.

"The purpose of Latin is to get the children to learn pages of Latin text off by heart to improve their memory."

I chose not to make a comment, as we were scheduled to meet his form-master next. The story became worse.

"Your son has no academic potential," he said. "I suggest you take him out of school and let him learn a trade."

"We're leaving," I said to Janet as we walked out of the school. I was infuriated.

"Where to?" she asked.

"Somewhere where he can attend a school that will appreciate his brains and, hopefully, where the sun shines more than it does here."

Despite this, Janet did not want to leave England. She felt that she and the children had put down roots: home, school and friends. She said she might consider going but only if I found a job and suitable schooling for the boys. I was determined to move. That very week, I located an employment agency in the West End specializing in advertising and left my portfolio of work with Jane, the owner. A week later she called me to say that someone from

Australia had been impressed with my work and wished to interview me. In a pub in Soho and after a few beers, Brian Cooper asked me a to join the company as a creative director in Melbourne on condition that I visit the city first, at my own expense, to get a 'feel' of it and if I could, find schools that would accept my sons.

"If you like it and you decide to stay, we'll pay for you and your family to come over."

I did as he suggested, immediately fell in love with the city and returned to London to hand in my resignation.

If emigration is born out of desperation or to embark on a new adventure, I certainly qualified on both counts. Two emigrations challenged my resolve and my resourcefulness. Just as my Zulu mentor had taught me to stay downwind and to be alert, so both experiences brought out my capacity to take stock and then take action. Many years later, Janet would say that despite her misgivings about leaving South Africa and then England, imposing my will upon her in this instance had been the right decision.

CHAPTER FOUR

On a sunny day in July 1981, I arrived in Australia to take up my position as a creative director at USP Needham now known as DDB Worldwide. My family followed a few months later and soon afterwards, my sons settled into their respective schools. After the series of difficulties they had encountered in the English public school system, they were now back on track and headed for their much-improved academic and subsequently highly successful professional careers.

One Sunday morning, after a lengthy spell of bowling in the cricket nets, my shoulder began to hurt. It was February 1983.

I rested my injured shoulder for a few days and, when the pain subsided, joined a friend of mine for our weekly game of squash. This aggravated the original injury. For a few days, I played no sport. I went to a physiotherapist recommended by our family doctor. His regimen of ultrasound therapy and deep massage did not help. A busy work schedule kept me from playing either cricket or squash for a few weeks. Despite the enforced rest, the pain persisted.

In the belief that continuing exercise was preferable to favoring my shoulder, I started playing squash again. I also went back to playing cricket despite the pain. To keep me going, I went to see more physiotherapists and kept taking painkillers. They did not help, so I decided to try acupuncture; years earlier, it had helped relieve the pain of back surgery. I contacted a well-known acupuncturist, Mr Wong. A gentle, slim, stoop-shouldered man, his quick smile and self-confident manner soon made me feel at ease. With the gentle sound of classical music, twice a week I yielded to the brief sharp stabs of his needles. The relief afterwards seemed worth it.

It was a crazy time. I'd go for treatment and feel better. Because I felt better, I started playing squash again. Then my shoulder hurt, so I went back for more treatment. The cycle continued unabated. After a few months, the pain became intolerable. I couldn't sleep. I couldn't drive my car. I couldn't lift my arm to brush my teeth. In desperation, I agreed to a physiotherapist's suggestion to have cortisone injected directly into the affected muscle. It made no difference. The pain was so intense that a week later when the physiotherapist suggested I have a second cortisone injection, I agreed. I had relief for two days; then the pain returned and seemed even worse. For a week or two, I gritted my teeth, stopped playing cricket and focused like a demon at work to distract myself.

I went to see an orthopedic surgeon. He suggested I undergo 'exploratory surgery' in order, as he said, to 'stop the tendon pressing on a nerve'. When he told me that there was less than a twenty per cent chance of the operation being successful, I demurred and went back to Mr Wong for more needle treatment. Again, relief was only temporary. By now, I was finding it hard to raise a spoon to my mouth. It seemed I had to make the hard decision to stop playing squash. I could not understand why my shoulder did not respond to any treatment. Nor could our family doctor.

I was working long hours and attributed my growing tiredness to the almost constant pain in my shoulder. On a few occasions, I woke up at night wet with perspiration. I thought that the painkillers for my shoulder were the cause, so I stopped taking them and made an appointment to visit our doctor. He was on vacation, so his partner agreed to see me.

Dr Unglik is a tall, well-groomed man with a cultivated grey, droop-edged moustache. Under his seemingly serious mien, he has a delightful sense of humor and a disarming manner. He usually greets his patients with at least two or three lengthy jokes to put them at ease. On previous visits, I had looked forward to hearing the latest from his apparently endless repertoire. On this occasion, my concern for my shoulder was not assuaged by his humor.

"There must be something you can do for my shoulder," I said.

"I am concerned about your paleness," came his reply. "I think you should have a blood test".

"How will that help my shoulder?"

"Let's first find out why you're so pale."

"I've always been pale," I replied.

"Not like this, you weren't."

"Yes, I was. When I was a child, my mother called me 'Paleface.' I never took the side of the Injuns."

"Don't be funny. Will you please go for a blood test?"

All I could think of was to find relief for the pain and fulfill my ambition to start up my own agency. I agreed to the blood test, convinced he would end up telling me that I all I needed was a tonic.

Dr Unglik phoned me a few days later. To my surprise, he asked me to see him at his office.

"What for?" I was working to a tight schedule. I couldn't afford the time.

"I have something to tell you, and I'd rather discuss it with you face to face," he said. It sounded ominous. It was.

"I want you see a hematologist," he told me looking across his desk the following day.

"Anemia?" I asked.

"I don't know. Maybe. Your blood count is a little lower than normal, and I'd like to know why."

That evening, I pondered at length on the possible causes of my lowered blood count, but could think of no answer. It never occurred to me for a moment that I might be facing a serious or even life-threatening disease. All I could think of was the pain in my shoulder.

In time, I would come to appreciate that most people faced with symptoms they have previously not experienced and which their doctors find puzzling to explain, delude themselves into thinking that, somehow, the warning signs will go away if they ignore them. I was no different.

The name I gave Dr Ironbark, the hematologist, was Dr Gloom. He had black hair, a black moustache and black-framed, tinted glasses that darkened whenever he faced the light. There was no lightness in his manner. Ever serious, he didn't smile much.

Every ten days I had a blood test. Every time I asked him what the results indicated, he said he did not know. Little did I know then that when a doctor says he doesn't know, he doesn't know. All he knew was that my blood counts – hemoglobin, white blood cell and platelet levels – continued to fall. Apart from my growing tiredness and the throb of pain in my shoulder, I felt fine. Something was wrong and no one knew why.

Ten blood tests and many months later, in the autumn of 1983, Dr Gloom sent me for a Computerized Axial Tomography (CAT) scan. The results were inconclusive. The only information I could extract from him was that my platelet count was a 'little on the low side'. I still thought I had anemia. I took iron tablets to no avail.

A week after the CAT scan and only days before my forty-third birthday, Dr Gloom suggested that as the blood tests were 'vague', I should undergo a bone-marrow examination.

"I think a bone-marrow is the only way to find out why your blood counts keep falling," he said.

To do the test, a long, hollow needle with a T-handle is inserted into the breastbone or the hip, and a sample of blood, bone and bone marrow is extracted. The sample collected is then observed through an electron microscope. A local anesthetic, usually xylocaine, is administered to numb the skin through which the needle is inserted. Two bouts of vomiting revealed I was sensitive to the drug. After that, the doctors gave me Valium injections to help relax me.

The test is harrowing. No matter how reassuring the doctors tried to be, nothing, but nothing, can mask the soft crunch you feel as the needle slides deeply into the bone and the marrow is sucked out. It feels like an alien invasion of nightmarish proportions. I never became accustomed to the procedure. By the time the doctors decided I had had enough, I was to have had no less than sixteen invasive bone-marrow biopsies.

Waiting for the result of the first test, I wondered what would happen if I had a serious illness. I didn't dare think the word 'cancer'. So fearful of what it might be, I pretended all was well and went ahead with my birthday plans for a dinner the following Friday with my family.

Denial can take many forms, and that dinner epitomized one of them. I did my best to avoid eye contact with everyone. As we had done on many other occasions in our life, Janet and I acted our parts so well no one suspected anything was wrong.

The weekend that followed seemed to me to be the

longest I had ever endured.

Monday brought the first biopsy result. Nothing. If the doctors knew, they certainly weren't telling. In fact, they didn't know.

Colleagues and friends began commenting on my paling complexion. One called me aside and asked me if I was suffering from anemia. I didn't know what to say.

"Maybe I'm not getting enough sleep," I suggested.

I went into limbo for the next five months, enduring several blood tests and two more CT scans. Week after week, I visited Dr Gloom, and week after week, his comment was the same. "We don't know why your levels keep falling. I suggest we keep testing you until we find out."

Tests, tests and even more tests! Suspecting it might be a virus he tested me for fevers found in countries I had never visited! There was still no explanation for my night sweats.

The harrowing and draining sweating had begun a few months earlier. I would go to bed, fall asleep and wake a few hours later soaked through. At first, these sweats were an inconvenience. I ran out of nightclothes, sheets, blankets and sleep; I became increasingly anxious about my condition.

My inner compass could not find true north. I knew of no one who could give me directions or where to go for help. To add to my growing sense of dislocation, a downturn in the economy resulted in staff cutbacks and my having to take on an ever-increasing workload. I suggested to my family that we all needed a holiday and a change of scenery.

"Let's go north," I suggested, hoping to reset my compass.

It had been a typical August in Melbourne: cold, damp and rainy. A plane flight away we found the warmth of the sun on the Sunshine Coast at Noosa. For my children it was three weeks of carefree fun. Try as I might, I found it hard to dispel my growing sense of foreboding. In vain, I hoped the holiday would never end but work for me and school for the children beckoned. As did the next scheduled blood test.

I decided to talk to my friend, Alan, a dentist I assumed had some medical knowledge.

"I've started coming out in boils, and these lumps in my armpits and groin seem to be getting larger," I told him. "My abdomen seems to be getting larger, too."

"It sounds as if you either have an infection or you're having a baby." he joked. "What does your doctor think it is?"

"He doesn't know." I dropped the matter.

Apart from his wife, no one knew that Alan had started treatment for high blood pressure. In his usual light-hearted and humorous way, he suggested I try some of his medication. "It's all the same junk. Doctors know nothing!" His wry, derisive and cynical wit apart, Alan also held some very passionate beliefs.

Of course, I didn't take his medication. Nor did he. Two months later, Alan suffered a sudden heart attack and died. He was forty-one. I was forty-three.

I was bereft at the loss of my friend and spent the next several weeks comforting his wife, Denise. Helping her to sort out Alan's will and financial affairs occupied much of my spare time, and I was able to put my own problems aside.

Winter had now turned to spring. Six weeks and six more blood tests later, Dr Gloom suggested that I have another needle biopsy. I could feel the pain already! But not in my shoulder – that was better. Enforced rest seemed to have healed it.

It was now the first week of summer, but for me there was still a chill in the air. I kept busy so I wouldn't have time to think about the problem. I waited two long days before Dr Gloom's secretary called me to say he had the results of the second bone-marrow test. As I had a busy schedule at the office, I deferred my appointment to see him to the following afternoon.

Driving across town to his office, my thoughts were elsewhere. He stared at me when I sat down. I expected him to tell me that more tests were needed.

As tactful as he was, what he had to say next may as well have been scripted for a B-grade Hollywood movie.

"Well," he said, after a lengthy pause, "we've finally got a name for it."

"And it is…?" I prompted him.

He paused again.

'It's a very rare form of leukemia, called Hairy Cell Leukemia. Also known as HCL'.

"Is it benign?"

His reply really shook me. "No, it's malignant."

I felt the blood drain from my face. Then, feeling as if I was still reading from a movie script, "How long have I got?"

His reply was equally badly scripted. "I can't say precisely. A few months. Maybe. I don't know. New drugs are being discovered all the time. Right now, there is nothing available for your type of cancer. You will have to have your spleen removed, though."

"Will that cure me?" I asked, innocently.

"As I said, there is no cure. Having your spleen removed may give you a bit more time. We don't want it to get too big or it will rupture."

I have no doubt he did not appreciate the ironic humor in that statement. He had just told me that I had a disease that was going to kill me but that allowing my spleen to grow would do likewise! I almost laughed. Instead, I asked him how the operation would affect my blood counts.

"They may go up a smidgen," was his discomforting reply. When I asked him to be more precise, he said: "The platelet count will probably go up marginally."

My platelet count was now 69,000. Normal range is between 250,000 and 400,000. Platelets are the constituent of blood that controls clotting.

"The white cell count will probably go up a little." My white cell count was .27. The normal range is between 7.0 and 11.0. White cells attack invading bacteria and viruses in the body, fighting infections. My ability to ward off infection was deteriorating. The glands in my groin were getting larger and larger.

"Hemoglobin will probably go up a notch." My hemoglobin count was 11.0. Normal is between 14.0 and 17.0. Hemoglobin is the oxygen-carrying component of red blood cells.

"But," he added, "I cannot give you guarantees for any of them."

I listened in a daze as he explained the operating procedure. To comfort me, he said he knew of a good surgeon who had performed several successful splenectomies.

"Many people have had their spleens removed and have lived normal lives. I've already spoken to a surgeon. We'll have you home by Christmas," he added for reassurance.

The only Santa Claus I ever believed in was my Dad, and he wasn't a doctor. Again, I asked him how long I had to live.

"Medical science is always making new discoveries. They'll find a cure for HCL someday." So saying, he wrote out a prescription for cortisone that he said was essential to give my blood counts a temporary boost. "Unless you take it, there's a chance you could bleed to death on the operating table."

I found his odd logic fascinating and terrifying. He had told me I had only a few months to live, as there was no cure, and my blood counts were deteriorating. He told me that if my spleen grew larger it could burst and I could die. He told me that the risks involved in surgery could also kill me. Whether it was my blood pressure or a distant echo, I could hear drum beats in my head. Simba, the lion, was on the prowl, and I wasn't armed. With no supporting impi, I felt defenseless.

"How low can my platelet count go before I strike real trouble?" I asked. I wanted to protect my back.

"If it gets below 20,000, you could hemorrhage, anywhere, at any moment. If you have a cerebral hemorrhage especially, you could die."

Dr Gloom undoubtedly felt he had to convey a sense of urgency to me. He certainly did - but not with the result he intended. To my amazement, I didn't panic or strike out in anger. Again, I heard a ringing in my ears, and for a few moments, I felt quite numb. Then I heard those words from long ago: 'Jwa, to be clever is to be still.' In that moment, that awful feeling faded. I felt I was downwind.

Leaving the arrangements for the operation to him, I took the prescription and drove directly to my pharmacist. A short while later, armed with a bottle of Prednisone tablets, I headed home. Rounding the corner near my house, I saw my wife coming towards me in her car. She had been on her way to the supermarket. We parked our cars. She slid onto the passenger seat next to me.

"Well?" Janet asked hesitatingly.

"I have leukemia." She burst into tears on my shoulder.

"Don't worry," I said, trying my best to comfort her. "Everything will be alright." I felt consoled by my own words. I was about to discover how uncomforted she was.

Our eldest son was working towards his school-leaving certificate. She was worried that the shock of my news would prevent him getting good marks. At her nagging, I agreed not to tell the family for the time being. From not telling the children or my father, it was a short step to keeping the facts from friends and colleagues. As the months and my health wound down, we were compelled to turn down several dinner invitations because of my tiredness. Instead of telling the truth, we made up different excuses. Our children were friendly with many of our friends' children and she was afraid the news of my imminent death would get out. As a result, she was insistent that we did not tell our friends.

"If we tell them, their children will tell ours. That must never happen."

At that moment it didn't seem important to me as to who knew what. I did not have the energy to argue with her. This decision caused me great distress in the first months of my illness.

I'd always thought that life was a cruel joke and that death the last act before the 'crack of doom'. No cosmic travel. No entering another plane. No afterlife. As kids, we used to sing:

The worms crawl in and worms crawl out.
They crawl in thin they crawl out stout.
A-oo, A-ee, A-oo, A-ee,
How lucky we will be-e.

It was funny then, but now as I heard the refrain in my head, those words didn't seem funny at all. I could not believe that I was going to die. But then, who does?

CHAPTER FIVE

I first became aware of my fear of my death in my teens.

I had never been afraid of doing anything involving physical risks. From leaping off the wardrobe in my bedroom as Superman when I was a child to leaping off rocky outcrops into mountain pools as a teenager. From clambering from window to window on speeding trains to scratching my name with a penknife on the buoys holding up shark nets 400m offshore, I survived all sorts of adventures. Like our comic-book heroes, my friends and I grew up as normal teenagers. We believed we were invincible.

One night when I was about sixteen or seventeen, as I sat watching the distant stars and the moonlight over the sea, I was suddenly filled with the most awful sense of dread. The blackness of my mother's words to me when I was four came over me. "Geoffrey's mother has gone to heaven, far away." Suddenly, I became aware that I was no more than a speck of dust in a dark and remote corner of the universe. In a flash, I knew that unlike the apparent permanence of the stars and the planets, I would simply pass away and be forgotten by the ones I loved; that I would be unable to remember them and what my life had been. I felt powerless. Where would all my thoughts go? And what about my feelings? Would they simply vanish with my dying breath into thin air signifying nothing?

This terrified me. Waves of helplessness overwhelmed me. For years and years, a palpable and overwhelming sense of existential dread came over me, mostly at night. I would wake up with all the symptoms of a panic attack. My heart would race. I'd perspire and, inevitably, hyperventilate. Dizzy with desperation, I would be filled with an insatiable desire to escape. Anywhere. Sometimes I would drive around aimlessly for hours in my car until I felt calm enough to return home to bed. Sometimes I would control my panic by reading a newspaper or watching television into the early hours of the morning when I would fall asleep, exhausted. I felt that if I could spend my sleeping hours awake, I could avoid that inevitable night.

These waves of dread would also sweep through me while watching a beautiful sunset, the moonlight over the sea or, as was often the case, while I was playing with my children. With each tidal attack, I felt an impending sense of loss and sadness. I was afraid I would be separated from the ones I loved. I was saddened by the thought of my children growing up without a father and that I would not see them blossom. Death seemed quite pointless and yet so terrifying I could not stop thinking about it.

The Bogeyman in the night was now the Grim Reaper.

I tried to discuss the matter with friends but they were discomfited, preferring to talk about anything else. Unable to discuss my fear, it lay submerged, painfully surfacing through countless poems I wrote. These expressions were my only escape valve, and I have no doubt that they helped me to maintain my equilibrium down the years.

Until I was confronted by my own mortality, the only person I knew who feared death with the same sense of dread as I did was a friend I had met in Israel several years earlier. Talya told me she had grown up on a kibbutz near the Syrian border. Whenever Al Fatah rained rockets down on them in the dead of night, she cowered in an underground shelter. The screech of the rockets, the subsequent detonations and the screams of the injured and dying left her shaken. She consumed large amounts of tranquillizers to maintain control. As Talya told me her story, she panicked and began to tremble. She was terrified. I did not know how to comfort her. It was not until I came so close to dying and a final acceptance of my death that my own dread finally faded.

When I asked Dr Gloom to explain Hairy Cell Leukemia, he referred to it as a type of 'non-Hodgkin's lymphoma'. I knew that cancer is a malignant disease affecting bone or tissue. I knew that leukemia is cancer of the blood, and that lymphoma is cancer of the lymph system, but 'non-Hodgkin's lymphoma' meant nothing to me. When Dr Gloom said I would have to have my spleen removed, all I could picture was the surgeon's knife slicing through my abdomen. Surgery seemed so drastic – all the more so as I knew it was not a cure.

As my wife sobbed on my shoulder, I realized that if I was going to stand any chance of overcoming my insidious foe, I had to stay alert and follow its tracks. To stay downwind, I needed a second opinion. That evening, I discussed the idea with her. She wasn't convinced.

"Don't you think the specialist knows what he's talking about? Our doctor wouldn't have sent you to someone who didn't know what he was doing."

"In the event," she continued, "I think you should see Sally Rather."

Six months before my leukemia was diagnosed, Janet had severe sciatica. She tried in vain to disregard the pain, but it persisted. Our doctor prescribed painkillers. When these failed to work, he arranged for her to be treated by a physiotherapist. This aggravated the problem. The pain in her back became so severe she could hardly move. She mentioned her difficulties in a letter to her mother who lived abroad and within weeks, she received a reply. Her mother advised her to contact her friend, Sally Rather, saying that she had successfully treated a number of people through spiritual healing.

Janet refused her mother's suggestion saying that as far as she was concerned it was all hocus-pocus.

She was in such pain; I tried my best to persuade her to go. Two weeks later, when she was bent over double with pain, she told me she was going to see Sally. "I can't bear this any more. Maybe she really can help me."

"I'll drive you there."

"No," she replied. "If I'm going to make a fool of myself, there's no need for you to do likewise."

I had read several books describing how faith healers and psychic surgeons, particularly in the Philippines, had treated people for a host of ailments. The large number who claimed to have been cured led me to believe that perhaps I should keep an open mind. It was just as well that I did. An hour later, Janet returned walking almost upright and in far less pain. A few weeks later, the pain returned but she never went back to Sally. Instead, after seeking the advice of our family doctor, she was admitted to hospital for treatment. Two weeks of enforced bed completely healed her.

Now she was adamant that I should visit Sally.

"She didn't cure you," I said. "You never went back to her."

"What I didn't tell you," she said, "Sally has, apparently, also successfully treated cancer patients."

At this point, like so many people in my predicament, I was prepared to try anything. I felt that I had nothing to lose. This was my first venture into the nebulous world of unscientific claims and false promises that beguile the new cancer patient. An hour later, I met a slim, slightly built woman of about sixty with curled light brown hair, softly spoken and with a gentle demeanor. She guided me into her bedroom and pulled up a chair for me. As I sat down, I noticed a picture on her wall of a man wearing a turban. What struck me were his smiling eyes. They resembled Sally's. In reply to my silent question, she told me that he was her guru and guiding spirit.

Standing behind me, she said: "Relax. Take a few deep breaths."

Slowly I became aware of a sensation of warmth spreading across my shoulders and down my back. I felt as if I was floating on a cloud. I was bathed in a white light that turned to blue, then gold. For a while, I lost all sense of time and space until I became aware of the scent of Sally's perfume and remembered where I was.

"You can open your eyes," she said.

"You must have warm hands," I ventured, in an attempt to explain what I had experienced.

"I didn't touch you."

"Then how did you do what you just did?"

"It wasn't me. It was someone else," she said cryptically. "You know, there is nothing to fear."

'I'm not afraid,' I replied. 'It's just that I don't know what to do next."

"Be patient. The answer will come."

Sally's words reached back down the years. I remembered the advice of John Ndmande. 'Jwa, to be clever is to be still'. In that moment, I felt that, somehow, things would turn out all right.

Even so, I remained sure that I needed another opinion. Sally had reminded me that healing comes from within. Who could I ask? The only person I could think of was the man who had treated my shoulder with acupuncture. The following morning I telephoned his secretary.

"I need to see Mr Wong urgently."

"How would next Thursday suit you?"

She was so polite and even though I didn't want to sound melodramatic, I said: "This is a matter of life and death."

That afternoon, I walked into Mr Wong's office. "Your shoulder must be pretty bad for you to want to see me so urgently?"

"It's not my shoulder I'm concerned about. I found out yesterday that I have leukemia. The doctor wants to remove my spleen before it gets too large and bursts. Anyway, he says there is no cure."

"How can I help you?"

"I want to speak to someone who can tell me about non-medical forms of treatment. There's no point in having surgery. I wonder if there is an alternative form of treatment I can try. It occurred to me that you might be able to offer some advice."

"Give me a few minutes." He opened his filing cabinet and, after shuffling through his cards, turned to me and said, "I have it!"

He scribbled a name and telephone number on a piece of paper and handed it to me. "I've heard of this Colin Jones," he said. "He's a homeopath. Why don't you give him a call?"

Why not indeed! I was primed by hope; logic had deserted me. I raced out of his office and into a telephone booth a few meters away. I wondered if I could change from Clark Kent into Superman. My head was giddy with speculation. The number I dialed was busy. After several frantic attempts, I finally got through. Then my call was put on hold. I was in a sweat. He eventually picked up my call.

"Can you please give me an appointment? I've just been diagnosed with leukemia. I have to see you."

"Sorry. I'm booked out for months."

I thought I had misheard him, realized I had not.

"Could you repeat that?" I was struggling to keep my voice calm.

"I can't see you for at least two months."

I felt the blood drain from my face.

I dashed out of the telephone booth and back to Mr Wong. I was agitated. He was relaxed. He looked through his files again and handed me another note. "Dr Vaughan is a doctor and a naturopath," he said. "Here, use my phone, this time."

I called and made an appointment to see him the following afternoon. "Good luck", said Mr Wong, as I turned to leave. "If things don't turn out, come back and we'll see what we can do."

This episode with Mr Wong was significant. Until that afternoon, I considered coincidences to represent chance occurrences, random happenings of no great significance. My assumption was about to be challenged. The note he handed me started a sequence of events it became harder and harder for me to believe were not connected. In retrospect, I now realize that when one is desperate it's easy to imagine there are connections to be made when none exists.

The following afternoon, as I sat waiting to meet Dr James Vaughan, I was filled with doubt. Perhaps I was accustomed to the somber surroundings of a doctor's surgery. This was different. The place was a mess. Toys were scattered around the floor of the waiting room. Behind a counter on one side of the room were shelves stacked with a variety of medications whose names I did not recognize. None of the people who came and went looked particularly ill. I felt so tired, I wondered if it was all worth it.

And then I met him. Dr Vaughan was of medium height, lean and bookish. He seemed friendly enough. This was not the time for small talk. I was direct.

"I have Hairy Cell Leukemia. My hematologist insists on my having a splenectomy, but I want to keep my spleen. Can you help me?"

Dr Vaughan was equally direct. "I don't know how to treat your problem. If my knowledge is correct, there is no treatment." He took a notebook out of his pocket and as he wrote, said, "I'm going to give you the names of four people who may be able to help you. One of them lives in India, so he may be a little difficult to contact." He tore the page out of his book and handed it to me. "The rest live here in Australia. Two of them are faith healers, so you don't have to go to the Philippines for psychic surgery. One of them, at least, should be able to help you. I'm afraid that's the best I can do. Good luck."

He also handed me a sheet of paper entitled *'Self-management for common infective illnesses'*. The articles were all about drugless treatments and the varying uses of vitamins. Calcium ascorbate and Vitamin A featured several times.

"I don't know to what extent these can help you," he said. "In the meantime, you may as well try them."

I bought several bottles of Vitamins C and A and took them for several months. I also bought a bottle of selenium and Vitamin E. According to the leaflet these were, in combination, powerful anti-cancer agents. I was prepared to take almost anything that claimed to offer me a cure.

I walked out of his rooms with the note he had written for

me. I glanced at it. The names meant nothing. Peter Evanston. Dr Singh. Peter and Jane Smith. They were to become signposts along the way as I struggled to find a cure.

That evening I telephoned the first name on the list. Peter wasn't available. Instead, I found myself talking to his wife, Sharon.

She told me that Peter had bone cancer a few years ago and had one of his legs amputated; when his cancer spread to his chest he decided to treat himself.

"He's now in total remission and runs courses for cancer patients. Why don't you come along next Tuesday afternoon and find out if he can help you?"

Later that night, as I changed my sweat-soaked sheets for the third time, I hoped I had made the right decision. The swelling in my groin had become more painful. I also had an uncomfortable lump in my right armpit. The boils on my bottom hurt. Should I have my spleen removed even though it will not save my life? Should I take another path? Questions with no answers coursed through my brain.

I did not sleep much that night.

I visited Sally every day for the next week, and discussed my doubts with her. I looked forward to those quiet moments in her room. I realize now that having her unquestioning ear and compassion were the reasons I found going to her so helpful.

"Whatever will be, will be," she said. "The decision isn't up to you'" There was such an air of serenity about her; I hoped there was some truth in what she said.

The next few days were a blur of unregistered images and confused thoughts. Walking down the road or through a shopping mall, wherever I went I felt detached from reality. Everything appeared two-dimensional. I felt as if I was on the other side of my skin. I felt no connection with the people around me. I was an outsider. Even the blue of the sky seemed remote and toneless. The sun was without warmth on my face. My sense of isolation was so complete I felt as if I was divided from the world around me by a wall of glass through which no sound could penetrate. I was numb.

On Tuesday, I met Peter Evanston. Although his wife had told me about his amputated leg, I was slightly taken aback when I first met him. He wore a robe that highlighted rather than concealed his disability. Evanston had been diagnosed with a type of bone cancer called osteogenic sarcoma and then developed secondaries in the lung. Chemotherapy and radiotherapy followed, but he later discontinued any further treatment. He tried acupuncture, yoga, psychic surgery, laying-on of hands and meditation. He travelled to the Philippines and to India – and, shortly thereafter, his cancer apparently went into remission. Somewhere in those methods, I hoped there was an answer to my problem.

What I did not know at the time was that he had responded, predictably, to surgery and chemotherapy. A number of cancer experts and his own doctor later asserted that his claim of secondaries was highly questionable. I was desperate to stay alive, so I was prepared to try anything to prove my doctor's prognosis wrong. I threw myself with enthusiasm into the most bizarre and scientifically unproven programs. It was not until I had exhausted every possible alternative and my life was being measured by the day that I was shocked to realize that even my skepticism had not overruled my despair.

As I entered the room, I was struck by his enigmatic smile, his sallow, deeply lined cheeks and his long, uncombed, straight black hair. I joined the group of about thirteen people seated in a circle. He asked us to close our eyes. In a slow, dreamy voice, he asked us to relax our muscles in turn, starting at our feet and moving slowly up to our foreheads. We then sat in silence for what seemed like ages. Fifteen minutes later, he told us to open our eyes.

"For those of you who are here for the first time," he said, "This is the technique you must use before meditating. I've made copies of an instruction tape you can buy after the session." He then launched into the topic of the day. I listened, totally fascinated as he and the rest of the group discussed the one subject I dreaded most: 'Death and Dying.'

A part of me wanted to escape by racing out of the room. Curiosity and fear of revealing my terror kept me glued to the chair. One woman wiped tears from her face as she talked about the way she felt when her breast cancer was diagnosed. One man was stoical; he had undergone radiotherapy for cancer of the prostate. He was as afraid of surgery as he was of cancer. When the doctors could do no more for him, he had come to Evanston to hear what he had to offer.

Everyone present was facing cancer either as a patient or a carer. They were wives and mothers, husbands and fathers, brothers and sisters. Most of them expressed the view that they felt let down by the medical profession. All of them were keenly aware that cancer had irrevocably changed their perspective on life. Directly and indirectly, they had stared Death in the face. Now they wanted to know more about him/it. As I listened to them telling their stories, I became more relaxed. Fear of death was not new to me. For the first time I was able to confront my own mortality in the presence of others. It made me realize I was not alone. I looked across the room at Evanston, remembered what his wife had told me about him, and said to myself: "If he could do it, so can I."

Slightly more than a week had passed since Dr Gloom had told me that I had a terminal illness. Now, as I made my resolution, I felt strangely calm. By recognizing my foe and realizing that it was up to me to outwit him, I had restored my courage. Simba was upwind.

Before I left the meeting with Evanston, I bought a tape recording of his on meditation. One side of the cassette tape described the relaxation technique he had shown us that afternoon, the other side outlined how this relaxation was a prelude to meditation and an essential part of his program. In passing, he mentioned the name of Dr Ainslie Meares, but at the time I attached no significance to it. I was still absorbing what people had said about death. The following afternoon I told Sally about my meeting with Evanston and the group.

"I told you the answer will come," Sally repeated. Her faith was rock-like. Her touchless healing still amazed me. I felt emotionally renewed. As my trust in her grew, so I confided in her. Even though I had resolved to track down and overcome my foe, I still needed reassurance that I had made the right decision. She lent me a book that afternoon entitled *The Mystical 'I'* by Joel S. Goldsmith.

"I think you'll find many of the answers you're looking for in this book."

I looked at her skeptically. "How bad can it be? At least he has the same name as you."

Over the following days, as I read his book, I realized that I had so much still to learn. I bought more of Goldsmith's books over the next few months, and discussed most of them with Sally. Goldsmith asserted that our spiritual awakening lies in having total faith in the presence of God. His view was that if God is indeed omnipotent, omniscient and omnipresent then we are, he suggested, only witnesses to the events in our lives. I wasn't sure about this: I wanted to cover all my options; I still felt I had choices. I stored this new wisdom for later use.

The topic the following Tuesday afternoon was 'Diet'. Evanston explained how he believed that additives and preservatives undermined our health. Among the undesirable foods he listed were coffee, tea, sugar, salt, rancid cheese and meat. He talked at length about the need to detoxify our bodies and rid them of impurities. He built a convincing case for avoiding man-made foods and protein obtained from meat. He talked about the high levels of cancer-causing nitrites in preserved meats such as sausages, bacon and salami, and that, if his claims were correct, I had to stop eating these. I knew this would be difficult, as they were the foods I loved. In my fragile state, I was ready to try anything. Of course, we now know that there are no foods that can either cure or prevent cancer. In 1983, faced with a hopeless prognosis, I was desperate and ready to try any alternative on offer. What did I have to lose?

"To fight off our cancers, we have to strengthen our immune systems," he explained. "Meditation and diet are essential to achieving this goal." Once again, he mentioned the name of Dr Ainslie Meares.

"Who is Dr Meares?" I asked.

"He's a psychiatrist who lives in Melbourne."

I thought: Why learn all about Ainslie Meares' technique from Evanston when I can go direct to the source? I decided there and then that I would telephone Dr Meares the following day. I had to force myself to concentrate on what those around me were saying. The discussion moved from meditation back to diet. I was drowning in a torrent of new information. Everything seemed so plausible; it would take some time before I realized just how gullible desperate people could be.

Then someone asked Evanston, "Why don't you recommend that we follow the Gerson program?"

"It's too hard to do on your own. You need someone to help you to do it properly."

"Who or what is Gerson?" I asked.

"Dr Max Gerson was a doctor who treated many cancer patients with a radical diet he invented. I tried it myself," said Evanston, "but Sharon and I found it too hard to follow. Dr Gerson's daughter runs a clinic in the USA. To go there is an expensive alternative that I don't recommend." I didn't understand why the Gerson diet was hard to follow. I thought: Why learn about these things second-hand? Why not find out for myself? I decided to buy Gerson's book.

The next day I telephoned Dr Meares to book an appointment. I then walked from bookstore to bookstore but could not find Gerson's book. Eventually I found a store that was willing to order a copy from the USA, but was told I would have to wait six weeks for delivery. In the meantime, I began following Evanston's dietary plan, and attended his classes.

I came to understand, much later, just how desperate I was in those first few weeks. My default position was what I knew as a creative director of advertising; in a business where you are only as good as your next project, my life had consisted of thinking up new ideas and finding new headlines, often at a moment's notice. Now I was trying to find a quick solution to the all-too real deadline I was up against. With no previous experience of the terrain around me I was prepared to try anything no matter how crazy. I had turned away from the highway leading to surgery that offered no cure and onto a path I had never trodden before.

The path I had chosen led to Evanston. Sustenance for this journey consisted of glasses of raw vegetable juice made up of carrots and a variety of green leaves: spinach, watercress, celery and parsley. I stopped eating meat, and gave up tea and coffee. To boost the immune system, Peter had told us, nothing works better than Vitamin C. He didn't tell us that taking too much can lead to stomach cramps and severe diarrhea. I found this out the hard way and modified the dosage. The combination of cortisone, Vitamin C and vegetable juice shocked my system. I felt nauseous. I decided to reduce the number of Vitamin C tablets I was taking and soon felt better. Despite warnings about kidney damage, I later gradually increased the dosage until eventually I was able to take forty 100mg tablets a day. What I did not know at the time was that vitamin C is water-soluble so the body retains only the small amount it needs and excretes the excess. Given the dosage I was on, I was producing very expensive urine.

Evanston told us that he had meditated for several hours each day and was convinced this had cured him. I tried meditating for as long as I could, but I was still working and could only manage a few hours a day. I found it exceedingly stressful to find enough time to meditate, to make juices, to spend time with my sons, and to work.

Two months had passed since my diagnosis. I was so convinced I would disprove my doctor's dire prediction; I continued to withhold news of my condition from my colleagues. Who, I thought, would make long-term plans with someone who is dying? The answer was so forbidding I dismissed it at once. I lost an entire support system by not telling anyone.

By now, I meditated for up to three hours a day. My children were bemused; I could not give them a reasonable explanation for what I was doing. They later told me they felt rejected by my lack of time for them.

I was about to leave the office one afternoon on my way to a meeting of Evanston's group. I was standing in the lobby waiting for the elevator when our receptionist called to me.

"Joel, please pick up the telephone on the coffee table. There's a call for you."

It was from one of our major clients. A conference had been arranged for the following day, and he wanted to know which of his directors I wished to have present. I tried to concentrate on what he was saying. A popular magazine lay open on the table in front of me. The word 'cancer' leaped out at me. I picked it up to get a closer look. The article was about the Bristol Cancer Help Centre in England and outlined the success its director, Dr Alec Forbes, claimed to have achieved using diet, meditation and exercise to treat patients.

"Joel, did you hear what I said?" my client asked. I had been so busy reading I hadn't heard a word. I turned my attention back to him, and as soon as our discussion was over, I picked up the magazine and told our receptionist I would bring it back the following day.

In the time it took for the elevator to take me down to the parking garage in the basement, I had finished reading the article. The Bristol Cancer Help Centre treated its patients with an unorthodox dietary regimen that excluded meat, fish, dairy products and all preserved food. They were required to drink large amounts of fresh carrot juice each day. The theory was that the Vitamin A in carrots acted as an anti-cancer agent. The story underlined what it claimed was the growing number of orthodox physicians in England who were practising some form of alternative therapy. I felt excited. I was clearly not alone in my decision to try another way of treating cancer. Countless patients had turned away from conventional medicine in frustration. In the absence of a cure for my cancer, I did the same. The Tuesday afternoon groups were my introduction to a new way of thinking.

Thirteen equally desperate people were present at the meeting that afternoon. Ten were women. I wondered whether there was any significance in this ratio. Was it because men are conditioned to maintain a macho image? Facing the knife is manly. Drinking juices and meditating is for wimps. Better, I thought, to be a live wimp than a dead hero. Appropriately, the subject of the day was 'How to adopt and maintain a positive approach'. This was something I could relate to. I had refused surgery. In doing so, I had made a positive choice. Most of the people present had done the same. Save for three who had undergone chemotherapy or radiotherapy, the rest had opted for non-medical treatment.

Arnold had been diagnosed with a brain tumor some months before. He was painfully thin and had a vacant look in his eyes. He had undergone surgery, and now his doctors had nothing more to offer. His wife, Maryanne, brought him to the group in a final attempt to save him. He didn't know what was going on or, if he did, he gave no impression that he did. He sat in his chair like a lifeless doll, his head lolling on his chest, his hands hanging loosely beside him. There was no look of recognition in his eyes from one meeting to the next. At times, he trembled. On one occasion, he toppled out of his chair and began convulsing on the floor. We all sat looking on not knowing what to say as Maryanne cradled him in her arms and patted his head like a child.

"It'll pass," she said. "Carry on without us. There's nothing you can do."

Evanston proceeded to discuss the benefits of maintaining a positive approach. By the end of the meeting, Maryanne was still sitting on the floor beside her husband. I was very disturbed by this, and found it hard to concentrate on anything that evening. I wondered if this happened to all cancer patients at some stage or other, or only to those with brain tumors. If there was nothing they could do to help him – or, worse, if there was nothing he himself could do – there seemed to me to be no point in him trying to carry on living. I didn't meditate that evening. And I hardly slept.

Arnold and his wife never came back to the group but I met her a few weeks later while I was out shopping for vegetables.

"How is Arnold?"

'I wish he had your approach,' Maryanne mused. "If only he had done more for himself. Unfortunately, he doesn't even know who I am anymore. I'm going to lose him." Tears rolled down her cheeks. I didn't know what to say. She went on. "Looking back, it was a mistake for him to have undergone surgery. They turned him into a vegetable." She looked around the store, recognized her black humor, and gave me a wry grin.

"It's ironic, isn't it?" I've learned so much from the group, I now know I'll be able to cope when he dies."

I couldn't believe I was discussing death with a relative stranger. This was a new experience for me. Now that it was in the open, I felt better. A little later, when I was with Sally, I told her about Arnold and Maryanne.

"He lost his faith," was her answer. "She found hers."

I felt as if something or someone was missing from my life. If I wanted to get better, I had to make changes that would be even more fundamental to the pattern of my life. Meditating and changing my diet was only a start. I needed faith. As yet, I didn't have it. Then my wife told me that she was joining another of Evanston's groups.

Janet had nagged me continuously to follow the medical route and have my spleen removed.

"What made you change your mind?" I asked her.

"I haven't," she replied. "I'm joining a different group; I want to help the spouses of cancer patients. They need just as much support as the patients themselves."

"What about me?" I thought.

I did not say anything. I remembered that to be clever is to be still.

CHAPTER SIX

A few days after Dr Gloom had told me that I had Hairy Cell Leukemia, I contacted Dr Unglik and asked him if he knew from whom I could get another medical opinion.

"I don't know anyone else," he replied. "But I will make enquiries."

Two weeks later he called me.

"I've found the name of a highly recommended hematologist. He is also an oncologist."

The following morning I made an appointment to meet Dr John Sullivan, but could only see him in three weeks' time. By then I had embarked on my journey of meditation and diet. Even so, the weeks raced by. Finally, it was time to meet him.

I looked at his thinning sandy hair, his gentle dark blue eyes and flared eyebrows. I saw a fresh rose in his lapel. I was to learn he picked one from his garden every day. I recalled our family doctor's words: "I hear he's the best there is." I wondered if he was also going to tell me to have surgery.

"What do you know about the your illness?" he asked.

"Not a lot," I replied. "All I know is that I don't want to have my spleen removed."

"Why not?"

I told him that I knew it was not a cure and that a spleen is a rather vital organ.

"I can't see how removing it can do me any good. If I'm going to die of leukemia anyway, why should I subject myself to unnecessary suffering?"

'So what do you want to do?"

For the first time, I was asked what I wanted to do.

I told him I was meditating for up to three hours a day and that I'd changed my diet and was now a vegan. I said, "I think if I maintain a positive attitude and believe in what I'm doing, I stand a good chance of recovering." I told him about the support group I was attending, and how it had encouraged me to continue along the path I had chosen.

His answer was unexpected: "I agree with you. I don't think surgery will make any difference. There are some drugs we could try - but I think your attitude is right. I wouldn't be one bit surprised if you're around in two year's time to share a celebratory drink with me."

"You've got a deal," I said. His mention of two years gave me something to aim for.

"If I don't have the operation, is there any point in still taking the Prednisone tablets? I was told that they also make you put on weight, and that's something I can do without."

"I agree. If you've decided not to have the operation, I can't see any point in continuing with them. But go off them slowly," he cautioned.

Dr Sullivan proved to be a breath of fresh air at a time when I was in a fog. My wife was perplexed at his support of my regime. "Are you sure you discussed everything with him?" she asked with suspicion.

"He had my report from Dr Gloom in front of him. He confirmed that I had Hairy Cell Leukemia. When I told him I didn't want to have my spleen out, he said I stood as much of a chance with my method as with any other." Janet didn't believe me.

It was obvious to me that if I wanted to overcome my leukemia, I needed to know as much about my condition as possible. I needed answers. What was causing the night sweats? Why was I getting boils on my bottom and lumps in my groin? Why was I so unbelievably tired? And why was my abdomen getting larger? I had begun worrying about this some weeks before and had gone on a diet, eating special slimming biscuits instead of meals, doing sit-ups as I watched television - all to no avail. "You're getting fat," Janet said. I'm not sure if she realized it was my spleen growing larger.

The diet suggested by Evanston seemed to be my last hope. If it didn't cure my cancer, it would, at least resolve the fat problem. It did. Over the next few weeks, I shed kilos, but my abdomen still kept growing. Dyspepsia was making me more uncomfortable with every passing day. It was time for me to find out more about Hairy Cell Leukemia.

HCL is an unusual and relatively rare type of leukemia that affects the bone marrow, usually of people aged between thirty-five and fifty-five. It had once been known as Reticuloendotheliosis when the nature of the disease was less well understood. Slowly, more and more cases became known. As these were chronicled, so scientists built up a clearer picture of its character. In 1957 Dr Robert Gallo, a medical researcher in the USA who co-discovered the human immunodeficiency virus (HIV) that leads to AIDS identified Hairy Cell Leukemia as being caused by a particular type of retrovirus. This made me consider the question: Can a virus cause cancer? As research later confirmed, viruses cause many cancers.

The name Hairy Cell Leukemia is appropriate. When viewed under a microscope, the cancerous white blood cells appear to have little, spiky projections on them and can be found in the bone marrow, spleen and blood. These cells breed in the bone marrow. As they spread through the body, the spleen and the liver try to filter them out of the blood.

Eventually both these organs become so laden with hairy cells they swell. I had found the answer to my expanding abdomen. I was not over-eating. I was growing hairy cells in my spleen!

An ever-enlarging spleen is one of the most visible characteristics of HCL. The traditional method of alleviating this problem is to remove it. Because the spleen is the major producer of T-cells, the white blood cells that kill bacteria and viruses, it is vital to the functioning of the immune system. Removing the spleen increases the risk of a whole host of other life-threatening infections. Initially, these are minor and can be controlled with antibiotics. Eventually, the infections become progressively more severe and are the usual cause of HCL deaths. Most HCL patients who have their spleens removed soon relapse.

I was pleased I had made the choice I did. I remembered the words of Dr Gloom: "Many people have had their spleens removed and lived normal lives." What he hadn't said was that most of their spleens had to be removed because they had been ruptured as a result of injury. They were otherwise healthy. They did not have the burden of leukemia.

As the cancerous 'hairy' cells spread throughout the body, the bone marrow loses its ability to produce blood. The platelet level also falls and thus the ability of the blood to clot, so the risk of cerebral hemorrhage is increased greatly. Now I knew why Dr Gloom had been so insistent that I take cortisone tablets to prop up my platelet level. He had told me I could bleed to death if my count fell below 20,000.

HCL also eats away the oxygen-carrying component of the blood, the hemoglobin. Though not life-threatening in the early stages, a falling hemoglobin level leads to shortness of breath and places an unbearable strain on the heart and lungs as they battle to carry oxygen round the body.

Unlike other cancers and leukemias, HCL does not respond to radiotherapy, conventional chemotherapy, or bone marrow transplant.

Now that I knew more about my disease, I decided to improve my battle plan. To keep track of what I was doing. I started to keep a journal. It was January 1984. I don't remember the Christmas before at all.

The day after I met Dr Sullivan, I took my second son, who had recently turned fifteen, to the local athletics oval. He was keen to improve his running and I had been coaching him for the past few weeks. Tired as I was, I felt that if I could share in some of their regular activities, my children would not suspect there was anything wrong. Although I clung to my hope that I would eventually win through, my greatest fear was that I would die without having had the chance to say goodbye to them. As I watched him doing wind sprints down the track, I thought that the boys would have to be told, with or without Janet's support. I hoped I would not leave it too late.

I was standing with my hands in my pockets when I felt something hard. I had forgotten to take my cortisone tablet at lunchtime. Here was a message I could not ignore: cortisone was not the answer to my problems. I had to do it my way, without immune-suppressing medication. I flipped the tablet into a garbage bin.

"How are we doing, Pop?" my son panted in front of me catching his breath. I pretended to look at my watch.

"Great," I said, referring to the decision I had just made.

"How about another lap?" I said.

The following afternoon, I met Dr Ainslie Meares. First impression: tall, white hair, ruddy complexion, patrician nose, and bony hands. Second impression: friendly, strong handshake. His eyes bored through me. It was as if he could read my mind.

"Evanston sat where you're sitting," were his first words to me. "I taught him how to meditate." I had not yet told him I had found out about him through my encounter with Evanston.

"The fact that you're here means you've decided to live." I couldn't have asked for a more positive affirmation of the choice I had made. "I can help you, you know," he added.

I told him how I had changed my diet and begun to meditate. He wasn't at all interested in my dietary program. Instead, he talked about meditation and maintaining a positive attitude. He also asked me if there was anything else that was bothering me. I didn't think it was appropriate to start talking about the conspiracy of silence at home and how distressed I was that Janet was helping the husbands and wives of other cancer patients instead of me.

"People who are negative are usually the ones who keep telling others that they must be positive," Ainslie Meares later said. He then told me a little about himself and his work. It confirmed what I later read about him.

A former general physician, he had worked during the Second World War with shell-shocked soldiers. Afterwards, he spent much of his time researching pain control. He then wrote a textbook on the subject: *'Relief Without Drugs'*. Practising as a psychiatrist for over thirty years, his experiences with pain control led him to make extensive use of meditation for the treatment of psychoneurotic and psychosomatic illnesses. In 1976, the *Medical Journal of Australia* first carried his report on intensive meditation resulting in the regression of cancer. For a while, his colleagues refused to acknowledge his techniques. Then, in 1981, the British medical journal, *The Lancet*, published his findings on the regression of cancer in the absence of conventional treatment. His peers could no longer argue with his results, although, with few exceptions, they didn't fall over themselves to endorse his approach.

Meares had travelled extensively through Burma and India, including Kashmir. In his travels, he talked to yogis and other wise men about the ways in which they were able to exercise mind over matter. In Nepal, in the foothills of the Himalayas, Meares met Shivapuri Baba, a wise man reputed to be 134 years old. Half-saint, half-yogi, he made a deep impression on Meares. "This man had about him such an air of serenity that one was immediately aware of his presence," he said

Meares questioned him on whether he had ever felt pain. Shivapuri Baba told him that if he stood on a tack he would be aware of it, but that it would not hurt him. He claimed that he had achieved this state of mind through many years of meditation and ascetic practices. Meares then asked him how he had achieved such control through meditation.

"You can show a child a banana," Shivapuri Baba explained, "but you cannot tell him how it tastes."

The lesson for Meares was clear: the way to understand mental relaxation and to achieve mastery over pain was to practise meditation. Meares found that fire dancers in Bali had learned to walk over burning coals without any long period of training. "So there is a short cut," he surmised. He began to experiment on himself.

Meditation, traditionally, involves concentrating on a sound, a fixed object or the nature of God. Instead, Meares concentrated on the sensation of calm and ease. To convince himself of the effectiveness of his method, he subjected himself to complex dental surgery without an anesthetic. The dentist who performed the operation was so impressed he reported the event in the *Medical Journal of Australia*.

Meares' concept was simple. In times of stress, the body releases greater quantities of corticosteroids, adrenaline and noradrenaline. These stress hormones depress the body's natural immune system. In a state of stillness where there is no tension or anxiety, the body's immune system is not inhibited by the production of cortisone. In such a state, he claimed, the body can heal itself.

At one of our later meetings, Meares told me that he believed our bodies continually manufacture cancer cells. Cells, by their very nature, die and are continually replaced, sometimes with abnormal, cancerous cells. The body's immune system usually handles this process well on a regular basis, killing any malignant cells. When the immune system is weakened, things start to go wrong. Had the cortisone injections I received weaken my immune system? Had they hastened the onset of my illness? There were so many unanswered questions.

"You're not sure if I can help you," Meares said.

"Come!" It was an order. I followed him into another office where he opened the drawer of a large filing cabinet and took out several photographs. Placing one hand over the faces of his patients to hide their identity, he showed me a number of 'before and after' pictures he had taken. If he was trying to impress me, he certainly succeeded.

I visited Ainslie Meares twice a week for several weeks to learn as much as I could from him. I was still working long hours on several projects, and to make up time visited him early in the morning before going to work. As I was also attending Evanston's cancer support group every Tuesday afternoon, I was able to avoid having to explain my absences to my colleagues by referring to my recurring 'dental problem'. Of course, I was lying through my teeth!

Meares' method differed only slightly from that of Evanston. Evanston seated us in a circle on hard-backed chairs. Meares had arranged several large, comfortable high-back leather armchairs in rows in his high-ceilinged, thickly carpeted library. Green velvet drapes framed the windows. The walls were lined with rows of leather-bound books. One by one, he guided his patients into their respective chairs. When everyone was seated, he commenced the session. I never saw the faces of his other patients.

I then realized why Evanston spoke in the slow, dreamy voice he did whenever he meditated. He had copied this directly from Meares. Not only was the tone of the voice the same, so was the wording! Slowly, he told us to focus, in turn, on our ankles, calves, thighs, buttocks, stomach, chest, arms, hands, shoulders, neck, face, and then forehead. By 'letting go' of all tension and tightness in this manner, I was able to achieve a state of calmness wherein I eventually lost all awareness of my self. Meares explained this phenomenon by saying that during sleep the mind remains active while the senses remain inactive, whereas in meditation the opposite applies.

Much later, I came to understand the metaphysical significance of Meares' concept of letting go. At that stage, I thought it referred to muscle relaxation only. Meares startled me at one of these sessions. I was at the point where I could feel all awareness leaving me when he put his hands on my chest. I waited to see what he would do next. He rested his hands there for a while. When my breathing became more regular, he lifted his hands and pressed his fingers lightly on my forehead. The sensation of calm I experienced was similar to that when Sally touched me.

I later heard that many people, particularly women, had stopped visiting Meares because of his 'laying on of hands'. I could not understand why. There was no impropriety involved so I can only surmise that his actions were misunderstood. At one of our discussions in his study, the thought crossed my mind that Ainslie Meares was probably a faith healer like Sally.

Over the next few weeks, I came to know him fairly well. When he learned I came from Africa, he talked about his adventures there and showed me many of the artifacts he had collected on his journeys. He was well informed about witchcraft. In particular, we discussed superstition and its effect on the mind.

"Pointing the bone really works," he remarked. "If a doctor tells a patient he's going to die, he will. It doesn't matter if he's a witch doctor or a medical doctor."

Over the following months, I bought most of the many books he had written. I found him to be more eloquent in the written word. His prose was compelling and revealing. According to him, surgery and harsh treatments destroyed cancer. They also destroyed healthy cells. His method was radically different. Stalking my foe with grim determination and quiet desperation was clearly not the answer. I realized I had to be more relaxed to keep my escape routes open. I continued to modify my diet, to take more and more Vitamin C and to read as much as I could whenever I could steal a moment.

I was killing myself by trying to create more time. Evanston at 5pm on Tuesday afternoons; Meares at 8am on

Tuesday and Friday mornings; Work 9am - 5pm every day. More work 8pm - midnight; Lunchtimes and weekends: meditation. I made a vegetable juice every morning and every evening. My night sweats had not abated. After changing pajamas and sheets, what little time there was left to sleep was becoming increasingly precious. To soak up the sweat I spread a towel or two under me before I went to bed. On some nights, I'd use three, four, even five towels. Even so, I'd wake up completely 'wrung out'. My sons were now on long summer vacation from school. I was hard pressed to explain why I could not spend more time with them. I also had to keep my next appointment with Dr Gloom. I wondered how he would respond to what I had to say.

CHAPTER SEVEN

January 1984:
Platelet count 67,000; hemoglobin level 11.0; White blood cell count 1.8.

"I've spoken to the hospital," said Dr Gloom. It was the first note of satisfaction I had ever detected in his voice. "The operating theatre's been booked, and I've even managed to get you into a semi-private ward."

"I'm sorry you've been to so much trouble."

"What do you mean?"

"I've decided I don't want to have my spleen removed. I don't want to have the operation."

"Do you understand what you're saying? You have a terminal illness with perhaps only a few months to live at this rate. A splenectomy is the only chance you have of saving your life."

"But not permanently."

He countered. "As I said, new drugs are always coming along. Having your spleen out could give you a little more time."

"But it's not a cure. You said so yourself."

"I know. But many people have had their spleens removed and lived normal lives."

"But they don't have leukemia. Anyway, I've made up my mind. I've decided to treat myself."

"How are you going to do that? You don't know anything about medicine."

I was staring at the face of medical paternalism. I felt

discomfited at having to defend my actions. I told him I had changed my lifestyle, changed my diet and become a vegan - and started meditating.

He listened intently as I told him about my visits to Peter Evanston and Dr Meares. He knew I had been to visit Dr Sullivan as Dr Unglik had arranged for him to send my medical file to him. It was now back on his desk. He looked down at the file, then at me.

"What did Dr Sullivan say?"

I told him. He grimaced. His authority had been challenged. He was not pleased.

"I suppose you were entitled to get another opinion. Everyone has a different approach. But I want you to keep taking the cortisone tablets I prescribed."

"I've stopped taking them."

For a moment, he was speechless. Then he scolded me as if I were a miscreant schoolboy.

"I told you to keep taking them. You can't simply stop taking the medication. Your platelet count is getting too low. You're taking your life into your hands."

"Precisely," I replied.

"Oh well, it's your choice. I still think I should monitor your progress."

Then I told him about the large doses of Vitamin C I had started to take. He almost choked with disbelief.

"Don't take too many!" he admonished me. "An excess of Vitamin C can damage your kidneys."

I was dying of leukemia. He was concerned about my kidneys. We clearly saw things differently. I never saw Dr Gloom again.

One day soon afterwards, my wife returned from one of Evanston's support groups all fired up.

"I met someone at the group today you should meet." Her name is Patsy Yates and, would you believe, she lives around the corner."

At that moment, the doorbell rang. It was Patsy, on cue. Prearranged, no doubt.

"I was passing by," she said, "so I thought I'd pop in to say hello."

"I'd like you to meet my husband," my wife said by way of introduction.

What I saw was a short, slim woman with a shock of snow-white hair. Her cheeks were rose-red, her eyes a bright, twinkling blue. At this point, protest was futile.

"Your wife was telling me all about you. I also had cancer. Breast cancer. I had a radical mastectomy, but I'm in remission now. I'm very careful about what I eat, but it's so hard keeping away from chocolates and other nice things. I follow a modified version of the Gerson program. Arthur makes me juices every day. Arthur's my husband. I expect we'll be seeing a lot more of each other from now on. Janet and I are going to visit a well-known jockey tomorrow. He has liver cancer, and he's so positive. And his wife is a darling. She does so much for him. Makes all his juices and changes his clothes for him."

In that moment, I discovered three things about Patsy Yates. Once she started talking, she was like a clock that would only stop when it had run down. The second was that, despite her incessant chatter, she was well intentioned. Thirdly, she had a need to please.

A day or so later, Janet told me what Patsy had said on their way back from visiting the jockey and his wife.

"There's a man living in Ballarat who once had melanoma. Apparently, he cured himself by taking certain herbs and by changing his diet. Patsy suggests you go and see him. She used to visit him, and found him very helpful. Why don't you call Patsy and find out?"

Patsy told me everything she knew about David Perth, so I decided to call him. I told him Patsy had recommended him and told him why I had called.

"Are you sure you have leukemia?" He sounded guarded.

"I wouldn't joke about something like this."

"Who is your doctor?"

I told him.

"I can't promise to help you. But if you're prepared to come to Ballarat I'll see what I can do." He gave me directions on how to get to his house, and I arranged to visit him the following Saturday. On a dry, dusty day, I set out on my own to the country town of Ballarat, a two-hours' drive away. Perth's directions were as precise as his questions. I soon found his house.

David Perth didn't look as if he had ever had a serious disease. He was about thirty-four and stockily built. With his dark hair and clean-cut, tanned features, he was a picture of health. He told me that he had been wrestler before his disease was diagnosed and that he still trained hard to keep fit. I listened intently as he told me how the doctors had been unable to help him. They had sent him home to die. He searched high and low for a cure, and then heard about a clinic for cancer patients in Germany. He went to visit Dr Issels at his clinic where he spent several months under his care. When I asked him what form his treatment took, he replied, "I'm afraid I'm not at liberty to tell you."

"The authorities in this country don't approve of the type of treatment I had. I could get into trouble if they discovered I was advertising it. In fact, I'm going overseas to work in

England. At least they have an open mind about alternative treatments. You'd do well to go there. I'll tell you this, though," he continued, "the site of my melanoma is in the same place I once had a smallpox vaccination on my arm."

I thought of the several vaccinations I had had in my life. Could the vaccinations I had over the years have affected me? I wondered.

He then took a bottle of dark fluid from his desk drawer, handed it to me, and said, "This is wonderful stuff. Try it. No promises, mind you."

I looked at the label. *Veld Goud*. It was written in Afrikaans. Translated it means Bush Gold. It was a Dutch folk remedy commonly used in South Africa, the land of my birth. What a coincidence! I could hear the rustle of the grass. Through the window, I could see the shadows lengthening across a paddock. I was back in Africa.

"This comes from my home country," I said, holding up the bottle.

"That's a good omen."

I asked him if there was anything else I should do. By way of reply he handed me a list that looked formidable, but I followed it to the letter. I stopped eating fish, rice, cottage cheese, rye bread and fruit, but kept drinking the juices on the Gerson diet. I cut out all sugars, including grape juice. Anything with wheat, rye, oats and barley was strictly taboo. For a time, I stopped eating oats, but as it was recommended on the Gerson program I started eating it again a few weeks later. David suggested I take half a teaspoon of pollen granules twice a day and drink several glasses of beetroot juice that he described as the best natural substance to enrich the blood in cases of anemia. With each meal, I was to take 200 mg tablets of hydrochloric acid and pepsin.

"Put a broom under your bed," he added. "But make sure it lies along the north-south axis."

"What for?"

"To channel your energies properly."

This sounded crazy, but I didn't challenge him. I knew that a common practice in South Africa among women of various tribes was to elevate their beds so they could not be impregnated by a *tokolosh*, a dwarf-size mythical sprite. My current state of mind deluded me into thinking that he looked too healthy to doubt. I agreed to visit him again three weeks later. I was mindful I was so desperate I had thrown reason out the window. Even so, I drove back to Melbourne with a sense of renewed hope. Evanston wasn't the only person who had thwarted cancer by following a different path. There was Patsy Yates and now David Perth. I was determined to follow suit.

'Where did you go?" my father asked me on my return.

"To Ballarat."

"For a drive?" He sounded incredulous. "It's a long way."

"I wanted to see the flower show." I couldn't think of anything else to say. The look in his eyes told me he didn't believe me.

My father and I always confided in each other. Since coming to live with us in 1970, I had come to understand him. I trusted him. He was my best friend. Now I was lying to him. This was something I had never done. My conscience pricked me. It felt I was betraying the complete trust we had in each other.

"I think we ought to tell my father," I said to Janet when we were on our own later that evening. She was strident in her determination to keep the news from everyone. Eventually, and to avoid further argument, I reluctantly agreed not to, but I was very distressed. I attempted to restore my equilibrium by meditating. It was impossible. I was too upset. I was still distressed the following day. Again, I tried to meditate. What happened next marked a turning point in my life.

I had shut my eyes, taken a few deep breaths, and started to picture all the tension leaving my body. I was letting go, when suddenly I felt as if I was floating down a long tunnel towards a very bright light. In slow motion, I felt myself drifting closer and closer to it. Slowly at first, the light closed around me and I became part of it. I had no bodily sensations at all. At first, I was a little frightened, but as I drew nearer to the source of the light, I felt more at ease. The brightness was so powerful it blinded me. I emerged from the tunnel and sank into what I can only describe as a cloud, if you could call it that, of total whiteness supporting me buoyantly. How it was possible, I do no not know, but the light became even more brilliant. I could see nothing except a totality of whiteness. It had a clarity that was startling. There was neither up nor down. I had no sense of space or time. In total silence, I experienced an incredible sense of peace and love. I knew that if I had died and this was death then it was all right. There was nothing to fear. I was filled with love for everything and everyone. I felt that if this was, indeed, the white light of eternity then I wanted to be in this state of bliss forever. As it was, I felt as if I was moving – moving back towards the way I had come. I tried to resist and so stay where I was, but my efforts were futile. In a flash, I felt myself heading back down the tunnel, the brightness growing dimmer. Sound returned. I felt compelled to open my eyes. Ahead of me, through the window, was a clear blue sky. I had returned to where I had started.

At first, I thought I had been hallucinating. I was at a loss to explain it, yet in that moment I knew I had experienced something quite extraordinary and quite beautiful, yet I know both words do little to explain the effect. I felt overwhelmed with joy. I wanted to share this news with someone. Later that afternoon, a little reticently, I told Sally about my experience.

"You too," she said, an enigmatic smile on her face.

"What do you mean?"

"I believe many people have had similar near-death experiences. Elsie, my youngest daughter, has also seen a vision."

"So you don't think I'm crazy?"

"On the contrary, I think you're very fortunate."

The memory of my journey down the tunnel and into the light left a vivid impression on me. The experience changed my perception of death. I felt a sense of peace no words can truly describe. Although the manner of my dying still disturbed me, I no longer saw death as a termination of life. I believe that in that meditative state I made 'a leap of faith' and that my near-death experience threw me into a new level of understanding. It is well known that under extreme g-forces, fighter pilots lose consciousness and that their description of their near-death experience is a real phenomenon. I was beginning to discover that being in control was largely an illusion. It would take some time before I truly accepted this as an article of faith. I still had much to learn.

Confirmation of this appeared in a subtle guise about two weeks later. Belinda, the widow of my friend Alan, asked my wife and me to join her for a talk by Dr Elisabeth Kübler-Ross who had arrived on a lecture tour from the USA. Coincidence, someone once said, is God's way of remaining anonymous. I had started reading one of her books, *On Death and Dying*, just the week before. I had finished it on the very day Belinda invited us to join her. I had been fascinated by Kübler-Ross's experiences with dying patients, and had reserved another one of her books at the library.

The following Saturday afternoon I sat in the audience at the Dallas Brooks Hall. Short and slim with greying hair, conservatively dressed and bespectacled, Dr Kübler-Ross walked onto the stage and stepped to the lectern. When she started to talk, I was riveted. She was compelling. Her sense of humor provided the perfect balance to the weightiness of her subject. She related many of her personal clinical experiences and the ways in which she dealt with dying patients and their families. She also talked about the many cases of 'near-death' encounters she had researched. I was fascinated. The experiences of those who had 'died' during surgery and who had been revived to tell their tales were all amazingly similar. Each story was a repetition of my journey down the tunnel. I felt the hairs rising on the back of my neck. I knew that I had not been dreaming or hallucinating. There and then, I signed up for her weekend retreat.

"Remember what I tried to tell you a few weeks ago?" I said to my wife. "She described it exactly as I did."

"But you didn't die."

As with others later, it was difficult to communicate to her just how real my experience had been; that perhaps I had died, in fact, and had returned.

Dr Elisabeth Kübler-Ross was a pioneer in near-death studies and how people coped with dying. She helped to demystify the experience of death. Her vast experience in dealing with cancer patients and their families laid the groundwork for further research and even more groundbreaking discoveries. I was fascinated by the way she described everything with such deep understanding and empathy. Despite her encounters with the dying, she had retained a radiant air of optimism and an infectious laugh. After my first experience in 'the tunnel of light' (I was to have another similar experience later), I had no difficulty in accepting that death is merely a transition.

Kübler-Ross explained that from her hospital studies she had observed that every dying person goes through several emotional stages before they die. She held that these responses are similar for anyone who has suffered loss. Kűbler-Ross identified these stages as Denial/Isolation, Anger, Bargaining, Depression and Acceptance. Over the years, many people have misconstrued her divisions and taken what she said literally. In fact, she herself stated quite clearly that these stages were not sequential and they could occur together. One stage could last a lifetime. In my case, the stages defined by Kűbler-Ross were not clear-cut but a little blurred. I travelled backwards and forwards through them and so I had the opportunity to examine dozens of different possibilities.

The Denial stage is best summed up by people saying, with variations, 'This can't be happening to me', or, 'There must be some mistake'. They often go from doctor to doctor looking for someone who will confirm their belief that the diagnosis is wrong or is not so serious. Some may accept the fact of being ill but deny they are seriously ill. Some may accept that it is serious but deny the diagnosis. Some may accept the diagnosis but deny that the condition is fatal. When they are finally able to express their feelings, they can usually move on to the next stage. Denial does have its advantages. It's not an all-or-nothing situation. It can act as a shock absorber to reduce the impact of a doctor's fatal pronouncement. It can help people defer dealing with their dying until they feel ready to do so.

According to Kübler-Ross, following Denial there is Anger – a more difficult response for a patient's family to manage. The feeling of the unfairness of it all is expressed in many ways. 'Why me? Why now? Why didn't it happen to someone else? It's so unfair!' These are common responses. Most people react against the facts and their anger tends to be directed at people and conditions close by rather than to the disease itself. It may be expressed as hostility to God: 'I pray every day, so why has God abandoned me?'

Kübler-Ross maintained that these feelings of anger, grief, anguish and rage should be allowed to be expressed without judgment. With a shoulder to cry on and someone to talk to honestly, she felt that the patient could begin the next stage: Bargaining.

I believe I was extremely fortunate to meet Sally when I did. In her presence, I was able to express my different moods without having them judged. Her calmness soothed my stress. Her wisdom gave me a fresh insight into my reactions. With her unfailing support, I was able to better manage the storm around me.

The next stage she described as Bargaining which, she said, is not unlike Denial: to buy more time a cancer patient will do anything, no matter how bizarre. Bargaining is often characterized by negotiating with reality as if, by so doing, the condition can be reversed. I believe Elisabeth Kübler-Ross was right when she said that in the bargaining stage people who have never acknowledged God start to bargain with Him/Her/It. Bargaining does work. Research has shown that where patients have a wedding or anniversary or some religious event down the line, they bargain for, and often get, the extra time.

This stage was the clearest for me. I had two reasons to want more time. The first was that I should be spared long enough to see my children complete their schooling. The second was that I would, at the very least, be spared until the end of the year. It was now January. My youngest son would turn thirteen in October and, according to Jewish custom, would then celebrate his barmitzvah or coming-of-age ceremony.

I hoped I would be allowed to be present at this momentous occasion in his life.

Depression is the next and one of the more evident stages. Kübler-Ross called this 'preparatory grief accommodating all our losses, past, present and yet to come.' It is quite understandable and natural. It is a sad time for everyone as the patient realizes he or she is about to leave their loved ones behind, while the family knows they are going to have to deal with their loss.

The final stage is that of Acceptance. I could only marvel at how quickly I had reached this stage. The tunnel of light had given me such a sense of peace and hope that I was at once both accepting and optimistic about my future. Embedded in my genes was the age-old belief of my forebears that hope conquers all. Indeed, I believed then, as I do now, that where there's hope, there's life.

As I reflected on what Kübler-Ross said, it occurred to me that she had not discussed the one thing I felt to be most essential to cancer patients: the need to be alone - to have time to think, in your own time, and without people gratuitously telling you what to do. Taking time out to meditate gave me this opportunity.

I was well aware of the realities of having leukemia. I knew I had to die. If not now, then later. I had hope. I had faith. Time seemed no longer to be important.

Kübler-Ross ended her talk that afternoon with these wonderful words of wisdom: 'The only reliable guide along the spiritual path is your intuition'.

Until my encounter with the tunnel of light, I had consciously suppressed my hunches. By allowing my intuitive sense of survival to prevail, I believe I saved my life. Then she said, "From all my experience with dying people, I've concluded our bodies die but the spirit or soul is immortal."

In time, I would discover that her work provided the basis for further and more expansive research even though many people still cling to her State Theory as if fixed in stone. In time, I would realize that I had placed my intellect on the backburner. I had all the convictions of the uninformed. My season of awakening still lay ahead.

That evening, as I lay in bed reading the Bible – for the first time in over twenty years - the words I read in Ecclesiastes mirrored what Elisabeth Kübler-Ross had spoken about that very afternoon:

'Then shall the dust return to the earth as it was:
and the spirit shall return unto God who gave it.'

Ecclesiastes also reminded me:

'To every thing there is a season,
and a time to every purpose under the heaven:
A time to be born, and a time to die,
a time to plant, and a time to pluck up that which is planted.
A time to kill and a time to heal ....
A time to keep silence, and a time to speak.'

CHAPTER EIGHT

February 1984:
Platelet count 67,000; hemoglobin level 10.8; White blood cell count 1.5.

It was now three weeks since I had seen David Perth. It was time to visit him again. I drove to Ballarat.

"Still keeping to the diet?" He asked.

"Yes." I didn't tell him I had stopped putting a broom under my bed.

"I can't obtain any more of that South African folk remedy for you. The authorities here won't let it into the country. However, I want you to increase your vegetable intake to about 80 per cent of your diet. I know you're on vegetable juices, but I don't think they're enough."

"What about protein?"

"Eat almonds. They're full of protein. If you feel you have to, eat a little fish or chicken. In your condition you don't need much protein."

He then suggested that I contact a friend of his, Alex Schmidt. "He's a naturalist who can show you how to use crystals to check which foods you're allergic to." I didn't realize it then, but I was being sucked into the alternative therapy circuit, being handed, ever vulnerable, from one to another provider of false hope, parting with cash along the way.

"You may not think so, but there could be some foods that are weakening your system," Perth said. His comments echoed Evanston's about the debilitating effect of some additives and preservatives, but it was some time before I saw Alex Schmidt.

"I want you to see your dentist and get him to x-ray your teeth and jaw."

"Whatever for?"

He told me that Dr Issels believed that when a dentist fills a tooth he could never be sure that the cavity is completely free of infection. In his view, a low-grade residual infection could, over time, weaken the body's immune system and allow other diseases to manifest themselves.

"Where can I get a copy of Dr Issels' book?"

"It's never been translated into English. I can get you a copy in German, if you like, but I don't think it's necessary."

"I can't read German that well, anyway," I replied.

"Don't worry about it then. More importantly, each case is different. What was right for me may not be right for you. Keep on with the diet. I'm sure it will make a difference." The possibility of a further consultation with him was immediately ruled out when he said, "I'm leaving for England to work at the Bristol Health Centre with Dr Alec Forbes."

I remembered the article I had read about the Bristol Centre and the alternative methods they used in treating cancer. I asked myself whether this was another random happening or synchronicity. I wasn't sure. Not at that stage, anyway. Everything was happening so quickly. Before I left, Perth made a cryptic remark. Only later did its significance strike me: 'The answer lies within you.'

In my effort to leave no stone unturned, I made an appointment to see my dentist a few days later. He confirmed David's comment about the possibility of residual infection and arranged a full mouth x-ray for me.

"If we do find a problem," he said. "I would be most

reluctant to operate on you. Your platelet count is far too low." A few days later, the results of the x-ray revealed no sign of neglected infection in either the tissue or bone. The entire exercise had been of academic interest only - and a waste of money.

For a while, I kept to the dietary regimen recommended by Perth. When I first saw Evanston, I had thought, 'If he can do it, so can I!' My two meetings with Perth left me with the same impression. He had also overcome the most difficult odds. He looked so robust. I felt confident that I would also succeed. When I later related the story of my trip to Dr Sullivan he said, "David Perth used to be a patient of mine. He had a grade three melanoma. He had radiotherapy, but then refused further treatment. Obviously, he didn't tell you."

It was the beginning of February 1984 and less than three months since Dr Gloom told me I had leukemia. So much seemed to have happened since and yet I felt as if I had been told about my disease only yesterday. I felt sure I had taken the right road, but maintaining my composure was becoming more difficult. The night sweats continued unabated. I wondered if I would ever get a full night's sleep without interruption. My spleen was getting even larger and this made me feel increasingly uncomfortable. My lymph glands were extremely painful. The painkillers I was taking did not help.

Normally, the spleen cannot be felt, as it lies in the peritoneal cavity against the diaphragm and the abdominal wall. As it swells, the lower end of it moves sideways to the right and downwards. An ultra-sound scan of my spleen earlier that week revealed that it had grown to a length of about twelve centimeters. I had no idea that it would eventually reach twenty-eight centimeters in length and become the subject of intense curiosity among doctors and medical students alike. As it was, I could feel my internal organs being compressed. I had great difficulty in swallowing food. With my spleen jammed up against my stomach, I was struggling with increasing dyspepsia. There were times when I couldn't keep my food down. I found it easier to eat less and less. My weight dropped and I was beginning to look quite gaunt. It was one heckuva way to lose weight.

The subject under discussion at the next cancer support group I attended that month was 'Stress, and how to reduce it'. As Evanston described the effects of this on the body, his words echoed what Meares had told me. 'Imagine,' Meares had said, 'walking down the road. Suddenly a large dog leaps out from behind a hedge. You're so startled you leap backwards, your heart racing. The owner of the dog appears and calls him back. The danger is averted. You let out a great sigh of relief.'

It's well known that when we are threatened by some danger or other, our bodies release a large amount of adrenalin to prepare it for a fight or flight response. It explains why some people in sudden, life-threatening situations are capable of performing feats far in excess of their normal ability. In everyday situations, too, our bodies release large amounts of adrenalin when confronted with stress-producing situations. The boss shouts at you. Your neighbor uses the lawn mower when you're trying to have a nap. A newscaster says something on television you don't agree with. Under these conditions, fight or flight is usually not the appropriate response. All that adrenalin is unused. It builds up in the body. Meares claimed that his technique of meditation dissipates stress and provides the same 'letting go' as that sigh of relief. I came to think of it more as 'the sigh of release.'

"Surely," I asked Meares when I visited him a day later, "if you can find the cause of your stress aren't you halfway to knowing how to cope with it?"

"Not always, was his reply. "Some people, when their cancers are so advanced, don't have time to dig and delve for the causes of their problems. My form of meditation is so much simpler and more effective." His solution seemed straightforward enough: meditate more. This was easier said than done. The boils on my bottom and the lymph nodes in my groin and in my armpits were growing larger and more painful so I was finding it more difficult to sit and meditate for any length of time.

"Dr Gerson's book you ordered has arrived," said the owner of the bookstore over the telephone. Had the solution to my problems arrived in the mail?

This was no small pamphlet with a little, sketchy diet in it. It was a book of over 400 pages. The detail in it was mindboggling. Everything seemed to be backed by scientific evidence. Dr Gerson's personal story proved to be equally fascinating.

Dr Max Gerson was a doctor who, in the 1920's, had successfully treated many patients with chronic degenerative disorders. He did so through a diet he originally developed to cure his own migraines, which kept him in bed for days on end. He received worldwide acclaim when he successfully used his treatment to cure 446 out of 450 cases of lupus vulgaris. In 1928, a patient asked him to treat her cancer of the bile duct using his dietary program. She even offered him a signed disclaimer absolving him of any responsibility if it failed. Within six months, she was cured. She sent two further patients to him. He cured them both. With the same diet, he claimed to have successfully treated patients with tuberculosis, asthma, arthritis and diabetes.

One of the best-known patients he treated for tuberculosis was the wife of the famous author, humanitarian, and Nobel Peace Prize winner, Dr Albert Schweitzer. After seeing the results of the Gerson therapy, Dr Schweitzer wrote, 'I see in him one of the eminent geniuses in the history of medicine.' Compelled to flee Nazi Germany in 1938, Gerson was licensed to practice in New York. He set up a clinic and, in 1946, became the first physician to demonstrate recovered cancer patients to a US Congressional Committee. The lobby for conventional treatment by surgery, radiation and chemotherapy defeated by four votes a motion to support extensive research into the Gerson program. Forty years later, the United States Cancer Institute and dozens of bodies around the world officially endorsed a healthy diet and good nutrition in the fight against cancer but not, as so many claim, to cure it.

The title of the first chapter of Dr Gerson's book, *'A Cancer Therapy. Results of 50 cases'* was 'The 'secret' of my treatment.' The first line says, 'Of course, there is none.'

I was seduced by the pulling power of his copy. Had I know then what I now know, I would have returned the book and asked for a refund. But I was desperate for answers and so I read doggedly on. The first mistake people made, he said, was to attempt to treat symptoms. According to Gerson, the symptomatic treatment of anything in nature, including human beings, was harmful. The second mistake was to believe that cancer was an incurable disease. The third mistake lay in the way dietary tests were conducted: one substance at a time is tried and its effect observed. Then another substance is tried, and so on.

Gerson's view was that 'a normal body has the capacity to

keep all cells functioning properly. It prevents any abnormal transformation of growth. Therefore, the task of a cancer therapy is to bring the body back to that normal physiology, or as near to it as possible. The next task is to keep the physiology of the metabolism in that natural equilibrium. A normal body has additional reserves to suppress and destroy malignancies. It does not act in that manner in cancer patients, where the cancer grew from the smallest cellular unit freely, without encountering any resistance. What forces can suppress such a development? My answer is that this can be accomplished by the oxidizing enzymes and the conditions which maintain their activity'.

According to Gerson, the ideal aim of a cancer therapy is to restore the oxidizing functions. This involves detoxification of the body, providing the essential elements of potassium, and adding oxidizing enzymes.

I now appreciated why Evanston said the Gerson program was difficult to follow, and why anyone attempting it needed assistance. It was a full-time occupation.

The list of forbidden items in the diet outlined by Gerson was formidable. As I read it, I realized the diet Evanston recommended was the one Gerson had prescribed to prevent sickness, not to cure it, a fact that over time I came to realize seems to have been lost on most people who followed his program. Fortunately, I had started avoiding some of the banned items. Tobacco was one of these. I had been a heavy smoker (up to two packs a day) but had stopped two years before my diagnosis. Alcohol was another. I enjoyed a good whisky, now that was out - as was chocolate, ice cream, canned foods, tea, coffee, and cocoa. All oils and fats were precluded, as was salt, so were all berries and pineapple (he said their aromatic acids cause unfavorable reactions), nuts and avocado (too much fatty acid) and cucumbers (too much sodium). Meat and fish were not allowed until I reached a point of recovery. I could not use a pressure cooker or any utensil made of aluminum. To make the vegetable juices so important to the diet, I had to find a juicer that would grind and press as a replacement for my centrifugally operated one.

The schedule outlined was too difficult to follow. There weren't enough hours in the working week to keep to it. On weekends, I was able to manage most of the dietary requirements.

8:00 a.m. Orange juice followed a little later by oatmeal.

9:00 a.m. Green juice (depending on availability, made from several of the following: lettuce, chard, escarole, watercress, red cabbage leaves, green pepper, endive, Cos lettuce, spinach, beet tops and one medium-sized apple).

10:00 a.m. Apple and carrot juice.

11:00 a.m. Liver and carrot juice.

12:00 p.m. Green juice.

1:00 p.m. Apple and carrot juice, followed by lunch.

My choices included raw salad, warm soup; a large baked potato, unsalted buttermilk, non-fat yoghurt and stewed fruit.

2:00 p.m. Green juice.

3:00 p.m. Liver and carrot juice.

4:00 p.m. Liver and carrot juice.

5:00 p.m. Apple and carrot juice.

5:30 p.m. Apple and carrot juice.

6:00 p.m. Green Juice

7:00 p.m. Apple and carrot juice followed by dinner.

I could choose from non-fat, unsalted cottage cheese, non-fat yoghurt, unsalted buttermilk, warm soup, a large baked potato, two cooked vegetables and raw or stewed, unsweetened fruit.

The soup had to be made from organically grown vegetables and cooked in a heavy non-aluminum pot. I had to add a variety of medications into it to increase the potassium level. I stopped taking the hydrochloride and pepsin tablets, and took acidol-pepsin tablets instead as well as raw linseed oil and niacin. I later added Lugol's solution (five per cent iodine, ten per cent iodide in water), when I was able to obtain it.

I had still not adopted the full Gerson diet program. One of the main ingredients required was a mixture of various types of potassium. I had no idea where to acquire these and wondered if I would ever have the time to track them down. As for a juice made up of liver and carrot. Yecchh!! Anything but that!

Another major part of the program was detoxification. What is eaten has to be eliminated. As such, Gerson maintained that detoxification was essential to the success of his treatment. This meant using coffee enemas. The thought alone was repugnant. I wondered where I would be able to purchase the equipment required to perform this bizarre procedure.

Whether it was because I was trying to do too much, or because of my deteriorating condition, I was becoming extremely fatigued. Not sleepy tired, but rather as if someone had pulled out the plug connecting me to my energy source. I had become aware of this earlier but ascribed it to my work schedule. Now I wasn't so sure. Then Patsy came to the rescue.

"You didn't look well when I saw you this afternoon," she said on the telephone.

"I'm not."

The following morning Patsy came visiting bringing with her 'healthy' cake she had baked. "If there's anything my husband and I can do for you, let me know. Arthur doesn't work, so he can drive you anywhere you need to go." She told me about how she also made vegetable juices and had found a green grocer who sold fruit and vegetables that were free of pesticides and fertilizers. She gave me the address. For the next few months, I bought my greens there. While I still had the energy, I saw no reason why anyone else should do my shopping for me.

CHAPTER NINE

March 1984:
Platelet count 66,000; haemoglobin level 10.8, White blood cell count 1.9.

Throughout this period, I was focused on starting up my own advertising agency. To do this, I had to secure enough clients to generate a reasonable amount of income for the short- and long-term. Even under ideal conditions, this would be time-consuming. It requires a healthy body. It demands stamina. I had neither. I was finding it harder and harder to breathe. My blood counts were falling. My spleen and lymph glands were getting larger. My gums had started to bleed spontaneously. To control the bleeding my doctor had prescribed vile-tasting blood-clotting tablets to suck. How I imagined I could start up my own agency, I don't know.

Fortunately, I was clearly still in a state of denial. It enabled me to continue attending Evanston's groups once a week and to visit Meares twice a week. I also visited Sally every evening on the way home from work. I believe her calmness raised my spirits and boosted my confidence through this energy-consuming period. Over a cup of herbal tea, accompanied by a biscuit or two she insisted I eat. Sally always listened attentively to my discoveries. Not a day seemed to pass when I did not find a new book or article on cancer.

It was the autumn of 1984. The days were getting shorter. The nightly sweats were exhausting me. It was becoming harder to get up early each morning in order to make my juice before going to work. After visiting Sally in the evenings, I prepared the vegetable juices I had to drink later on. Finding time to meditate was becoming harder. My wife insisted I find a hypnotist to help me maintain a positive attitude. To appease her, I telephoned Dr Vaughan the following day and explained the situation to him.

"I know a doctor who practices hypnotherapy," he replied.

Dr Sam Gordon was fascinated by my reason for seeing him. He listened to the program I had adopted and how I was attempting to fit this into a heavy work schedule, and questioned me at great length. He then said: "I don't understand why your wife feels the way she does. I think you are being very positive. I also think you're being very brave."

He then asked me where my mother was. I was face to face with the past. At that moment, I could not see the relevance of his questions.

"Why do you want to know about her?"

"You've told me all about yourself, your problems with your wife and about your wonderful father. You've told me how you adore your sons. You haven't told me about your mother."

"There's nothing to tell."

"I don't believe that someone who occupied so much of your life can be left out of your life story?"

"I believe she died four years ago."

He leaned forward and he asked me, "Don't you know for sure?"

I explained how she and my father had separated and how my father had come to live with my wife and me. Briefly, I outlined the circumstances surrounding the split between my mother and me ten years earlier. I explained how she had finally rejected me. I stopped seeing Dr Gordon after two more visits. I was disconcerted by his constant discussion of my mother. I felt it had no bearing on my leukemia and my fight to stay alive. I was doing the best I could in the most positive way.

I had never grieved over my mother's death, never come to terms with our relationship. It was to remain unresolved until I was ready to deal with it, years later. Digging up my past did not seem a productive way of managing the moment. I wanted to stay downwind. I was prepared to try anything that would give me a fighting chance. I am ever grateful for the profound lessons in survival John Ndmande had taught me as a child. Attack was one. Defence was another.

The evening after I saw Sam Gordon, I drove with my wife to fetch our youngest son who had been to visit a friend. As we sat in the car waiting for him to come out, I spoke about Sam's constant references to my mother. I could not contain myself. For the first time since I received that shocking letter from her, I gave way to my pent-up anger at how she had rejected me and how she had believed I had failed to understand her motivations.

The following morning I still felt shaken. I was undecided whether I should attend Evanston's group that day. But I went. As if I had channeled the subject of the meeting, he talked about forgiveness. He stressed the need to remove negative influences from our lives.

"How can you forgive someone if you're not face to face with them?" I asked.

"Write to them," he replied.

"And if you don't know their address, then what?"

He suggested that when we meditate, we need to picture the face of the person we want to forgive in front of us so we could tell him or her we forgive them for all the sins they committed against us. Then, he added, we need to ask them to forgive us for all the sins we committed against them. He continued: "Visualization can have the most dramatic impact on the course of a disease. It's quite easy. Relax your body as if you were preparing to meditate. Then visualize what I suggested." It seemed simple enough, but I wasn't quite ready to try it. Not yet.

A few days later, I was browsing the shelves in a bookstore when a title caught my eye: *'Getting Well Again'* by Carl and Stephanie Simonton. It was the very book Evanston had talked about when referring to visualization. I scanned the pages and read that Carl Simonton was a radiation oncologist; his wife, Stephanie, a psychotherapist. The book described the results they had achieved using visualization with cancer patients at their Centre in Fort Worth, Texas. Their belief was that patients should not depend entirely on medical treatment to get better. They maintained patients have to participate in their own recovery, and can do this through their beliefs, feelings and attitudes. They recommended that they also follow a sensible diet and exercise regimen.

Their argument followed an obvious question: 'why do some people recover and others die when the diagnosis for both is the same?' The Simontons asserted that some people recovered because they felt they could make a difference to the course of their disease. They had a stronger will to live than others. I was equally fascinated by their next claim that there was a direct link between the occurrence of a serious illness and a highly stressful 'life event' such as divorce, loss of a child, immigration, loss of a job. Hans Selye at the University of Prague had undertaken much work linking stress to illness as far back as the 1920's. Later, in 1967, Dr Thomas Holmes and his colleague Richard Rah at the University of Washington School of Medicine devised the *Holmes-Rah stress scale* (you can Google this) that assigned numerical values to stressful events in one's life that alter established patterns of behavior. How people responded to change was the key: those who adapted well were far less likely to develop disease. They found that 49 per cent of the people who had scored more than 300 points had a high risk of getting a serious illness within twelve months. Only nine per cent of those with scores below 200 reported illness during the same period. Using the table indicated in the book, my score was 388.

I believed I had coped reasonably well with changes in my life. I was shocked to think that the opposite was possibly true and that the resulting stress may have made me susceptible to leukemia. Later, I realized that their claims were hypothetical and that not everyone reacts to stress in the same way.

The Simontons had also found that many of their patients had suffered severe depression long before their cancers were diagnosed. If having the blues as I did while living in England several years earlier was an indicator, then I certainly qualified. The similarities between my experiences and those quoted by the Simontons seemed close to the bone. Perhaps they were in the bone!

Instinctively, I felt that if what they said was correct, they offered me another potential weapon with which to keep my foe at bay. Working with cancer patients, they had found that people could play an active role in controlling or driving their cancers from their by bodies using strong imagery. Their technique was similar to that suggested by Evanston except they relied heavily on the imagery of an army of your own white blood cells attacking the cancer cells, and that you should view any radiotherapy or chemotherapy you were receiving destroying the cancer cells in the same way.

The feeling of wellbeing produced by this method was similar to that of the color healings I received from Sally. As I sat in her chair, she would ask me to take three or four deep breaths.

"Relax," she would say, as she placed one hand on my shoulder. "Picture a color, preferably gold, scarlet or red. Imagine yourself being surrounded by it. Feel it going through you." As she guided me into the color I had selected, she massaged me lightly with her free hand across my shoulders and down my back and arms. She then lightly massaged my temples and my forehead. Eventually she would tell me to open my eyes when I was ready.

Ten minutes of Sally's simple daily healings were the equivalent of a daily bottle of tonic!

Despite their apparent recorded successes, I discovered that the American Cancer Society did not endorse the Simonton method. Many years later, their research was even further discredited and fell into their category of 'unproven treatments'. I was unaware of this at the time. But how, I thought, could I fit in another twenty minutes? I decided to alternate between meditation and visualization.

Evanston had said visualization could be used in order to overcome long-held resentments. I found the technique for doing so in the Simontons' book. It seemed to me that Evanston had borrowed all his techniques from Gerson, Meares and the Simontons and promoted them as his own. I decided not to return to his groups.

The Simonton method of visualization to remove negative feelings was easier said than done, but I persisted. Over the next few weeks, I found it easier and easier. It seemed to work. Instead of pushing all thoughts of my mother aside, I began to feel a lot more comfortable thinking about her. Even so, it would take some time before I came to see how my mother's influence on my life could not be ignored. I could no longer downplay the part she had played in my life. I had to try to understand why she had acted the way she did. It would take a journey back in time to Africa many years later to uncover facts of which I had been unaware. Only then would I come to understand my mother. Only then would I know why I had felt so uncomfortable when Sam Gordon questioned me about her. I had never seen my mother's actions in any light other than how they were related to me. It was not until I was able to comprehend why she was so insecure and how her attitude towards men had been shaped and hardened by life with her husbands, her strict upbringing and her sense of shame at the behavior of her wayward brothers. When I finally realized this, I understood why she was so unrelenting with me and why she set higher standards for me than for anyone else and tried to fast track me into maturity. I believe that when my mother insisted that my father come to live with me, she embarked on a self-fulfilling suicide mission. If I had refused, she would have concluded that I was innocent and knew nothing of my father's ongoing and clandestine relationship with his first wife. If I accepted what I thought was my responsibility as a son, which I did, my mother would have assumed I knew about and condoned his activities. There was no question of redemption. While I have no doubt that our perceptions influence our judgments there are, at core, some truths of which we are completely unaware or which, even though they stare us in the face, we do not see. I was only able to find it in my heart to forgive her many years later when I finally found out that she had not imagined my father's activities at all.

My friends, Arthur and Patsy, had dropped in for a visit. I told them I had been for a blood test earlier, and that the results were disappointing.

"You're not following the Gerson program properly," Arthur said.

"I don't have time."

"Then stop work."

"I can't afford to."

"You can't afford not to," he replied.

His words jolted me. I had tried to fit my recovery program into my normal schedule. It was exhausting. It wasn't successful. I didn't know it then, but the answers to some of my questions lay just around the corner.

CHAPTER TEN

April 1984:
Platelet count 45,000; haemoglobin level 10.8; white blood cell count 1.7.

NATURAL HEALTH FOODS AVAILABLE HERE.

The sign above the pharmacy caught my eye. I was sitting in my car, parked in front of the shop. "What am I doing here?" I asked myself. I had no answer. I had passed this shop daily to and from work over the past few years, but I had never been aware of either the shop or the billboard. I decided to follow my instinct. I walked into the shop. A man in a white coat approached me.

"May I help you?" he asked. He had a friendly face with gentle, rounded features.

'I don't know," I replied. "In fact, I don't know why I'm in your store, I'm sure there's a reason. If I look around, I may find the answer. Do you mind if I do?"

"Go ahead," he replied quietly.

At the rear, I found a rack full of books. The titles covered a host of cancer cures about which I had never heard. I started speed-reading one of them: *'The Laetrile Story'*. I read how Laetrile, also known as amygdalin or Vitamin B17, had apparently been used very successfully in treating cancer. Its name derived from its chemical name, Laevomandelonitrile-beta-glucoside, or mandelonitrile glucuronide. Dr Ernesto Contreras in Mexico had explored its use and opened a clinic using it to treat patients from around the world. I discovered that laetrile is found in the kernels of stone fruits, beans, nuts, berries, grains and grasses. In high doses, it is very toxic and has to be medically administered.

"Do you know someone who has cancer?" the friendly chemist asked.

"I do."

"What type of cancer do you have?" he asked casually. I told him. "Well," he said, pointing to the book I was holding. "There's part of the answer to your problem."

"Laetrile? Where can I get it?" I asked.

"You can't get it in this country. It's illegal."

"I notice here," I said, "that the actor Steve McQueen tried it, but it didn't save him. Yul Brynner, too."

"Yes, but they had to go to Mexico to get it."

"There must be some way to get it here?"

"No," he replied. "But you can do the next best thing."

"What's that?"

"You can chew apricot kernels."

"Where do I get them?"

He squinted at me for a moment, and then said, "I can get you some." He paused. "What about coffee enemas? Are you taking them?"

It was a decisive moment. I had been trying to avoid them. Purging wasn't new to me. When I was a child, my mother used to force me to drink castor oil and orange juice. It was her panacea for everything from a sore stomach to a cold. The very thought of them was repulsive, but everything happening to me pointed towards my using them. Evanston had used them. My friend, Patsy, was still taking them. Several other people I knew were doing likewise. They were integral to the Gerson program in order to detoxify the liver. According to him, the caffeine in the coffee is absorbed through the colon and carried to the liver, which, in turn, is stimulated to produce more bile. Bile removes toxins. It seemed there was no way I could avoid them now. Coffee by mouth has a different physical effect and was forbidden.

"How?" I didn't know how to broach the subject.

The chemist, whose name was Jack Thompson, handed me a carton. In it was a plastic jug with a tube leading out of the closed end. The end of the tube was attached to a hard plastic nozzle specially designed to be inserted into the rectum. A tap on the nozzle controlled the flow. He handed me a pamphlet entitled *'Colon Cleanse, the Easy Way!'* By Vera Burnett and Jennifer Weiss.

"You'll also have to fast for eight days," he said.

"Where can I get these ingredients?" I asked as I flipped through the pages.

"I have them here."

"Do I need all of them?"

"Yes, I believe it doesn't work if you don't do it properly." As I had already discovered, nothing I was doing was working. So far, I had only partly followed Gerson's dietary recommendations. I was not adding the potassium compound required to the green juice. I wasn't even drinking the required number of juices. I wasn't taking all the medication prescribed. I thought that to give myself a better chance I had to include more of the Gerson requirements in my regimen. It was all or nothing now. I hoped my gamble would pay off.

"What's all that?" My wife asked, as I unloaded the many items I had bought at the chemist onto the kitchen table.

"I'm going on an eight-day fast," I replied. "I'm also going to take coffee enemas."

She looked at me as if I had gone mad.

"Don't worry," I said, "If the children ask, I'll tell them I've gone on a special diet. If they ask any more questions, I'll think of an answer."

I read the pamphlet, which explained in detail the basis of this cleansing diet. Five times a day I had to drink a mixture of juice, water, bentonite (a clay that absorbs water), psyllium seed and chlorophyll. The bentonite and psyllium were to bulk up and absorb toxins accumulated in my body. I had to take cascara tablets for their laxative effect, and chlorophyll, calcium, herbs and vitamins to keep up my strength while on the fast. According to the plan, I could not eat, but I could drink herbal teas, vegetable broth or juices. I had to drink at least five glasses of water a day. Last, but not least, I had to take the coffee enemas. The method was similar to that prescribed in Gerson's book, so I followed his recipe.

To prepare the coffee, I boiled three tablespoons of ground coffee in slightly over a liter of water and allow it to simmer for twenty minutes. When the brew had cooled to body temperature, I strained it into the special jug. I let gravity have its way by slinging the contraption over the doorknob in the bathroom. I then placed an old towel on the floor. This was as much to keep me separated from the cold floor tiles, as it was to mop up any spills. And there were some! There wasn't much room for error. I lay on my right side, and allowed a little of the mixture to flow into my rectum by controlling the tap at the end of the tube. At first, I thought I would burst, but managed to control it. Eventually, when all the coffee had drained out of the jug, I lay as still as I could for fifteen minutes. I was sure that if I moved even one centimeter, it would all pour out of me. There were times when I thought I was going to explode. Painful cramps came and went. Somehow, I managed to bear it. At the fifteen-minute mark, I leapt up and plonked myself on the toilet. The relief was incredible! The sight is best left undescribed. I masked the smell with a deodorizer.

There was a humorous consequence to all this. Whenever friends came visiting, they were greeted with the smell of freshly brewed coffee, but were invariably puzzled as to why I never offered them any.

For eight days, I took an enema every morning. This was always a lengthy process, taking almost an hour. Retaining the brew and releasing it took long enough. To keep the appliance germ-free, I washed it out before and after each procedure with a powerful chemical antiseptic, chlorhexidine. I boiled enough coffee for at least four procedures, but still had to warm up what I needed each time. I then prepared the vitamin and mineral mixture, and drank a glassful of this before leaving for work, and also prepared two further bottles of juice to drink at work, packing these very carefully so they wouldn't leak in my briefcase. When I returned in the evenings, I took another enema. Before retiring for the night, I would drink two more glasses of the mixture. My timing was not perfect. The chairman of our company had chosen that week to entertain as many clients over luncheons as possible. Somehow, I managed to make excuses as to why I could neither eat nor drink. I pretended I had sworn off the sizzling grilled prawns and succulent beefsteaks being passed under my nose. I allowed my glass to be filled with chilled white wine, but I didn't drink it. Watching everyone eat and drink, I was sorely tempted to give it all up and start again the following week. I held firm.

For the first two days of the diet, I felt extremely uncomfortable. I developed a throbbing headache that grew in intensity. I could feel I was becoming weak. By the fourth day, my headache had disappeared. I was feeling much better. My hunger pangs had subsided, I no longer felt like eating. By the eighth day, I felt positively elated. My senses were ultra-sensitive, and I was filled with an incredible sense of vitality. I decided to extend the diet for a further three days. It was with great difficulty and a certain reluctance that I eventually stopped. I was so euphoric I was sure I could fly. On the eleventh day, I started eating a little fruit, and did so for two days. On the thirteenth day, I ate a little rice, and then returned to my original diet.

The blood test I had a few days later showed no improvement. I had been a little too optimistic about the result. I felt deflated for a few days, and then my mood lifted. I had lost much of the weight I had hoped to lose.

"I was once on that fast," Patsy said to me when I visited her and Arthur the day after I ended it. "I thought I told you all about it? It was a long time ago."

"No, you didn't." I replied. "Did it help you?"

"It was good, but it doesn't last long enough to be of any use."

I told them that my latest blood test had shown no improvement. My counts were still falling.

"You're not following the Gerson program properly," Arthur said. He had told me this before. "Patsy could never have followed the program if I hadn't retired from work to help her."

"What happened?" I asked.

He told me how Patsy had been diagnosed with breast cancer thirteen years earlier. She had undergone a radical mastectomy. Two years later, she suffered a stroke. She recovered. All was well for five years. Then a visit to her physician confirmed she had secondaries in her hips and spine. Hormone therapy was prescribed. She joined Evanston's support group and started an intensive course of meditation. She started taking coffee enemas and followed Evanston's dietary program. Five months later, she was told she was in remission. Much to Arthur's distress, Patsy eased up on her diet, reducing the number of enemas she was taking. She was still meditating but doing so less often. And she was drinking only two or three juices a day.

"It's the church that keeps me going," she said, the excellent effects of the hormone therapy notwithstanding.

"What church?" I asked.

"I go every Saturday afternoon to St Aloysius's. Father John is the reverend there; he's such a nice man. He really makes you feel welcome. And the healing I get there! Why, it's fantastic! I feel so much better. You can come with me, if you like."

Attending church on a Saturday afternoon did not appeal to me. I was using time over the weekends to catch up on what I wasn't able to accomplish during the week: to make more juices, take more enemas, meditate more and spend time with my children.

"No thanks,' I replied.

"Can't blame you," Arthur whispered. "I think it's a load of hogwash."

I tried to keep an open mind. I had always regarded 'healing' and suchlike activities as quackery. I still do, but I was desperate. It was clear that Patsy had a childlike faith in the church and in healers.

"I'll stick to what I can do in the meantime," I replied. "Maybe some other time."

"You should get a juicer like the one we use," said Patsy.

"They're very expensive," said Arthur. "It'll cost you about $500. But I reckon it's worth it. It's similar to the type Gerson recommends for his program."

"Wait a moment," Patsy interjected, "Joel doesn't have to buy a new one. Mary (who was Mary?) bought one for her mother, but she died before they could even use it. I wonder if she still has it?" She bounced out of her chair and raced to the telephone. She returned a few minutes later and told me that her friend still had it. "If you're prepared to drive to their house, they'll sell it to you for $300."

I had been on my version of the Gerson program for a month. I now understood why Evanston had said it was the most demanding regimen to maintain. Gerson himself stated that it was advisable not to start the treatment if for any reason strict adherence to it was not possible. I wasn't drinking the prescribed thirteen juices a day. I wasn't taking the coffee enemas needed every four hours. I had still not obtained all the supplements that were required. Getting the right juicer was a beginning. Three days later, I bought it, still in the original packing. As I walked into the house with it, my father said, "Will you please tell me what is going on here?"

"This is a much better juicer," I replied.

The look in his eyes told me he didn't believe me. "Why are you on this crazy diet? Is something wrong?"

I was in a dilemma. Should I tell him? He knew something was amiss but couldn't put his finger on it.

"This is the same kind of juicer as the one Patsy uses," I said.

My father looked puzzled. "I understand. But why does she use it?"

I couldn't tell him. I tried another approach. "This machine grinds the vegetables so the juice is squeezed out. The old one is simply a high-speed grater."

"I see," said my father. "Sounds sensible to me." He looked at me askance.

I read what Gerson said about raw liver juice as part of his therapy. I could not ignore this issue forever. He considered fresh calf's liver to be 'the most important weapon we have in the fight against cancer.' He admitted that the most difficult part of his program was to restore full liver function. To do so, liver and Vitamin B12 injections had to be administered. Defatted ox bile and pancreatin tablets also had to be taken. I decided to follow the program one step at a time, the first of which was to buy the liver.

"Do you sell calf's liver?" I asked the first butcher I called on.

"Calf's liver, ox liver, what difference does it make?"

"I'll need a fresh supply of calf's liver every day."

"Get out of here!" He said, angrily. "Are you some sort of weirdo?"

The reactions of the butchers I saw after that were only slightly less antagonistic. For the most part, they said they couldn't guarantee the age of the liver. When they asked me why it had to be so young, I said I was 'on a special diet.' The looks on their faces said it all. They thought I was crazy. They had no idea how desperate I was. Then my luck changed. I called in on a butcher's shop close to where I lived.

"Why do you want such fresh liver?" he demanded. I looked at him. He was in his sixties, short, stocky and very pugnacious. His thin, greying hair was combed neatly backwards. The wrinkles that creased his kind grey eyes were at odds with the sharp, clipped tones of his voice. I decided to tell him.

"I have leukemia," I said.

"What's that got to do with wanting fresh calf's liver?"

I told him I had refused to have surgery, as it was not a cure. I explained that I had opted for an alternative, non-medical way of treating myself through diet and meditation. As I spoke, his eyes filled with tears.

"My first wife developed cancer several years ago," he said. "They took her spleen out, but it made no difference. She died. We had tried meditation and a diet given to her by a friend. A part of that diet included drinking a juice made of carrot and raw liver, just like yours." He took a handkerchief out of his pocket to wipe his eyes. "Please accept my apologies. Listening to you has quite unsettled me. My name is Jim. What's yours?" He jabbed his hand towards me. His grip was like a steel vice.

"I'll get you your livers," he said, after I told him about their role in the Gerson program. "I'll try my best to get them for you every day." He did. He said he would not accept payment from me. "If you insist on paying, you can get your liver somewhere else." Jim was a real help. He demanded that I keep him apprised on my progress. I did. And I paid him back for the free livers by buying all our meat for the family from him. Until he was compelled to sell the shop some time later and left town, Jim and I remained firm friends.

"Now what are you doing?" my father asked, as he watched me unpack a fresh liver.

"I'm going to juice it."

"You are crazy," he said. I decided there and then that I could no longer lie to him.

"Dad, there is something I have to tell you."

In the privacy of my father's bedroom, I told him of the events leading up to and including the diagnosis. I explained the reasons for the juices and the theory behind them. "I do wish you had told me sooner," he said, a grimace on his face, tears in his eyes. "I knew that something was wrong. You know, you look terrible. Your skin is yellow, your eyes are sunken - you're as thin as a rake. Who did you think you were kidding? I've known you all your life."

We hugged each other and we cried. The relief was intense. For my father, knowing that I would undoubtedly die before him was the cruelest of blows. He kept repeating, "This isn't how it's supposed to be." I don't know how long I rested my head on his shoulder, but it was long enough to re-establish contact after all these months of secrecy. Time shrank. Once again, I was that four-year-old child riding shoulder-high on the Sherman tank that was my father. He reminded me how Dr Melle had told him that with a chest like mine, I could survive anything.

"Jakey," he said, "if you think you'll pull through this, I know you will. You've always done what you said you would." He took off his glasses, wiped his eyes, and took charge.

"I'll make the carrot and liver juice," he said. "At least I don't have to drink it."

The strength that carried him through the Russian Revolution and two world wars had not waned. He had enough sap for both of us. I was getting wearier by the day. I was grateful for his help. I don't know how I would have managed without my eighty-two-year-old Father Christmas.

As soon as he had juiced the mixture, he turned to me and said: "You'll please also do me the favor of drinking it where I can't see you." I took the glass outside and stood on the patio. This was it. It looked like chocolate mousse. It smelt like carrot and liver. Did I sip it or what? I decided to get it over with as soon as possible. I quaffed it in one go. Then I threw up into the garden.

"It needs more carrots," I told my father.

"Okay", he said. "I'll make you another glass." The

addition of more carrots made the mixture slightly more palatable. Still, it took some time before I got used to it. At least, I thought, I had added another arrow to my quiver.

"Jakey," Dad said, "I have every confidence in you. You do whatever you feel is right to get yourself better. I'll help you every way I can."

I made a green juice every morning; Dad made me a green juice and a carrot and liver drink every night. On weekends, I was able to have three drinks a day. I had to believe I had taken the next important step in my struggle to heal myself.

CHAPTER ELEVEN

May 1984:
Platelet count 44,000; haemoglobin level 10.2; white blood cell count 1.3.

I followed the modified Gerson program for the next few weeks. Gerson maintained that recovery could take up to eighteen months. In some cases, it had occurred in as little as a week, but I was not following the program to the letter. I felt I was doing the best I could under the circumstances. In the meantime, the tablets Dr Sullivan had given me to stop my gum bleeds had been successful. I continued visiting Sally every day and drew great strength from her. My courage came from the lessons John Ndmande taught me as a child. "Listen well," he would say, waving a prophetic forefinger to the sky, "and you will hear."

When I was learning to ride my bike, I kept crashing into Mrs Poxen's rose bushes. I was scratched all over. John watched me for several minutes.

"No time to cry," he said. "Impi never gives up."

I never forgot Johns' words. I was, if nothing else, always determined to succeed. If getting into the water-polo team meant swimming longer laps, I did so. If being selected for the athletic team meant training longer hours, I did so. I wasn't about to give up. I was going to keep tracking my foe until I found out how to overcome it. I was determined to ride that bike even if I kept falling over, even if I bled to death doing so.

I read voraciously. I bought several books and borrowed

dozens more from the library. I clipped every article I came across in newspapers and magazines. I asked Patsy to do the same. I built up a library and a reference file. The more I discovered, the more complex I found the cancer puzzle. Each author told a different story. Every success was attributed to something different. No two doctors seemed to agree on anything. As far as dietary recommendations were concerned, I tried everything: garlic pills, selenium, thymus sweetbreads, biotin, desiccated liver, papaya enzyme and Vitamins A, C and E. There seemed to be no end to what was on offer.

Then I reread Gerson's book. He placed emphasis on the importance of potassium. His potassium mixture had to be added to every drink except the liver juice. I decided to visit Jack Thompson, the chemist.

"I need potassium to add to my concoctions," I told him. "Can you please order these for me?" I handed him the list: 33.3g potassium gluconate; 33.3 g potassium acetate; 33.3 g potassium phosphate (monobasic); all to be added to 900 g water.

It took him several weeks to obtain them. One had to be imported from Germany.

"I also need to make up a Lugol's solution," I said.

"What's that?"

I explained that it consisted of five per cent iodine and ten per cent potassium iodide that were supposed to restore the electrical potential of cells and accelerate the healing process. I told him that Dr Gerson considered it another key element in his diet.

"I'd check it out with your doctor first," he said. "Iodine can do strange things to you."

I decided to wait. In the meantime, I bought several

packets of peppermint tea for good reason: Gerson's book had warned that coffee enemas could produce varying reactions. I had experienced severe spasms in my abdominal area some time after I had taken one. I had also suffered nausea and agonizing headaches. To add to my discomfort, my tongue had become coated. Peppermint tea, according to Gerson, mixed with brown sugar and a little lemon, washes out the accumulated bile from the stomach and the duodenum. I drank several cups a day; they became my anodyne. The coating on my tongue disappeared.

Slowly a pattern began to emerge from the information I was building up. A common theme was that the environment in which we live is so polluted it wasn't surprising that I, like many people, was suffering the effects. Everything I ate seemed to be bottled, canned, preserved, powdered, sprayed or frozen – almost all with added coloring and flavors. In as many ways as I possibly could, I tried to avoid all these apparent no-no's including artificial sweeteners. I stopped using fluoride toothpaste and threw out all the naphthalene flakes we used to keep moths out of our clothes. Ghee doesn't burn, so I bought this to use instead of butter for cooking. I persuaded my sons to limit their intake of peanut butter. Peanuts are legumes not nuts. They grow underground so they can be contaminated with fungi. Emulsifiers are added to keep them soft when they are made into peanut butter. Some cola drinks contain phosphoric acid, while commercial ice cream contains invert sugar – both, according to Gerson, highly carcinogenic.

"Why can't we have them?" my sons asked.

"You can, but cut down on them. Some of these things can cause cancer," I told them. "You don't have to stop eating them. Just to be aware of them and reduce your intake."

"But our parents never told us," my wife piped up.

"Right," I replied. "And just look at me."

In a further attempt to keep my head above water, I decided to make sure it was as pure as possible. If chemicals are added to water to make it potable, what happens to the chemicals? I learned that chlorine is added to water to remove bacteria. By some accounts, chlorine produces free radicals that can cause cancer, as well as forming chloroform and carbon tetrachloride, both acknowledged carcinogens. Fluoride is added to water to help prevent dental caries, but according to some of the books I was reading, there was no proof that it does not cause systemic damage. I decided to buy a water purifier. But which one to get? The first one I bought had to be fitted over the tap outlet. The tap in our kitchen had a slight flange on it. No matter how hard I tried, it would not fit. I returned it to the store. A few days later, I found another brand, but saw that hot water passing through it turned the water cloudy. I wondered whether it had destroyed the filter inside it.

I asked Arthur. As an engineer, he knew a thing or two about these matters. He told me he had tried several brands, but none seemed to be effective for long.

"Hot water will almost certainly destroy any filter in a short space of time," he said. For the next few days, I drove from health-food shop to health-food shop. I telephoned cancer support groups, and spoke to several people. They confirmed what Arthur had told me. About two weeks later he telephoned me to say he had found a water purifier that seemed to be the best available.

"It's sensibly made," he said. "It's made with several filters in it so it will presumably provide better filtration. It's not a permanent attachment, so it can't be affected by hot water. I have one here I've bought for Patsy and me. Come over and have a glass." He was right. The water from it tasted as fresh and as clean as spring water. I ordered my own. The company that made it charged a fee for renewing the filter once a year. A small price to pay, I believed, for an assured supply of uncontaminated water.

There was a side benefit to all this. The taste of a good whisky is unaffected if it is diluted or cooled with ice cubes made with pure water. I had sworn off alcohol but my visitors commented so favorably on the taste of the Scotch I offered them, I revealed my 'secret'. I'm sure the company's turnover rose since I became their unofficial advertising representative!

Patsy was a mine of information. She phoned me a few days later. "Jack has Bach flowers," she said, "and I've bought a bottle of the rescue remedy." Patsy always assumed you knew who and what she was talking about. Bach flowers sounded like a flowery cantata. I was fascinated. Flowers to cure cancer? What next? It was necessary for me to visit Jack to restock my supply of vitamins so I asked him about Bach flowers.

"They're drops made from the juice of flowers. There's one for every problem."

He handed me a pamphlet. "That'll tell you all about it and which ones you need. There are six essences to choose from. I make them up from those," he said, pointing to several large, pear-shaped flasks behind the counter.

An English physician, Dr Edward Bach, promoted flower remedies as a combination of herbalism and homeopathy. He claimed that certain emotions produce chemicals that remain in the brain unless they are removed. The natural substances that will eliminate them are the extracts of certain flowers. I scanned the list. Some seemed to match my needs, others hinted at covering my options, so I chose Hornbeam for mental and physical weariness and Star of Bethlehem for the after-effects of shock or trauma. The Rescue Remedy was mandatory. This was a composition of Cherry Plum, Clematis, Impatiens, and Star of Bethlehem.

To make up the required selection of six, I took a bottle of Olive (for mental or physical exhaustion), Vervain (for loss of faith or extreme anguish) and Gorse (for despair). As Jack decanted my selection into glass vials, I read the accompanying pamphlets he had handed me. Positive affirmations were to be said before taking each lot of drops, 2 – 4 in a teaspoon of water at least four times a day.

The list of affirmations seemed simple enough. Many of them reflected much of what I had been through, and would still face. To name a few: 'I deserve love... I no longer need to get even with my parents in order to succeed ...I can best fulfill myself in my own way, doing what I choose, always coming from my own center ... I let go of the illusion that anyone else's decisions have power over me without my full agreement,'

The list raised several issues. I was desperate for love. I hadn't resolved the issue with my mother completely. For another, Sally, Patsy and Arthur apart, I seemed to be surrounded by people who kept insisting that I should develop a positive attitude. What did this mean, really? The pact of silence meant I couldn't talk to anyone. The affirmations convinced me of one thing: some unseen force was driving me on and wouldn't let me surrender. Ultimately I would appreciate my instincts had been correct: positive thoughts without positive actions are meaningless.

It was May. My forty-fourth birthday was upon me.

Would it be my last? Based on the doctors' predictions, at the rate I was going, it would be. Janet and I took my father and children to one of our favorite restaurants. It was with a hollow feeling that I watched the tableau before me. Would I ever celebrate another birthday with my children? I was saddened to think that their world was about to change and I couldn't prepare them to face it. I tried to lighten the mood by jesting with my sons. My father understood and joined in. There was such an air of unreality about the situation. I was glad when dinner was over.

Later, I considered my options. It was six months since my diagnosis. Despite Dr Gloom's dire prognosis, I was still alive. I continued visiting Sally every day but had stopped seeing Meares. His rooms had been badly damaged by a severe fire the week before. He told me he would not be seeing anyone for a while. I had stopped attending Evanston's groups. In any event, I had learned all I possibly could from them. I remembered the list of names that Dr Vaughan had handed me. I had seen Evanston. Dr Singh lived in Bombay. That left Peter and Jane Smith. I remembered his words: 'You don't have to go to the Philippines for psychic surgery.'

There is nothing quite like good dose of skepticism to compel you to doubt the apparently plausible claims of alternative practitioners. I had never seriously entertained the idea of psychic surgery. I had read a couple of Lyall Watson's books so I was familiar with the subject. A friend of mine had travelled to the Philippines for treatment of her varicose veins. Evanston had claimed some amazing results when he went there with his wife, Sharon. She had, apparently, filmed his operation. Even though Peter had been 'opened up', there was no scar. As skeptical as I was, I still wondered what psychic surgery could do for me. I had leukemia with no solid tumors. Maybe I wouldn't need surgery. In any event, how could I explain an overseas trip at this time to my colleagues and friends - or to my children for that matter? Going interstate was different. I could always pretend I had to film a television commercial where we could be assured of a daily supply of sunshine.

"How do I contact the Smiths?" I asked Patsy.

"I can tell you," she said. "I went to see them with Evanston. They were wonderful. We stayed in a little motel close by, and went to visit them every day. I see them whenever they come to Melbourne, every few months. I don't know when they're coming again."

I wasn't prepared to wait for their next visit. I had to stay downwind. I had to examine every option. I was getting more breathless by the day as my hemoglobin levels continued to fall. My swollen lymph glands were a constant and painful reminder that my body was under attack. And I was so, so very weary.

I wrote a lengthy letter to the Smiths, explaining my condition and circumstances and asked them for their advice. Their reply came a few days later. It was, they said, a good time to visit them; over the next few weeks they had a light schedule and could add me to their current list of appointments. They said I should allow for a week of treatment. They explained that a one-off healing would not be sufficient. In any event, such a long journey would be tiring, and I would need all the rest in between I could get.

I put my long-held plan of forming my own advertising agency into the 'pending' tray in my mind. I stopped moonlighting. I didn't have enough energy to work, meditate, make my juices and still spend some time with my family. I also looked extremely tired. This made it easier for me to tell everyone I had decided to take a week's holiday and fly to the sun. Nobody seemed to care. I had cut myself off from my colleagues by not lunching or having sundowners with them. Much later, I would learn they all thought I was having an extra-marital affair.

I soon discovered what it must be like to be a secret agent. I had become paranoid about anyone finding out the true object of my mission. I now needed to find a travel agent who was both obscure and reliable. A few, furtive days later, I found an agency close to my office. I confirmed a return trip, leaving in seven days. To find accommodation, I telephoned the Smith's secretary. She suggested I stay at a motel close by.

"It's only a five-minute taxi ride away, so it's really handy," Susan said. "It's also inexpensive." As tired as I was, I managed to find the inner strength to travel.

It was an uneventful journey. The flight provided me, in the physical sense, with much needed space to reflect on what I had done and where I was going. I had to try something different to arrest my falling blood counts. By now, I had convinced myself that part of the problem lay in the fact that I wasn't following the Gerson regimen to the letter. To do so would have meant giving up work. I realized I still had to deal with the unresolved issues with my mother as well ending the conspiracy of silence I had bought into. I was keenly aware I could die before I had sorted out these matters. Although my experience in the tunnel of light had reassured me about life after death, I felt uncomfortable about the manner of my dying. I didn't want to die in pain. I didn't want to die in a sterile hospital ward surrounded by strangers and attached to life-support machines to no avail. With so much still undone, I simply wasn't ready to die. Not yet.

The plane landed. I came back to earth. From the motel,

I telephoned the Smiths. Susan, advised me to rest. It was mid-afternoon. "Jane and Peter prefer to see patients in the mornings," she added. I took a nap. I meditated. I went for a walk on the beachfront. I was tired. My falling hemoglobin level meant I was constantly breathless, but the thought of something new occurring in my life gave me strength. For an hour or more I reveled in the sound of sea, the salty taste of the surf, and the going down of the sun. I slept well that night.

The following morning, at ten o'clock precisely, I arrived at their home. Susan asked me to complete a personal details form. Under the heading of 'problem', I wrote 'spleen cancer'. My somewhat cynical mind was up to its old tricks. Susan asked me to wait in the reception area. I looked at the four people around me: three women, one man. Listening to their conversations, I noted that two had cancer, the third Parkinson's. I couldn't tell whether the woman had been successfully treated or not. The man was a sugar farmer. I gathered he had returned for the umpteenth time. 'Something' was working for him, I thought.

Then it was my turn. Susan led me into a room, asked me to strip to my underwear and lie under a sheet spread over a couch. She stepped out of the room. As I changed, I wondered what I had let myself in for. I lay down and waited. Minutes later Jane Smith entered the room. In her early forties and trim of figure, she had long black hair and an oval, strikingly handsome olive-skinned face. She stood behind my head and closed her eyes. I could hear her praying. She stepped to the side of the couch on which I was lying and placed her hands over my spleen. She seemed to go into a trance. Almost immediately, I felt a strange vibration, as if a tuning fork had been struck and placed on my abdomen. She asked me to turn onto my stomach, and placed her hands over the spleen area on my back. Again, I felt that strange vibration. She told me that she could feel no lumps.

"You don't need psychic surgery," she said after a while. "There are no hard tumors. You don't have a solid cancer."

She hadn't been fooled by my description of spleen cancer. I told her I had leukemia.

"The answer to your problem is in your mind," she said.

"What do you mean?"

"You know what I mean," she shot back at me. "Your personal problems with your wife are getting in the way."

How did she know how close to the truth she was! Had Patsy told her?

"You must meditate," she said.

I led her briefly through my experiences over the past six months. I told her how I had modified the Gerson diet. I explained how I meditated according to Meares' method. I described how I practised the Simontons' method of visualization. She nodded in approval. I told her about my tunnel-of-light near-death experience. She smiled.

"You're fortunate to have had that experience. You should also pray. Faith can help you through the most difficult times. As far as diet and meditation are concerned, your attitude is extremely positive, but you're not attacking the main problem." She tapped her forehead. "We'll talk about that when I see you next. In the meantime, go back to your hotel and have a good rest. You'll want to sleep after this healing."

I returned to the motel. I slept for the rest of the day. She was right. The treatment had left me completely exhausted. From the second day fate intervened so I never had a chance to rest directly after my healings. Jane had obviously told Susan about the diet I was on. After my second visit, Susan handed me a juice extractor.

"I managed to borrow this from a friend," she said. "I'm sure you don't want to miss out on your juices while you're away from home." I was grateful for her concern and her caring. I started making my juices as soon as I returned to the motel.

Jane and I talked a lot. She kept referring to what she described as my 'emotional problem'.

"It's all very well to have a positive approach," she repeated. "But you must surround yourself with positive people. Negative people and negative words drain your energy. You have to be single minded. Don't be swayed from the path you've chosen. Love will come your way. Be patient. God loves you. Your family loves you. Learn to love yourself a little."

Jane's advice challenged me to consider how freely I was exercising my choices. At one level everything seemed so random and beyond my influence, and at another I was making my own decisions based on my frantic efforts to stay alive. Was it a combination of the two? Either way, I was aware how I was denying the urgent need to address the relationship issues with my wife, pretending to be the breadwinner by working crazy hours, and imagining that my sons and friends would never find out.

This state of pretense was shaken by events that started on the second day I visited the Smith's home. Jane had completed her healing on my spleen. I was sitting in the foyer waiting for a taxi to take me back to the motel. I was in a reverie, half-thinking about the much-needed rest I was going to enjoy, when I realized I was eavesdropping. I could hardly avoid hearing the speaker. He was highly voluble. He was also highly agitated.

"What's the point of carrying on?" He was addressing the man seated next to him. His voice was so loud I was sure he intended us all to hear. Or else he simply didn't care. "I'd be better off going home, getting out my gun and shooting myself." He paused. "No one can do anything for me. Not even these people!" he said as he jerked his thumb in the direction of the unseen Smiths.

"If they can't help me, who, in God's name can? You're all wasting your time here – and your precious money." His voice had risen even higher. He was now shouting.

I didn't stop to think. I blurted out, "You can help yourself, you know."

He turned to me. "What would you know?" He glowered at me. "I have cancer, you know. What's your problem? Why are you here?"

The look on his face switched from a mixture of anger and resentment to one of disbelief when I said, "I have leukemia. I also want to get better. That's why I'm here."

"I could do with a few words of help, friend, if you have the time."

"Can do," I replied. I did have the time. I had planned to return to the motel to rest, read and meditate. Fate had intervened in the form of a fellow cancer patient.

"Right. Cancel his taxi!" he shouted at Susan. "This bloke is coming to my house for lunch and a talk." There was a collective sigh of relief as I left with the source of agitation. We walked out to his panel van parked in the driveway.

"Here," he said. "Let me open the door for you. It's hard to open if you don't know how."

As he opened the sliding door for me, I looked more closely at him. His right arm was missing! He saw that I had noticed.

"Lost the bloody thing in a lathe just after my honeymoon," he said.

I spent a lot of time with Bruce Dougan that week. He was in his early fifties, short and, I suspect, at one time had been stocky. Now he was thin. Under his wavy greying hair his eyes were a bleary blue. He looked so tired. The pain showed on his face. Bruce had advanced cancer of the liver.

I marveled at the way he drove his van. Whenever he had to change gear, he took his hand off the wheel, changed up or down, and then grabbed the wheel again. He did it so quickly he hardly missed a beat.

"Hope the cops never catch me," he laughed. "They'd take my license and my livelihood away."

Bruce had an infectious laugh. He was a genial man who tried his best to mask his pain. He turned the van into his driveway. "Come on," he said. "I'll show you what I've achieved. This is what I'll be leaving for my wife and son." He waved his arm towards his house. It was a modest dwelling set in surroundings of great beauty. His back lawn ran gently down to a jetty on the river. There was no boat. A neat, fully equipped work shed stood to one side.

"I run a caravan repairs business with my nephew. I took him on when the doctors told me I only had a few months left."

"When was that?"

"A few months ago," he quipped. "They said I should have radiotherapy. When I asked them if it would help, they said 'No'."

"That's bloody stupid," I told them. "Why make me undergo treatment if it isn't going to help?" He turned to me and added, "That was when I decided to give the Philippine witchdoctor and his wife a go. They haven't helped me yet. I don't suppose they ever will. It's too late. I'm going to die." I looked at him. He wasn't joking. He was deadly serious. "I've made arrangements to leave the business to my wife. She'll manage it with the nephew." It was a sobering experience for me to meet someone in such a sorry state. He was in a lot of pain. No matter how hard he tried, there were times when he could not hide his grimaces. "I'm trying to drink lots of carrot and vegetable juices, but it doesn't help."

"Why don't you give up work and concentrate on getting better?" I asked him. I had just asked the question of myself.

"I'd have to sell this place," he replied. "If I do that, I'll have worked for all this for nothing."

"But if you don't, and you die, you'll have worked for all this for nothing, anyway."

"What can I do?" he asked. His plaint sounded familiar. "I've been given so many different and conflicting pieces of advice; I don't know what to do. I'm in such pain I couldn't be bothered to try them all. Come on!" he changed the subject. "Come and meet my wife and son. Let's have lunch."

Blonde, close-cropped curly hair turning slightly grey, a round face with pink cheeks, a big woman, a large smile. There was no way Liz could hide the inner pain she was experiencing. It had almost erased the laughter lines around her eyes. She was extremely polite. She asked me how I was coping. I said I was trying to meditate. I added that I wasn't doing enough of it.

"I can't find a quiet enough place to meditate," Bruce interjected. "Liz is always banging pots and pans."

"What am I supposed to do?" she asked. "I can't move the kitchen."

"So what do you want me to do? Die?"

As we ate I watched Bruce, Liz and Andrew, their blond,

handsome ten-year-old son. It was a pitiful sight. Liz believed Bruce was about to die. Andrew was too innocent to understand. Life for him was his peanut-butter sandwich. Bruce was trapped between fear and despair. He was hoping for a magic wand. In my ignorance, I tried to help. I talked to him at great length about the benefits of meditation. Me, the expert!

"If it's too late to save your life," I said. "At least meditation may help you manage the pain." I also thought it would help him work through his anger.

"I really miss having my beer and pork scratchings with the blokes down at the pub," he muttered. "What have I done to deserve this?"

On the fourth day, he agreed to try meditating. "Only if we do it together."

We sat in the garden and I led him through Ainslie Meares' technique. Slowly, the pain lines seemed to ease. After a while he looked at me and said, "I feel better than I have in quite a while. I wish you could stay up here with me. It's easier to meditate with you around."

The following day, as we were driving back to his house, he turned to me and said, "Forget about going back to the bloody house. Let's go to the beach."

The beach was crowded. Bruce managed to park the van near enough so we didn't have far to walk. We were dressed in shorts and short-sleeved shirts. We found a space on the main beach. We spread out towels and lay back in the sun.

'How ironic!' I thought. 'This is quite bizarre! Here I am with leukemia. Bruce has liver cancer and one arm. We're lying here as if we don't have a care in the world. Sooner or later neither one of us will have anything to worry about.'

Bruce must have read my thoughts. He turned to me and

said, "Look at all those people. They think they're never going to die. Just look at them!"

We couldn't stop laughing. It didn't matter that people were staring at us. We knew something they didn't!

We swam. I had been a strong swimmer once. Now I could barely hop over a wave. Bruce simply rose and sank as each wave came and went. Our laughter was hysterical. Back on the beach, we talked. Bruce was adamant that unless he was given space to enjoy peace and quiet, he would never be able to meditate. I didn't have an answer. We talked about death.

"I'm afraid of dying," he admitted, with look of pain in his eyes.

I replied that I had also been afraid of death for so long. I told him about my panic attacks. I described my experience through the tunnel of light. As I talked, I felt more comforttable about the subject. My growing ease conveyed itself to Bruce. He also became more relaxed with the idea of dying.

Then it was time to say goodbye. My week was up.

"Can't you stay on?" he pleaded.

"I wish I could," I replied. "We'll stay in touch."

"I'm taking you to the airport. I won't let those bloody cab drivers rip you off."

"I'll go by bus."

"No you won't!" he snapped. "If you're going to leave, I'm going to make darn sure you go!"

We hugged each other and said goodbye. For months afterwards, we kept in touch by telephone. He wasn't able to maintain a program of diet or meditation. In quiet desperation, Bruce started attending church services.

"He's an honest priest," he told me. "He hasn't promised me anything. I respect him for that." The quality of his life improved, but not his time. In between bouts of excruciating pain, he found some peace in that church. Bruce died shortly before Christmas that year. He left with the understanding that his death was not the end. He finally accepted that life was eternal.

My encounter with Bruce Dougan was a turning point and the first of many more intimate experiences with someone whose life was in transition. It was my first exposure to someone who was facing the same angst as I was. I saw reflected in Bruce so much of the anger, denial and resentment I had felt. I saw so many of my own domestic conflicts reflected in his. It made me aware, far earlier than I would otherwise have experienced, of the changes I needed to make if I was going to stand any chance of surviving. It gave me a head start in regaining much of my lost self-confidence. I made, and lost, a very special friend that year.

CHAPTER TWELVE

June 1984:
Platelet count 40,000; haemoglobin level 9.7; White blood cell count 1.2.

I believed that the healings I received from Jane had given me the strength to spend time with Bruce. By late afternoons, I was drained. I rested to regain my energy. On three or four occasions, I had managed to stroll down to the beachfront at sunset. It was in moments like these that I took the opportunity to reflect on what I had learned. Improving the positive aspects of my life would take a little time. In the meantime, I had to correct a number of omissions.

While I was away, I had been unable to take any coffee enemas. The water I had been drinking wasn't purified. The juicer Susan had lent me was of the high-speed grater type – not the kind I'd want to use for too long. According to Gerson, this process destroys natural enzymes. I had made up a green juice every day, but not the crucial liver and carrot combination I still believed in.

"The potassium gluconate I ordered for you has arrived," Jack said as I walked into his chemist shop. It was my second day back. I had come to restock my supply of vitamins and supplements.

"There's enough here to last for ages," he added. "I made it up for you just as you requested. Where are going to keep all these bottles?" He pointed to several one-liter bottles.

"May I leave them here with you and get you to refill my bottles when I need them?"

"You certainly can. By the way, in your absence I located a source of liver-extract tablets. There're quite expensive though. And you'll need a prescription to get them."

An integral component of the Gerson program was the need for a daily intramuscular liver injection. Such medication was unavailable, so liver-extract tablets would have to suffice and it was very doubtful if I would ever persuade Dr Gloom to write a prescription for them. It was time to find a doctor who would be more tolerant of my approach. It was time to find a positive influence - a Dr Light. I remembered my visit to Dr Sullivan and the open attitude he had shown to my approach. I telephoned his office and made an appointment to visit him two days later.

A blood test confirmed the increasing severity of my symptoms. My gums had started bleeding again so Dr Sullivan prescribed more of the vile-tasting coagulant tablets. A normal spleen cannot be felt. By now, mine felt like a small pumpkin. It was about fourteen centimeters long and was hurting to the point where I needed to take stronger painkillers. I was still breathless. It wasn't a case of having to take an extra breath or two. I had to concentrate on forcing the air into my lungs. Walking was getting harder. I had to stop every few paces to catch my breath.

Anemia is one of the symptoms of leukemia. I was most unhappy about this. I felt the answer to my difficulties was to get back on the diet, such as it was. I believed I had to try harder, if possible, to follow the Gerson plan even more closely. I also needed advice on an ongoing basis. I came to an agreement with Dr Sullivan. I would attempt any method of treatment I thought appropriate. He would monitor my progress and answer any questions I put to him, and he would tell me if he thought any of my methods were life threatening.

He agreed that it would always be my choice as to what I did. I asked him for a prescription for liver-extract tablets. "They can't do you any harm," he said, as he wrote out the prescription.

"What about iodine?" I asked. "Gerson's program calls for Lugol's solution. Can I take it without harming myself?"

"Send me the details and I'll let you know."

I made photocopies of the relevant pages from Gerson's book and gave them to Dr Sullivan. He later advised me that he could see no danger in using Gerson's iodine solution.

"If you find yourself developing any unusual symptoms, though, please let me know."

With the potassium brew, the liver-extract tablets and the Lugol's solution, I had obtained almost all the ingredients I needed to comply with the requirements of the Gerson program. Near enough, but not good enough. I was not drinking as many juices a day or taking as many coffee enemas as called for in the program. Working as I was, I simply didn't have the time. I felt I was doing the best I could under the circumstances. I wondered whether it was enough.

I wrote to Dr Gloom and told him of my decision. I thanked him for his concern and interest in my case, I explained that I had decided to switch my care to Dr Sullivan and asked him to forward my case history to him. His reply indicated he would still be willing to see me should I decide to seek his advice. I have no doubt that every cancer patient owes it to himself to find a doctor with whom they feel more than just comfortable. They must believe they can trust them. They must find a doctor who will always tell the truth - and accept that the patient, not the doctor, owns their life.

Visits to my doctor were no longer filled with gloom. I had met someone with whom I could discuss a range of issues not necessarily medical-related. Most importantly, Dr Sullivan expressed great interest in the program I was on. His attitude gave me confidence to persevere with the course I had taken. Best of all, he listened – and he answered my questions. Over the next few months, I must have driven him crazy. His solution was simple. One day, as I was about to leave his office he handed me a large book.

"Here, take this," he said. "It's not that latest edition, but I think you'll find it useful in answering some of your questions." From this weighty tome entitled *Hematology. William J. Williams, Ernest Beutler, Allan J. Erslev, and R. Wayne Rundles. 1972. McGraw-Hill Inc.* as well as many other journals, I learned a great deal about cancer and blood disorders in general, and more about the symptoms associated with Hairy Cell Leukemia in particular. I needed a different sort of book, however, to provide me with the answers to my emotional problems. That would have to wait until I took on that task myself.

I was engaged in an endless round of continuously boiling up coffee and then taking the enemas behind closed doors. I was making vegetable and raw liver juices as well as vegetable soup, to say nothing of the actual preparing and cleaning up. I had to keep track of and take countless tablets. I went for healings. I meditated. I did visualizations. During all this time, I still managed to read in order to learn more. And I was still working.

It is undoubtedly painful for a family to find themselves thrust into a situation where they are compelled to watch the often bizarre and always desperate attempts of someone they love trying to heal themselves in the face of a life-threatening disease. Had Janet been able to see the benefits of what I was doing she might have been supportive. Evanston had claimed he could never have succeeded without the help of his wife Sharon. Patsy said she could never have done it without Arthur's help. The closer the family bond, the easier it is. My sons found it highly rewarding when they eventually took an active part in my program. But that was later. My advice to loved ones: give all the help you can, but don't take over.

Shortly after my return from visiting the Smiths, my gums started to bleed again. To staunch the flow, I pressed my thumb and forefinger over the bleeding area. The pressure eventually stopped the blood. When this didn't work, I resorted to sucking my blood-clotting tablets. They didn't always work either. Then one night I woke up with a slimy, salty taste in my mouth. I switched on the lamp next to my bed. My pillow was soaked in blood. It happened again the following night. I was in serious trouble.

"I think I must stop working," I said to Janet the next day. "I'm not getting any better. To have any chance of recovery I need to do everything properly. I have to give my recovery my best shots. The Gerson plan, meditation. I need to rest. I'm so beat. The night sweats and bleedings are keeping me up most of the night. I can't carry on like this."

Janet was concerned about our financial situation if I stopped working. I pointed out that we had one insurance policy to cover lost income due to illness and another that would safeguard her and the children if I died. She would not agree. My isolation was exacerbated by the odd looks my children gave me when I made my mysterious brews and took coffee enemas for no apparent reason.

Everyone thinks his or her own situation is unique. As long as they maintain this belief it isn't easy for them to realize they are not alone in their dilemma. I came to know many people faced with a life-threatening disease whose spouses or families were unable to cope. Not everyone has the emotional resilience to deal with a dying loved one. Equally, there are many patients who cannot face the prospect of altering their lifestyles or rearranging their priorities even though they are aware that by doing so they stand a better chance of recovery. By placing other people's wishes before their own, they deny themselves their last chance to regain control over their lives. I talked to Sally about Janet's resistance to my plan.

"Have faith," Sally said to me a few days later. 'Trust in yourself - and God."

"When you were in Queensland," my wife said to me a week later, "I told Mike and Julie that you had leukemia. They kept asking so many questions. Anyway, they're our best friends. It's only right that they should know. Julie used to work for a radiotherapist. She knows about these things."

The ring of conspirators had been widened. A few days later, my dear friend Mike asked: "Why don't you have your spleen removed?" Janet had clearly not told them the whole story. I explained my reasons for refusing surgery and attempting alternative approaches. He understood at once, and so he and his wife, Julie, supported me in every way. From that day on, Mike visited me at every opportunity. He hardly missed a day. With his ready smile and firm belief in my approach, his visits were a source of great comfort. They certainly strengthened the bond between us. Later, when it became harder for me to drive my car, Julie ferried me on my weekly visits to and from the hospital.

I remembered the healings I received from Jane when I was in Queensland. I recalled her words and so added prayer to my daily routine. My prayers were answered, after a fashion, some days later.

"I find massage very helpful," Patsy said to me. She had come to visit me carrying a plate of lentil pie. Whenever Patsy tried out a new healthy recipe, she usually made an extra serving for me. Patsy's meals-on-wheels kept me going. I listened carefully to what she had to say. She was a mine of information. Through her, I was discovering an extensive and diverse underworld devoted to alternative treatments of healing.

"'I've been going to this man for several weeks," Patsy said. "He's really helped me. He understands my problems better than anyone else. Why don't you try him?"

I was skeptical even though Evanston had talked about the beneficial effects of massage on cancer patients. Much later, I was to find I had overlooked Gerson's objection to this tucked away in a sub-section near the end of his book. Patsy was sure it had helped her. She made the necessary arrangements for me to visit Alistair Jones.

On a cold winter's day in June 1984, I rang the doorbell of a house in a tree-lined street in an inner suburb. An attractive, slender woman in her forties opened the door. Her name was Carmen. As she ushered me in she informed me that Alistair was upstairs and would be down shortly.

I wondered why Alistair had not come to the door. I wondered who she was. She had long, dark, wavy hair. She glowed with health and radiated a sense of great calmness. His wife? In response to my unasked question, she said, "Alistair and I work together." She showed me into a small, sunlit room. A doctor's examination couch stood in front of the window. A double bed and dressing table completed the furnishings. She asked me strip to the waist and handed me a sheet to cover myself, as it was a little chilly. Telling me to rest on the couch, she left the room to fetch Alistair.

I was puzzled. Where was he? I stripped and lay down on the couch. I heard someone enter the room and I turned my head. I saw a slightly built man of medium height dressed in an open-neck, brown shirt, brown shorts and long brown socks. His attire struck me as a little odd. After all, it was the middle of winter and the house wasn't warm. There was something else about Alistair that was different: even though he was looking towards me he was not looking at my eyes.

He had close-cropped, light ginger hair. His face was pale and slightly drawn. It was a friendly face. The pale eyes stared without seeing. I found out later that he had been involved in an industrial accident and had lost 90 per cent of his sight. He could discern shapes and outlines but no detail. At first, this disability seemed at odds with his occupation. Alistair had been an agronomist. His competence and knowledge stood him in good stead. Verbal descriptions of crops and environmental difficulties had enabled him to continue identifying and solving problems brought to him by his many clients.

"Now let's see what's wrong with you," he said. He took a pear-shaped crystal attached to a slender thread and held it over my body. Immediately it began to swirl round and round. It was close to my face, I was sure it would knock my nose off.

"This will help me establish the levels of energy in different parts of your body," he explained. "Once I find where your levels are at their lowest, I'll know where to treat you."

I told him I had leukemia. He didn't ask me how my symptoms had manifested themselves. After about twenty minutes, he put the crystal aside and held out his hands in front of him above my body. As I watched, he moved his hands as if he was massaging me. He then lowered his hands, and began to massage me. One and a half hours later I felt as if I had been run over by a steamroller.

Carmen stood at the foot of the bench. She saw me grimace. "Alistair isn't just massaging your physical body," she said. "He's massaging your psychic body too."

I thought this was all crazy, but my experiences with Sally and the Smiths in Queensland, plus what I had read, compelled me, with great effort, to keep an open mind.

"He's massaging away your problems," Carmen added.

I hoped he was. "'But why does it hurt so much?"

"They're very deep-seated," said Alistair. "They're hard to get at."

"A-choo!!" Without warning, Alistair let out the loudest sneeze I had ever heard. I almost leaped off the couch. I could feel my heart racing.

"What was that?" I asked.

Carmen leaned forward. "He has to release the build-up of negative energies he's drawing out of you," she explained. I felt confused. If Alistair had, in fact, tapped into the source of my emotional pain his sneezing reaction was a far from silent affirmation. I thought that if Alistair's violent 'sneezes' could remove the causes of my woes I would continue to try to tolerate his outbursts. They were so loud and sudden I never got used to them.

"You'll need to come back a few more times," Alistair said as he finished massaging me. "I haven't been able to remove all your negativity."

As I left, Carmen handed me a card. I looked at it: Get the bends out of your road.

"I'm a clairvoyant," Carmen said. "That was a very clear message I picked up."

As I was about to drive away, I turned the card over. On it, she had scribbled another message: Be positive at all times.

"Ever since I lost my sight, all my other senses have become highly sensitive," Alistair had said while he worked on what he called my 'troubled soul'. "While I agree with everything else you're doing, your home and work situations are part of the problem."

As with Jane Smith, Alistair and Carmen were convinced only I could cure myself. By passing the success of my recovery entirely onto me, it was obvious that they and other practitioners of alternative treatments absolve themselves completely if they can't help or if anything goes wrong. I rejected the notion that I should take the blame for my disease. I had enough to cope with, anyway.

I was determined to see what might happen, so I returned to Alistair on Saturday mornings for a few more weeks. After each painful treatment, Carmen handed me a new card. Each was a variation on the same theme: my problem was my 'dis-ease': it was causing me great unhappiness. My unhappiness was killing me. In his own way, Alistair seemed to have pinpointed part of my dilemma. To help me, he gave me massages. Carmen gave me messages. He was a technically blind man of the soil who had, it seemed, unearthed my problems. More and more it seemed to me that I had to take a new direction.

My friend Patsy was still going to church every Saturday. I noticed how well she looked for days afterwards. One day I asked why she went. She and Arthur didn't seem to be the religious type.

"I go for healing, because I feel so much better afterwards. And there's such a lovely atmosphere. It gives me strength. The church gives me hope."

"Are you going this week?" I asked

"Yes. Do you want me to take you?"

"Yes, please."

"Arthur," she called out excitedly. "Joel is coming with me to church this Saturday."

"Not you, too! So, she's talked you into it as well. Humph! I thought you were going to Alistair? Now he's got something to offer."

I told him what Alistair had said about my problem.

"I don't know what else to do," I said. "There has to be an answer to all this somewhere. I'm obviously looking in the wrong direction. Perhaps I need guidance of a more spiritual nature."

"It's your business if you want to go to church. It seems to help Patsy. Maybe it'll help you. But I still think you ought to go onto the Gerson program properly. If Janet goes to work - as she had been considering – you can easily do it. Your father's helping you make the juices, so that's a start. I think you've wasted valuable time following some of these other crazy diets."

Little did he know how true his words were.

CHAPTER THIRTEEN

July 1984:
Platelet count 36,000; haemoglobin level 7.9;
White blood cell count 1.2

The Thursday before I went to church with Patsy, I experienced my first attack of palpitations. It was frightening. Without warning, my heartbeat shot up from around 68 beats a minute to almost 200. I felt a burning sensation in my chest. In panic, I telephoned Dr Sullivan. He advised me to breathe slowly and to lie down and to call him back if I didn't feel better.

Some time later, my heartbeat returned to normal. I had never experienced anything like this before. It was terrifying and I had no way of controlling it. The following day I visited Dr Sullivan. He gave me a blood test. The result confirmed that my hemoglobin level had fallen even further and that, as a result, my heart had to pump harder to get oxygen through my body. At least there was an explanation for what had happened the day before. Dr Sullivan had clearly not wished to alarm me.

The night sweats continued. The antibiotics I had started taking had alleviated, but not eliminated, the boils. My spleen was growing larger. The headaches were getting more severe. The sight of the church as I drove up with Patsy on a sunny, afternoon did little to raise my spirits. It was mid-winter. I wondered if I would ever see the blossoms in spring again.

St Aloysius's was an independent Catholic Church of Healing. It stood on the corner of a quiet cul-de-sac and a busy, major thoroughfare leading downtown. The houses surrounding it had a same old look about them: redbrick fronts, stuccoed porches and red-painted galvanized iron roofs. Looking up from the cracked paving stones beneath my feet, I saw a modest church in need of much repair. I entered the vestibule and the busy street sounds faded. I was embraced by an overwhelming sense of peace, a sense of calm. To keep the chill out of the air, bar heaters had been located at several points along the walls. From a pile of numbered cards on a table at the rear of the pews, Patsy took two. She handed one to me. She then placed a dollar coin in the plate. I did likewise. I couldn't help noticing there wasn't much more in it when we left.

"They call out each number in turn, so it's best to be at the top. I don't like waiting around all afternoon for a healing. I usually want to get straight back home to have a sleep. It can make you very tired." Her words reminded me of my experience with Jane Smith in Queensland. It was clearly a common response. I looked at the cards Patsy had taken. I had taken number 2, Patsy had 3. I couldn't imagine anyone jumping the queue in a place like this. Still, I kept quiet. We took our seats. Then I saw something I had never seen in a church before: arranged in front of the altar were four leather-topped couches of the type used for examination in doctors' surgeries. Then, in ones and twos, people entered the church until there were about twenty of us. From a doorway to one side of the altar, the vicar stepped forward and stood in front of the pulpit.

Reverend Bishop was a tall, gaunt, white-haired man in his seventies. His long white beard offset his ruddy complexion. His eyes sparkled. He smiled and greeted the congregation. After a short address on a verse from the Bible, he led us in singing several hymns. This pattern was repeated every Saturday. From not attending synagogue, I was now attending church and, as time went by, I would also go to Baha'i and Hindu gatherings.

"Will all healers present please step forward," he asked.

Two men and two women rose from their seats and took their places at the head of each couch.

"Will the first four numbers please come forward for healing," said Reverend Bishop. My healer asked me to sit on a low stool at one end of the couch. He placed his hands on my head, closed his eyes and prayed for my healing. He then asked me to lie on the couch on my back. He placed one hand on my head and another on my abdomen. Gently, he began to massage my whole body. As he moved his hands over my arms and chest, around my shoulders and down my arms, I felt as if I was bathed in the soft, warm glow he had asked me to conjure up in my mind. It was the most pleasant sensation. I felt safe. After about ten minutes, he asked me to clasp my hands behind my head. For the next several bone-clicking minutes, he manipulated my back. I wondered if he was a trained chiropractor. If he didn't know what he was doing, I felt sure I would never be able to walk again. Then it was over.

"When you're ready, you can get up. In the meantime, rest a while."

I lay absolutely still for a few minutes. Was he a very good masseur? Was it the spirit in the place? Was it simply contact between one human being and another? I didn't know the answer, but I felt calmer. I now knew why Patsy laid such great store in coming to St Aloysius's for healing. Just as she had predicted, when I arrived home I slept soundly for a couple of hours.

I visited St Aloysius's every Saturday afternoon with Patsy for the next few months. By the time the weekends rolled round again, I was so drained from my efforts during the week all I wanted to do was sleep. I was still determined to follow this path although I had no idea where it would lead me. The healings I received at the church seemed to make me feel better. Getting back and forth was a problem simply overcome. Patsy took me in her car. I was curious about the church and its methods, so I asked her but she didn't know.

"Why don't you have a talk to John Bishop?" she said. "I'll arrange it for next time. We'll go a little earlier."

Patsy was as good as her word. On our next visit to the church, I met Reverend Bishop shortly before the service. He led me into a kitchen behind the altar. We sat down.

"Did you know I once had cancer?" he asked.

"No."

He lifted his shirt to reveal a huge scar across his back.

"They operated on me. It was a very large melanoma. I'm all right now. But I played a key part in my own recovery. It was a mixture of medicine and faith." He leaned closer. "Life is terminal. Cancer is not. Here, have a look at this!"

He handed me a typewritten sheet of paper: *'Professional Services Available'*. The headline was followed by a brief outline of the services offered by the church: marriages, christenings, funeral services, and deep relaxation with spiritual healing, numerology. The next headline grabbed my attention: *Green Vegetable Juice Therapy*. The synchronicity of events was never more vivid to me than at that moment. I had first heard of juice therapy from Peter Evanston. I then found he had based his plan on that of Dr Gerson. David Perth also advocated vegetable juice, basing his diet on that of Dr Issels. Now Reverend Bishop was doing the same - with one difference:

he was not as adamant about the type of juicer used. It seemed to me as if everyone knew about something I did not.

Bishop's outline reflected the same principle the others had stated: they believed that incorrect eating causes most of our physical problems. Bishop's spiritual message echoed Jane Smith's message to me: 'as a man thinks in his heart and mind – so is he. To find a real cure from our ills, we must look further than the mere physical reality of our complaint. Positive thinking combined with correct eating and several glasses of the Green Juice a day 'offers quick relief and a possible cure from all our ills.'

"I'm doing almost all of this already," I said, reading his diet.

"That's good. Have you ever had a numerology reading?"

"No," I replied.

He took out a printed sheet of paper, wrote my name on it, and then asked me when I was born. Armed with this information, he proceeded to evaluate my present character, my developing character, and the character I would have when I finished my moral lessons. The outlook was promising.

"According to this," he said, "you will live to be eighty-eight. You will achieve a high moral level. Keep going. And don't be put off by negative people."

I was still skeptical, and yet as far-fetched as all the claims I had read and heard about were, I was still prepared to consider any option I hoped might help me. I was perturbed by my falling blood counts. Gum bleeds were upsetting enough, although I had more or less accepted them, but I found my recent spontaneous nosebleeds distressing. I found it hard to come to terms with waking up to find my pillow soaked in blood. My swollen lymph glands were becoming increasingly painful. The one in my right armpit was now the size and hardness of a golf ball. I was experiencing pain in my spleen; sudden razor-sharp thrusts that came and went. As the months wore on, they lasted longer. No painkiller was strong enough. And I was so very weary - a problem that would become worse and worse.

Eventually, I was even too tired to go with Patsy to the church. I thought I had reached the end of my endurance. How much more could I take? Had I arrived at Heaven's door without a prayer and without a blessing? I decided it was time to consider more deeply those issues I preferred to avoid. Events over the next two weeks convinced me I could no longer ignore them.

"Why are you so yellow?" I looked up. It was Peter, a colleague of mine at work. "You have jaundice, you know. Hasn't anyone told you how bad you look?"

"If I had jaundice," I replied, "the whites of my eyes would be yellow. Look! They're white."

He looked at me in bewilderment. "So what is wrong with you?"

"Nothing", I lied. "I'm on a new vegetarian diet. I have to drink liters of carrot juice every day."

"I can understand that. But why are you so yellow and so thin? You know, everybody's talking about how gaunt you look!"

The concern in Peter's eyes told me he knew something was wrong. I now had no doubt that everyone was discussing me. I had withheld the truth for so long, the situation seemed irretrievable. To tell everyone at work so long after my diagnosis seemed ludicrous! I kept quiet. And I did nothing.

Many years later, I bumped into Peter at a restaurant. He looked as if he had seen a ghost.

"We all thought you had died," he exclaimed.

"I guess not," I replied. I told him what had happened. To this day, I am not sure how much he understood of what I told him.

A low hemoglobin level is an indication that the oxygen-carrying capacity of the blood has been reduced. In order to compensate, the heart pumps faster to make more efficient use of the existing cells. The sudden palpitation attacks that resulted were becoming more frequent. They were scary. They always started without warning. From a normal and steady 65 – 70 beats, my heart would suddenly hammer out a tattoo of 200 beats. I was sure my heart could not withstand these assaults.

I later learned that regular palpitations of this intensity could easily result in a fatal heart attack. In that last week of July and first two weeks of August, I had at least eight such attacks. During one of them, my temperature also rose to 39°C. That might not seem very high but my normal temperature is 35.5°C. I started to shiver as much from the cold as from anxiety. I felt as if I had been left lying naked in the middle of an Arctic blizzard. I could not stop my teeth from chattering. The pain in my spleen was unbearable. I was soaked in perspiration. Patsy came to visit. She had dropped by and had no idea of the state I was in. As soon as she saw me she asked if she could call John Bishop. I must have agreed, because half an hour later, he came through the door. He sat next to my bed and took my hand.

"'Pray with me," he said. We recited the Lord's Prayer. I then followed him through Psalm 23. He placed his hands over me and prayed for me. I vaguely remember looking at him through a hazy mist. Then I fell asleep.

A week later, it happened again. In desperation, my wife

telephoned Patsy. Patsy phoned John Bishop. He came to minister to me on a miserably cold winter's night in the pouring rain. It was past midnight. He held my hand. He prayed for me. I made it through the night. It was a most terrible time. I am forever indebted to him for those visits. The following week, as we sat in church, I was reminded of John Ndmande's words as Reverend Bishop recited these words from Psalm 107:

'Then they cry unto the Lord in their trouble, and he bringeth them out of their distresses.

They are glad because they be quiet; so he bringeth them unto their desired haven.'

CHAPTER FOURTEEN

August 1984:
Platelet count 36,000; haemoglobin level 7.2; White blood cell count 1.1

"It's time to stop work," I said to Janet a few days later.

It was the second week of August. My prospects were as bleak as the weather. I had to do something to change direction. I wasn't prepared to die. Not yet. I had been on the Gerson program for eight months, on a part-time basis. Dr Sullivan pointed out that my blood counts were falling at an alarming rate. I felt that to give me a better chance I had to increase my intake of juices from three to the prescribed thirteen. I needed to meditate for about seven hours a day instead of only two or three. I needed much more time. I was dying fast.

I told my wife, "I'm not prepared to give in without a fight. I feel as if I'm battling against enormous odds with my hands tied behind my back. At the moment, it's a no contest. I'll tell the children I'm working from home. That shouldn't be too hard for them to accept."

The boys were excited by the prospect of my being at home. They believed we would spend more time together. We certainly saw more of each other, but the year was ending, and exam time fast approaching. My eldest son was about to sit for his school leaving-certificate in November and spent most of his time studying. At least, I thought, whatever time I had left, I would be with my family.

The following day, I confided in my managing director.

"Are you sure it's not pernicious anemia" he asked, after I explained my reasons for having to stop work. He was most upset.

"I wish it was otherwise, but there's no doubt I have Hairy Cell Leukemia. I've had every test you can think of."

"Is it terminal?" he asked.

"There is no cure. I refused surgery because it offered me no hope. Instead, I decided to follow a dietary program. I believe that unless I follow it exactly, it will offer me no hope, either."

"How did you manage to keep it from us for so long?" he asked. "It must have been terrible keeping it to yourself."

I explained to him how I used to meditate during my lunch breaks. He now understood why I raced home every day after work.

"'If there's anything I can do before you leave," he said, "please let me know."

It sounded like polite but empty patter. I couldn't have been more wrong. A few days later, Alan approached me. "I've been thinking," he said. "What you're doing is extremely courageous. I agree that to give yourself any sort of chance, you must concentrate on getting better. Do it. And don't worry about money. We'll take care of that."

I was flabbergasted. The advertising industry is everything anyone ever said about it. It's creative, it's fun, it's hard work, it's rewarding. After twenty years in the business, I also knew there was little room in it for affection, even less for compassion. Alan proved to be a rare exception to the rule. I shall always be grateful for the help he provided. For several months afterwards, the company paid me as a full-time consultant.

"'What are we going to do about school fees?" My wife

asked, a few days later. Our youngest son attended a well-known all-boys grammar school. The fees were extremely high.

"I noticed," I said, "that some of the other grammar schools are offering full scholarships. Why don't we let him sit their entrance exam? With his grades he's bound to get in to one of them!" She agreed. Our son wrote the examination shortly afterwards and was accepted by all of them. We advised his school that he would be leaving. The headmaster called Janet and asked her to visit him. She told him I had leukemia and had stopped working, so we could no longer afford the fees.

"You don't have to send him to another school," the headmaster, Reverend Sligo, told her. "We're prepared to offer him a full scholarship. We need more students like him."

We were extremely grateful and highly appreciative. Until he finished high school four years later, he received a scholarship award at every annual prize-giving ceremony.

It was now ten months since my leukemia had been diagnosed. I was still alive. Now that I had stopped work, I planned to do what I thought I should have done much earlier. I hoped I hadn't left my move too late. I had been playing with my life.

A few days later, Patsy phoned. "The Smith's are coming to town," she said, excitedly. "I'm going to make an appointment for a healing with Peter. Do you want me to make a booking for you with Jane? I believe they will only be here for about two days. They're driving down." I accepted her offer gratefully. I felt I needed more than moral support. Jane might just be the tonic I needed.

The Smiths were working in a scout hall on the other side of town – a distance of over 30 km. My concerns about driving so far were quickly dispelled when Arthur offered to drive me there. When we arrived, there were dozens of people ahead of us. Eventually, it was my turn.

"How is the path of positive thinking?" Jane asked as she rested her fingers on me. I told her that I came to the view that positive thinking did nothing – but that positive action did. I told her I had stopped work and was now engaged in pursuing a full time program of diet and meditation. She listened attentively and then started her healing on me. It was the same as when I last saw her. I could feel her hands vibrating on my skin. I could feel the warmth surge through me. I felt a sense of great peace. A while later, she said, "I think I've done as much as I can for you to this point. It's up to you." With the onus on me, I believed that unless I tried to follow the diet as diligently as possible, I was unlikely to slow down the approach of my death.

CHAPTER FIFTEEN

September 1984:
Platelet count 34,000; haemoglobin level 7.6; White blood cell count 1.3

All I had was hope. I pinned it on following the Gerson program as closely as possible. I no longer had to place my get-well schedule as a footnote in my work diary. To give me time to meditate, my father offered to make four of the thirteen juices I needed every day. At ground level, my battle plan was taking shape.

I carefully followed the schedule set out in Gerson's book, adding the Lugol's solution and potassium mixture to many of the juices. As the potassium made the juice very sour, leaving it out of one of the Green juices was a real treat. I was now doing four coffee enemas a day.

Unfortunately, some of the ingredients I needed for the program– the liver injections and some recommended tablets – were simply not available. Of those that were, one caused me some initial difficulties. I was supposed to take a 50 mg niacin tablet with each of my meals. I swallowed the first one without food in my mouth; within minutes my face became extremely hot and flushed. My body felt as if I had been dusted all over with itching powder. It was a most unpleasant sensation. I never tried that approach again.

At my next visit to Dr Sullivan, I asked him about thyroid tablets. Unusually, he suggested I omit these from the program. "I think your condition is somewhat different. If you can manage without them, I think you should. I think the liver extract tablets you're on are enough."

Now that I could focus my full attention on getting better, two things became apparent. Without my father's help, I could not have managed. He had his own health problems to contend with. I didn't want to burden him but he was determined to help me. I accepted his offer. Gratefully. I hadn't quite appreciated how much effort and time it took to shop for the ingredients for my juices. Now that I had the time, I decided to drink as many liver and carrot juices as prescribed on the program. This meant getting into my car every day to buy fresh liver, and a weekly trip to a health food store to stock up on all the supplements, vitamins and minerals required by the diet. Fresh vegetables for the soups and so many juices meant I had to buy these on a daily basis. I needed over 3 kg of carrots a week alone. It was tiring. My wife did not help as she had now found employment from 9am – 5pm.

My blood counts were fluctuating but were still on a downward trend. My spleen was getting larger: it was now 18 cm long. Even if my diet had allowed me to eat a great deal, my compressed abdomen would now allow it. I had increased the number of juices and coffee enemas. The result was exactly as Gerson had warned so I used liberal doses of room freshener to clear the air. The 'flare ups' he spoke about were more severe than I imagined they would be. The headaches were intense and painful. I felt grumpy and out of sorts. I perspired profusely. To help overcome the problem I drank copious amounts of peppermint tea.

Sleep was a luxury I had dreamed of for the past ten months. Lack of sleep distressed me and made me irritable. I desperately wanted to sleep. I needed sleep. My body craved it so much it overtook me whenever I tried to meditate. As I relaxed each part of my body before meditating, I found myself nodding off.

"Don't fight it," my father said to me. "Sleep is the best medicine."

I tried to heed his advice. I felt so good after a long sleep, I eventually decided not to rail against it. I made sleep my ally. Several authors I had read stressed the need to restore the body's metabolism. The metabolic rate slows down during sleep. Meares' form of meditation was designed to still the mind. According to him, this reduced stress levels which, in turn, allowed the body's immune system to recover. The very nature of his method suggested that every other function also slowed down. I wondered whether his method also produced a similar response in slowing down cancer growth. It seemed logical; I gave in to my body's desire to sleep.

Before I stopped work, it had become harder to make excuses as to why we were accepting fewer social invitations. To maintain the illusion that everything was normal, my wife wanted us to keep seeing friends, to accept invitations to dinner, or watch a movie over weekends. By the time the weekends came round, I simply wanted to see more of the children, meditate more, and drink more juices. Finding time to do everything was not possible. And I was so very, very tired.

"You can't shut yourself away from people," Janet argued.

"If we don't tell our friends what is wrong," I replied, "then we'll have to make excuses for why we can't join them. I need to sleep. I need to meditate. I have to make juices. I must prepare and take coffee enemas. I don't have time to waste." Defending my position was becoming as tiring as the demands of the program and my declining health. My priorities were different from hers.

Within a week or two of my stopping work, however, my wife worked out her plan. She told our closest friends that I was 'ill' and that I was not keen on making too many social arrangements, but she swore them to secrecy to protect our children from the truth. To them and the rest of the world she said I was "working from home." I have no doubt that Janet made things harder for herself as well by struggling to keep up the façade.

As a result, she invited friends to our house so I didn't have to drive home after an evening out. It made things a little easier for a while. As soon as our guests had left, I tumbled into bed. I was so exhausted from the chitchat and maintaining the pretense that all was well with the world. There was an elephant in the room and she was pretending it was not there. My increasing weariness made me less and less inclined to be with people.

On the way home from church the week before I stopped work Patsy asked me, "What are you doing on Thursday night? I'm asking because I used to invite cancer patients to come to our house for tea and a chat in the afternoons. Patients find it so much easier to talk about their problems with other cancer patients. But it's hard for many people to come during the day. Either they work, or their husbands and wives work. Arthur and I think we should have these meetings on Thursday evenings so more people can come. You've stopped work, so it doesn't make any difference to you. We're just around the corner, anyway. You'll be in bed by half past ten." It sounded like a good idea. I accepted her offer.

Later, Patsy invited Reverend Bishop to attend these get-togethers so others could benefit from his healings. Over the next few months, I learned a lot from meeting these people. I didn't say much. I listened.

Without exception, everyone who attended these evening meetings was pursuing an alternative non-medical treatment. All of them were facing cancers of various kinds: breast, prostate, uterine, lung and pelvic. They were all keen to hear what Reverend Bishop had to say. From Aileen I learned about *Iscador* made from mistletoe and which, she claimed, had been used with great success in Switzerland. She also told me how she affirmed her positivity with her mantra: 'every day, in every way, I'm getting better and better.'

Almost all of them had tried modified versions of the Gerson program as well as other diets. They had all tried meditation. None of them would have anything to do with medical treatment. All of them died.

"There's one doctor who is different," Patsy said. We had been discussing the negative responses of the group to the medical profession. "He practices orthomolecular medicine."

I had read that orthomolecular medicine strives to restore the body's strength and build up the immune system's defenses through a program of vitamin and mineral supplements. I made an appointment to visit him.

A few days later, I came face to face with the full cherubic face of a short, plump man. He gave me a physical examination. As I was getting dressed he said, "I'm going to prescribe a number of things that should bolster your immune system." He wrote out a prescription for several vitamins and minerals. The list mentioned Thymus sweetbread, Formula Four, papaya enzyme, Vitamin E, Vitamin B3, Vitamin B12, garlic capsule, riboflavin.

"These are not contra-indicated for the regimen you're on. In fact, they should help you."

Wherever I went, whomever I spoke to, the underlying message I kept getting was that cancer was considered a direct result of a weakened immune system. The thinking of the day was that apart from stress and emotional strain, poor nutrition weakened this intricate structure. The orthomolecular message was similar to that suggested to me earlier by Dr Vaughan. I was prepared to try anything that might safely and painlessly arrest my falling blood counts. I was already taking selenium and had raised my Vitamin C intake to 25g a day. I was still taking the medication prescribed by David Perth as well as those needed for the Gerson program. There was the high financial cost to this belief in alternatives and it was mounting. I had thrown rational thought out of the window and was clinging to every alternative route others with cancers recommended.

The additional medication did nothing to prevent my falling blood counts. Every time I saw the orthomolecular doctor, I was struck by how overweight he was. I felt disheartened. I lost confidence in him. His fees were high as were the cost of the medications he prescribed. I stopped seeing him but continued taking the tablets he had prescribed for a few months more.

It became important for me to manage my time in between juices, enemas and meditation. I tried to read as widely as I could, to find out more about cancer and the hundreds of different treatments people had tried to conquer it. When I felt so tired I could hardly breathe, I simply sat and watched television. This distraction never seemed to last long. Suddenly it was time again to take an enema or make a juice. Or meditate. Time had become even more precious as I weighed how little I thought I had left. When the boys came home from school, I tried to spend as much time with them as I could without disturbing my schedule. It was one thing to pretend to the world and to them that I was working from home – quite another to make believe I was busy when they were around. I explained away all the juices my father and I were making as 'another one of 'Pop's fads.' As far as meditation was concerned, Janet told them I was doing this to overcome the stress of my work. When I stopped work, I continued meditating. I felt sure that they were aware of the contradiction. I doubted if they believed their mother's explanation. I eventually found out I was right. My middle son's acuity led the way.

"Why are you so yellow?" he asked.

"From all the carrot juice I drink."

"But why do you have to drink so much?" he persisted. I could not think of a satisfactory answer. "I'm a vegetarian," I replied. "I like carrot juice."

He looked bewildered.

"I can't tell you now, but I will explain all this to you one day."

At the time I thought that my answer had satisfied his curiosity. I would eventually realize how I had deluded myself and how the conspiracy of silence I had bought into had negatively affected everyone around me.

Most of the diets I came across struck me as variations on the Gerson theme. I made some minor adjustments. I eliminated tomatoes, red and green peppers, parsnips and egg plant from my diet. I stacked kilos of carrots, spinach, celery and parsley into the trunk of my car. Eventually, as my tiredness and breathlessness increased, I allowed Arthur to make these purchases for me. The one chore I felt I could not ask him to carry out for me was to visit Jim to get fresh calf's liver for my juices. By now, Jim and I had become friends. He looked forward to my visits to find out how I was doing. I enjoyed his abrasive humor and the chance to talk to someone about something other than my many problems – including my distress over my wife's insistence that we keep the news of my illness from the children.

I spoke to Sally about this. She listened to me carefully and then said, "I watch a program on television every Sunday morning. I think you may find it extremely helpful. If you can get Janet to watch with you, it'll probably help even more." That Sunday I rose earlier than usual, prepared my coffee and juice, and switched on *Hour of Power*, an internationally televised program of worship led by a charismatic leader, Robert Schuller. The address that morning was 'Courage'. His message struck a responsive chord in me.

"Courage is not an absence of fear," he said. "Courage is an act undertaken at great risk with total awareness that failure can result."

If this was courage, it was no big deal. I wasn't afraid. I was aware of the path I had taken and the risks I was taking. Somehow, I thought, everything would turn out all right if only I could stick to my plan without distraction. It wasn't easy. Week after week, my blood counts kept slipping lower and lower. With every passing day, I felt my energy levels dropping as well. To complicate the problem of my gum bleeds (the nosebleeds, mercifully, had become infrequent), I developed mouth ulcers. My falling platelet count meant I couldn't heal. The ulcers were to be a source of great discomfort for weeks. I hoped I had the courage to persevere.

CHAPTER SIXTEEN

October 1984:
Platelet count 34,000; haemoglobin level 6.7; White blood cell count
1.5

I stopped going to Alistair on Saturday mornings.

Shortly afterwards I stopped attending the church with Patsy on Saturday afternoons as well. A politically sensitive dispute had occurred between Reverend Bishop, his wife and several of the healers at the church. The atmosphere had become emotionally charged. I had received a circular from the church asking me to take sides. I had no desire to become involved. In any event, however good the healings made me feel, they did nothing to arrest my falling blood counts and increasing weariness. Patsy continued attending for a while, and then stopped too. Reverend Bishop and I maintained contact through the Thursday evening groups until they came to an end towards the end of October.

"I think they're draining Patsy of her energy," Arthur commented.

"Our numbers are also starting to thin out," I noted.

"That's because they originally came here to talk to you, Patsy and me. When Patsy started offering them John Bishop's healing services, they shied away. Some of them have died. I know you and Patsy lay great store in healing. I think some healers are honest, but as for the rest, well they are..." He left his sentence unfinished.

The death of the group was a little sad. I had learned much from it. In particular, I realized that I had been fighting too hard. It was weakening me. Looking at the failure rate in that group made me realize I had been right to rearrange my priorities. It occurred to me that most of them could have reacted differently to their situations. They all suffered from fear of the word 'cancer'. They all believed that cancer was a terminal illness. With one or two exceptions, they believed that if they did what they were told they would get better. Few decided to take responsibility for their therapies. They had all succumbed to the lure of quackery, myself included. Patsy apart, all of them had lost the one ingredient I felt was key to recovery: hope.

I needed all the hope I could muster. It was mid-October. My sons were hard at work preparing for their end-of-year exams. I was in a terrible state. My boils were so painful I could barely sit for more than a few minutes at a time. I now had to meditate lying down. The hard lumps in my groin and under my arms were sore and uncomfortable. I was still getting short, sharp stabs of pain in and around my spleen. Every time I put my head on my pillow, I became aware of a hollow, thumping sound in my ears, a clear sign of a falling hemoglobin level. Knowing what it was made no difference. I still found it terribly disturbing. It was a beating reminder that my heart was pumping harder and harder to drive the remaining oxygen-carrying cells around the body. At times, it was so loud it would wake me.

I reflected on my current condition and decided I had to do something. I remembered my visit several months before to Dr Vaughan and took out the piece of paper he had given me. Four names. So far, my voyage of discovery had led me to two: Peter Evanston and Jane Smith. I looked at the list again: Dr Singh, the homeopath in Bombay was the next. The prospect of a long and tiring journey made me shudder. I decided to find someone closer to hand.

After several enquiries, the name Mary Glenn kept cropping up. I decided to see what she had to offer.

Mary was an attractive woman in her early thirties, medium height and build. She had short black hair framing a serene face. Seated across a desk from me, she asked me to outline my problem. I explained to her all about Hairy Cell Leukemia. I told her how I had refused surgery. I gave her a lengthy explanation of the program I was on. She didn't prescribe any medication. Instead, she said, "I'd like you to write out your life story. I can only work out what you need if I know more about you." I found her request very unusual.

"Are you a psychiatrist?" I asked.

"No, but I have a feeling you know what I'm getting at. I'd like you to detail those aspects of your life that have been the most distressing. Try not to leave anything out."

I made an appointment to visit her a few days later. I remembered what Meares had said: "Finding the root cause of your stress is all well and fine if you have the time - and the money. Most cancer patients can't afford the costs of lengthy therapy. You need expert guidance and total commitment on the part of the patient to do whatever is necessary to correct the problem. Cancer patients want their doctors to do everything for them." Instinctively, I felt he was right. I heard the first inner murmurings that whispered that there was a link between resolving my deeper conflicts and recovering from my disease. Alistair Jones had stressed the need to alter my circumstances. To follow that route would take more courage than I now had. Meares' simple approach of meditating and so letting go of all fears seemed much easier. As to whether it would cure me of cancer, well that was another matter.

I started to write. I filled several pages outlining my childhood as well as my relationship with my mother. Reluctantly, I touched on some of my current difficulties with my wife. I tried to reconcile what had happened in my past to my illness. I realized that we fear most that which we do not understand. Facing the truth isn't easy. I pushed these invasive thoughts to the back of my mind. I was still looking for some help from the outside. A week later, I handed the notes to Mary.

"Your problem is complicated, to say the least," she said. She handed me a bottle of tablets. "Take these in the meantime. I'll be writing to Dr Singh in Bombay. I'll ask him what he suggests."

She said she had studied under Dr Singh in India and explained that she was still his student. She planned to visit him the following year.

I talked with Mary regularly over the next few weeks. The tablets she gave me didn't help. Then one day she called me.

"Can you come next Tuesday at two-thirty?" she asked. "The doctor will be here and he wants to see you."

"Who? Dr Singh?"

"Yes." She told me that he was en route to the USA and had agreed to give a few lectures to students in Melbourne. Mary had persuaded him to see me.

Dr Singh was a well dressed slightly built man in his early sixties with a gentle demeanor. He examined me and expressed amazement at the size of my spleen. It was now well over eighteen centimeters long and hard to the touch. I described my symptoms in detail.

"I want you to take these tablets," he said. He scribbled some names on a piece of paper. "Mary will arrange to get them for you. This is a temporary measure only. I can't treat you on one visit. If it is at all possible, I'd like you to come to

Bombay. I have a hospital there. If I had you under my care for a while, I believe I could help you."

I didn't have enough energy for the trip. I also wasn't totally convinced he could help. I tried the pills he prescribed but I was reluctant to try out all his dietary recommendations – some of which were at variance with the Gerson diet. He had told me that a little baked fish for protein, honey and boiled rice could do me no harm. What did I have to lose? Following his suggestions gave my diet some variety, but after a few weeks, there was still no improvement in my blood counts. My symptoms were not alleviated. I felt that carrying on with his program was a waste of time. I discussed the matter with Mary. She agreed. Unless I could go to India, there seemed no point in continuing with Dr Singh's regimen.

I saw Mary for several weeks more. She was attentive and extremely compassionate. At each visit, she handed me a bottle of pills. I took them religiously. Slowly, I began to realize I was drawing more comfort from her support than from her pills. I decided to take yet another path.

A few days later, my constant friend and mine of information phoned me. "Did you know that Placido is coming out?" Patsy asked. For a moment, I thought she had been a closet opera buff and was referring to the world-famous tenor, Plácido Dominga.

From what I had read, Reverend Placido Palitayan was one of the most renowned psychic surgeons in the Philippines, even rumored to have been a consultant to the late President Marcos and his family. Placido was the founder of the Christian Spiritual Regeneration Movement. Among its many beliefs, it holds that the Bible is the inspired word of God that Christ is the only true God, and that divine healing comes through faith and obedience to Christ. CSRM also believes in resurrection and the Last Judgment. Stories concerning Placido's surgical successes had already been told to me. His name has been mentioned in every article or program on psychic phenomena in the Philippines.

"You'll have to phone and make an appointment," Patsy said.

With great trepidation, I made my way several nights later to the address I had been given by a local member of the CSRM movement. I was ushered into one of the bedrooms where I was greeted by Placido and an assistant who was also his translator.

He was a small man. I am not particularly tall but I towered over him. He stood with his hands clasped in front of him and gave me a slight bow as I entered. I returned the greeting. His assistant asked me to strip to the waist and to lie on the bed. Placido and his assistant closed their eyes and prayed in what sounded like Spanish. After a few minutes, they washed their hands in a basin placed on a side tables.

I had read many stories about psychic surgery. I couldn't resist glancing down at my body to see what they were doing. I was both apprehensive and fascinated. I could scarcely believe what I saw. Placido approached me and seemed to lower his hands into my abdomen. I thought I could feel his hands moving about in me. I could see blood welling up on my body. His assistant wiped the blood away. Placido appeared to extract something from me. I could hear it thud as he threw it into a bucket placed beside the bed. He repeated this procedure three times. Each time I saw his blood-smeared hands seem to withdraw something from me and throw it into the bucket. I felt no pain. I craned my neck harder. There was no blood on my abdomen! There was no more blood on their hands. He placed his hands on my forehead and together he and his assistant prayed. I still don't know how they did it.

After the prayer he said, through the interpreter, "I have cleaned you out as best I can. Your problem is in your blood." I was amazed! I had not told him I had leukemia. I made an appointment to visit him a week later. He repeated the same procedure. He told me he could find nothing more to remove. His message was similar to the one before: "Your problem is in your blood." Only later, much later, did I come to understand the deeper meaning of his words.

A close friend of mine, who I can best describe as a 'skeptically doubting cynic', told me he had watched Placido operate on his wife. He had seen him expose her spine in order to remove secondary growths. I have read several books and articles on this phenomenon. I had undergone two 'operations' by this man. Some people suggested to me that I have been duped by sleight of hand and chicken livers. Others told me I was gullible and that my despair laid me open to the power of suggestion. Still, how did he know I had a blood problem?

In time I would come to realize that even though I had lost my fear of death, I was prepared to try anything to stay alive for as long as I could, no matter how bizarre or unscientific the programs were. I trod paths leading in different directions. I was in a maze with so many dead ends. Eventually, I would come to appreciate just how capricious and deluding hope can be.

CHAPTER SEVENTEEN

November 1984:
Platelet count 51,000; haemoglobin level 5.9; White blood cell count
0.9

It was now a year since my leukemia had been diagnosed. Amazingly, I was still alive. I had no idea if I was on the right path. A host of treatments were available to me: surgery (which offered no cure), diet, detoxification, meditation, visualization, spiritual healing, and psychic surgery (none of which had worked so far). Dr Sullivan made it clear that although gamma globulin to boost my immune system and lithium to increase the production of white blood cells could give me some respite, they could not cure me.

On the other hand, so many people had suggested to me that only I had the answer to my illness. I was not sure what that I was. Could I be truly responsible for my disease? Guilt was a burden I felt I could happily live without. I felt helpless. Peace of mind was a distant call. The answer, in spite of all the meditating I was doing, seemed unreachable. I was bone tired. My symptoms continued unabated. My headaches were getting even more severe. However, my hope for a recovery remained undimmed. No matter how bad I felt, I had an inner sense that if I could just hold on something good would happen. I had always been an optimist. I had always been determined to win through. My body seemed to be on another track. I felt as if it was being subjected to a road test. It was being shaken, rattled and rolled out of control.

My lack of concentration became a source of amusement

for my children. On several occasions I put a pot of water on the stove, added the coffee needed to make the brew, and then forgot to turn down the heat after it had started boiling. The result was coffee splatters all over the stove and the floor.

Was there anything else left to try? I was about to find out. Patsy had been drinking wheat-grass juice for several months. She had even used wheat-grass enemas. I had listened to her and Arthur's explanations of why she drank it and how they prepared it. It seemed as if everyone she knew had tried wheat grass. Some had sworn by its success. I wanted to know more, so I spoke to Jack, my friendly pharmacist, who told me to buy a book entitled *'Be your own doctor'* by Dr Ann Wigmore who had devised wheat-grass therapy. I found her story fascinating.

She was born in Lithuania in 1909. Although a sickly child Ann helped her grandmother, a naturalist, nurse people who had been wounded during WWI. Ann's parents were almost prevented from emigrating to the USA because of her ill health, but her grandmother cured her using unusual methods of treatment. In 1925, the family finally emigrated. Some time afterwards Ann was involved in a car accident. Gangrene set in and her doctors wanted to amputate her legs. She refused. She remembered her grandmother's ideas. She ate all the green things she could find growing outdoors. The doctors were amazed at her recovery.

When she was about fifty, continuing health problems plagued her: arthritis, migraines and colon cancer. She began eating weeds and grasses. She experimented with growing greens indoors. Her health improved so dramatically she founded the Hippocrates Health Institute in 1963. She co-lectured with Dr Paul Dudley, a famous heart specialist, and was later given many awards for her services to the field of cancer and other degenerative diseases, including a citation by the commonwealth of Massachusetts. She seemed to me to have sound credentials, and offer another path to recovery

Ann Wigmore asserted, as had Dr Gerson, that no known disease can attack a strong and healthy body. Cooked foods, additives and preservatives, pollution and drugs create nutritional deficiencies and a build-up of toxins. The result, she said, was constipation. By not eliminating toxins on a regular basis, cancer – especially intestinal cancer – was, in her view, bound to result. Her solution to all these problems lay in restoring the body's natural balance. 'By keeping the body clean and free of toxins, the body's natural immune system is strengthened. The body is its own best healer. We spring from the earth. We return to it. We are inextricably linked to it. We need the elements of the earth to sustain us. To do this we must eat 'live' food such as sprouting seeds, grains and greens, fruit and vegetables. The emphasis must be on enzyme-, vitamin- and mineral-rich foods. Correspondingly, our diets must be low in protein, starch and fats.' The answer, according to Wigmore, was to be found in grass and sprouts.

Sprouts, she maintained, are nutritionally superior to any other foods. They are economical to grow. They cleanse the blood. I generally don't like eating green foods so I liked her idea that one salad serving of sprout legumes could furnish all the daily requirements of protein and cell-building vitamins and minerals. Wigmore stated that she had discovered that chlorophyll in grass was the Great Restorer. She experimented with varieties from all around the world and claimed that wheat grass was the best and most palatable source. She also found that if it was introduced rectally, it was absorbed even more effectively. As an equally beneficial result, it acted as an enema to cleanse the body.

There seemed to be nothing in Wigmore's regimen that was at odds with Gerson's program. I was taking enemas so I didn't have constipation. I was drinking raw vegetable juices so I was obtaining most of the nourishment I needed. I had nothing to lose so I decided I would now grow sprouts. I borrowed and bought several large glass jars. Into these, I spooned mung beans, fenugreek, alfalfa, lentils and sunflower seeds. I soaked them overnight. Old stockings, elastic-banded over the necks, helped to drain the water and prevent the seeds from falling out when I rinsed them twice a day. I placed the bottles along the windowsill to catch the sunlight. Within a few days, I had all the fresh sprouts I needed. In order to maintain a steady output, I would repeat the process whenever we finished a bottle of sprouts. I say 'we', because everybody in the family enjoyed eating them. Sprouts became an integral part of every salad we made.

Growing wheat grass was to prove a little more complicated. I bought bags and bags of wheat and two dozen plastic trays. I used about one sack of potting mix every two weeks. I started growing wheat grass under the veranda, then wherever else I could find a space. It takes about seven days for the grass to reach its cutting height of about 10 -15 cm, so I had to maintain a steady crop rotation to ensure a regular supply. Laid out as they were, the trays resembled miniature fields of waving bright green grass. Their visual appeal, combined with the inclement weather, was too much for Babe, our cat, who decided to urinate on my grass rather than on the damp stuff outdoors! I had to throw everything away and start all over again. Ingenuity was required to relocate the trays. We used bookshelves to keep them off the ground and the cat off the grass. I also used the wheat grain I bought to make Rejuvelac, another essential part of Ann Wigmore's program. Rejuvelac is a fermented juice made by soaking wheat grains in water. Its function is to aid digestion. I drank at least three glasses a day. Its slightly sour taste was not unpleasant.

Extracting juice from the grass, though, was more difficult than I imagined. Wigmore's instruction was to use a special hand-operated juice extractor, which, she explained, preserved the enzymes from damage by electrical interference. There was a more practical reason for using a hand juicer: the grass wrapped itself around the cylinder of my electric machine. The smell of burning grass made me soon realize I would burn out the motor. After several futile attempts to find someone who sold a hand juicer, I eventually found one for sale in a health-food shop.

As soon as the grass was at the optimal height, I harvested it. It was now ready to convert into wheat-grass juice. I tried several times to turn the handle but it was useless. My strength had left me.

"I'll do it for you," my father said. But I knew he often found it difficult to push the harder vegetables down into the electric juicer, having already washed, scraped and cut them. When he had made the vegetable juice, he would clean the machine. This involved dismantling it. He would rinse out the filter, with a brush scrape the fibrous matter off the grinder and wipe clean the various other parts. He would then lubricate the drive shaft with vegetable oil and reassemble the whole contraption. Our kitchen seemed to be in a permanent state of mulch. It was too much for him. My eldest son came to the rescue.

"Can I do it for you?" he offered.

My initial reaction was to refuse. His exams were just

around the corner. I didn't want to burden him with this tedious chore.

"I want to do it," he insisted. I agreed. As it was, without his strong right arm to turn the handle – and it wasn't easy – I would have given up. I didn't have the energy. I felt terrible.

Wheat grass looks like it tastes. Grassy green. Arthur could quaff a glassful without flinching. Patsy grimaced as she sipped it, slowly. I gagged. After several attempts, I swallowed the lot. It is slightly sweet but very harsh. I never got used to it. I also found wheat-grass enemas more difficult to cope with than coffee ones, harder to retain. They also gave me the most terrible cramps. I persisted, though, and managed to do at least two a day.

Adding the Wigmore program to the Gerson one was an act of desperation. To maximize the effects of both required time. Again, time was a resource and a fuel I felt I was running low on but I was determined to go down fighting. I was not prepared to end up at the end of an unfeeling tube in my arm in a sterile environment.

My daily schedule was starting to have an effect on the boys. My eldest son had been at home for the past few weeks studying for his end of year exams. The two other boys were also nose-deep in their books. It was obvious to them that I wasn't working. If I wasn't meditating, I was taking enemas. If I wasn't preparing and drinking juices, I was reading or sleeping. Growing grass, sprouting seeds and drinking sour juices had turned me into a creature from Middle Earth, a Gandalf with carrot-colored skin!

I discussed the situation with my father.

"You have to tell the children," he said. "It's only right that they know."

I knew there was one final exam left to write that Friday.

"When will you tell them?" he asked.

"On Saturday."

"Good," my father replied. "This secret business has gone on far too long. You should have followed your own feelings in the first place."

On Saturday morning, the children were in the kitchen having breakfast.

"I'd like to have a talk with you when you're finished," I said.

"There's a cheap guitar being advertised in the newspaper," my youngest son said. "Please can we go and see it?" The moment wasn't right. His attention was elsewhere.

"Okay," I replied, "but can we sit down afterwards? There's something I'd like to talk to all of you about."

The interlude to view the guitar was opportune. I was together with my sons. I kept the mood light.

"The cheap guitar is a loss leader," I told them. "They'll tell us it has already been sold. They want you to buy a more expensive one." My son didn't agree. We bet on it. I won. I hoped I had established the mood I wanted them in: optimistic in the belief that I knew what I was talking about.

As soon as we returned home, I called them into our bedroom. "Do you think I've been acting strangely over the past few months?" I asked. My question produced a torrent of responses. I had been right. They had talked about me among themselves. My eldest son summed up their feelings.

"We thought you were going round the bend. But why?"

"I'm not well," I said.

"You're sick, aren't you?" My middle son's question was rhetorical.

"Yes."

"I knew it," my eldest son said.

"Why didn't you tell us?"

"Your mother didn't want you to know."

"We though you had something terrible, like cancer," my youngest son said, fighting back tears.

"I have leukemia. But I'm determined to get better."

I put out my arms and we embraced. We all cried. I don't think I had ever faced a more difficult or pain-filled moment. I told them all about the events leading up to the diagnosis. I explained in detail how I had refused surgery. I told them I had decided that since surgery offered no cure, I was not going to allow anyone to cut me open. It was my body, and I could choose to do with it as I liked.

My approach was so upbeat I achieved the response I had hoped for. We talked about the diet, the wheat grass, and my interstate visit to the Smiths, the Philippine faith healers, the church, coffee enemas, and meditation. I left nothing out.

"I want to beat this problem," I said. "If I don't succeed – and there's a chance that I may not – at least I'll go down fighting."

"Good on you, Pop!" said my middle son.

"I'll keep making the wheat-grass juice," my eldest son added.

"I'll help Grandpa make your juices," my youngest son offered. My middle son cradled my hand against his cheek.

At that moment, my wife walked in. She looked at me and confessed: "My psychologist said you were right to tell them." As I found out much later, he was convinced I was going to die and told Janet I was in denial.

CHAPTER EIGHTEEN

December 1984:
Platelet count 29,000; haemoglobin level 5.39; white blood cell count 1.0.

Once our children knew about what was actually going on, there was a different mood in the house. Whereas they had previously been reluctant to do more chores than necessary, now they fell over each other to help. It was all I could do to prevent them taking over completely. I had three new allies. Knowing that they supported me gave me great strength.

Despite this, my blood counts continued to fall although the levels occasionally rose from one test to the next. My spleen was now 20 centimeters long. I felt bloated and uncomfortable. I couldn't take more than two steps at a time before I had to stop to recover. This usually took about five minutes. I gulped in great breaths of air to offset my oxygen deficiency. Deep breathing didn't help. I asked Dr Sullivan if I could hire an oxygen cylinder.

"It won't do you any good," he said. "You need hemoglobin to carry oxygen around you body. You don't have enough red blood cells to hold any extra oxygen you inhale."

"Then how come I'm managing the way I am?" I asked.

He explained to me that there are so many red corpuscles in every milliliter of blood. This number, known as the Mean Corpuscular Value, is constant for everyone. In my case, the leukemic cells in my bone marrow were destroying the immature blood cells. As the number of these cells became fewer and fewer, there were fewer corpuscles left to carry oxygen around my body. Amazingly, blood tests revealed that nature had compensated, in part by increasing the size of what few red blood cells I had left. But it wasn't enough. I felt quite depressed. As always, this feeling did not last long.

All the self-help books I had been reading made the same point: the only way to overcome a problem is to think positively. Almost everyone I had spoken to concurred – except other cancer patients. To think positively all the time was impossible. Everybody has up-days and down-days. Cancer patients have a lot more down-days. There were some days when I felt completely distraught. There were dog days when I felt it would be so much easier to die. But from the outset I had decided to take responsibility for my disease and its treatment. I knew I was taking positive action. I knew I was maintaining it. Even then I understood that action is more important than mere words.

When I was child and crashed my bike into Mrs Poxen's red rose bushes, I persisted and so learned to ride. Forty years later nothing had changed. Now, as then, I was still determined to keep going, even if it meant bleeding to death in the process! It was just as well I decided to keep going. My headaches and spleen pains continued to be a constant source of discomfort. I was still suffering from night sweats and constantly looking for dry sheets. My gums were bleeding more often. Every morning I woke up with the salty taste of blood in my mouth. The tablets Dr Sullivan had prescribed were no longer effective. It was time to change medication.

"Cocaine is on of the best vaso-constrictors," he told me. "It's also safer than the tablets. I'm going to prescribe a cocaine mouthwash for you. Rinse your mouth out with it every time your gums bleed. It should help."

For a while, it did help to staunch the bleeding. On a couple of occasions, I inadvertently swallowed some of the mixture. The result was most pleasant. Whenever my spleen pain increased, I swallowed a little more. As a pain-reliever cocaine was far, far better than a mouthwash! Some time later, I asked him whether he had been concerned that I might have become addicted

"It would have been the least of your problems," he replied.

I plugged back into the alternative cancer network and telephoned Mary shortly afterwards to ask her if she could suggest anything to help, other than following the modified Gerson-Wigmore program.

"Have you tried wheat grass?" she asked.

"Yes."

"Lots of it?"

"As much as I can cope with."

I was now drinking three to four glasses a day as well as the twelve glasses of juice required by the Gerson diet.

We discussed the Wigmore program in detail and came to the conclusion that it was time to take an even more aggressive approach. There is a school of thought that cancer increases the need for protein. The answer, they say, is to 'starve' the cancer by keeping to a low-protein diet. I discussed this with several people. I checked all the reference material I could find. I stopped eating what little poultry, fish and eggs I had re-introduced into my diet. I stopped munching almonds. If the almost total avoidance of any protein was going to help me, I was prepared to try it. I felt desperate.

My ankles were swollen from poor circulation. Instead of

my heart maintaining a steady 70 beats a minute at rest, it was around the hundred-mark. The palpitations recurred with greater frequency, each one a more terrifying experience than the one before.

I meditated longer. Instead of two to three hours a day, I meditated for four. It was hard to stay focused. My wife's sister had arrived from overseas to visit us so there was non-stop bustle in the house. As much as I would have preferred a quieter environment, circumstances dictated otherwise. Arthur and Patsy helped me to conserve my strength by continuing to buy my vegetables for me.

A few days later on my way to purchase more fresh calf's liver, my left eye became blurred. I stopped the car. I wiped my eyes. It made no difference. I could see nothing except a red mist. I telephoned Dr Sullivan.

"I can't see properly through my left eye. It's all blurry."

"Come and see me tomorrow morning. I'll tell my receptionist you're coming in." His voice was calm. I was concerned. As the evening wore on, I became completely blind. The next morning he told me what had happened.

"You've had a retinal hemorrhage. I think you should have a platelet transfusion. As soon as your eye clears up, you should also have a full blood transfusion. Your counts have become too low for comfort or safety." Keeping his cool kept me cool.

I had tried to avoid medical intervention that did not offer the chance of remission or a cure. To refuse now would have cost me my life. Reluctantly, I agreed. He telephoned the Day Centre at the Royal Melbourne Hospital. He wasn't wasting any time. Dr Sullivan's rooms were attached to the hospital but a long walk away to the main part of the hospital and the Day Centre on the third floor. Blinded as I was in one eye and with no energy, Dr Sullivan escorted me as I shuffled slowly towards my first transfusion.

It was a room about five meters square. My first impression was that it was a cheerful place. Posters depicting capital cities around the world adorned the walls. The notice boards were covered with postcards sent by patients on overseas travels. There were bulletin boards with notices from edge to edge. A large refrigerator marked 'Cytotoxic Drugs. Keep Shut.' stood against one wall. Several easy chairs lined the other walls. Dr Sullivan introduced me to Cynthia who asked me to sit down. I felt detached from my surroundings. This wasn't happening to me. The smiling faces of the other patients seemed at odds with the place. I was sure this was all a bad dream.

Cynthia asked me to put out my arm. The prick of the needle brought me back to the here and now. It occurred to me that I didn't even know to which blood group I belonged. Dr Sullivan explained that there is more to a transfusion than simply matching blood types. Rhesus (RH) factors have to be accurate as well. Fiona, another nurse, offered me a cup of tea. They sat with me as we waited for the blood to be delivered from the Blood Bank. Dr Sullivan left me to attend to some of his ward patients. He returned a short while later, inserted a needle into my arm and connected this to a saline drip. As soon as the platelets arrived, Fiona exchanged the saline bag for a 250ml bag of platelets. I was surprised to notice the color. I assumed they would be red but they were brown. I closed my eyes. I didn't know what to expect.

"You'll be okay now," Dr Sullivan said. "I'll leave you in the capable hands of these lovely ladies."

As I lay back in the recliner, I marveled at the fact that an ingredient of a complete stranger's blood was being used to save my life. I felt a surge of gratitude. I also realized that I had, perhaps, left everything too late. I couldn't see any benefit in gaining a few extra months. If I was going to spend my remaining days attached to a tube, what was the point of carrying on? I was going to die anyway. A time would come when the transfusions would no longer help. As I later found out, platelet transfusions cease to have any effect after the fifth or sixth time.

I reflected on what I had done. I was sure I should have stopped working sooner. I would have had more time to follow the Gerson program properly. Suddenly, the reason for my existence seemed beyond my comprehension. If I was meant to continue living, the choice was now out of my hands. I then had the most fearful thought: 'If I don't die from leukemia, I'll probably die of AIDS.'

The newspapers at the time were full of stories about patients who had contracted a new disease called AIDS as a result of a blood donor carrying the HIV virus. I had read all about it but had accepted my platelet transfusion admittedly with some trepidation. I knew transfusions were not a cure. They usually signaled the end. To die from an infected palliative seemed ironic. I felt despondent.

"May I call a taxi for you?" Cynthia asked me about an hour later. She smiled. "You're done. Doesn't take long, does it? Your eye will clear up pretty rapidly."

She was right. The following day, the mist lifted.

The nurses at the Royal Melbourne Day Centre were refreshingly different from nurses I had previously encountered. They were young. They were friendly. The ward sister, Cynthia, was in her late twenties. Long blonde hair framed her cheerful face. Her eyes twinkled from behind her large-framed glasses. She always had a ready smile. She was gentle. She was caring. Most of the nurses there shared her passion for working in oncology. I don't know how I would have coped with the physical intrusion of the transfusions if they not been as efficient and compassionate as they were.

A few days later, I had a further blood test. My platelets had shot up to 38,000. My hemoglobin was at 5.2.

However, Dr Sullivan was not satisfied. "I think you can't afford not to have a full blood transfusion," he said. "You're putting too much strain on your heart. You're at great risk of even more severe infection."

"Can we wait until after my son's barmitzvah?"

"When is it?"

"The Saturday before Christmas."

"You've lasted so long, I suppose a few extra days won't make that much difference. Still, if you don't feel right, please phone me."

"Can I have an AIDS test?"

"I wouldn't worry if I were you," he replied. He told me later that if my time was so limited, being infected with AIDS was low on the agenda.

"My wife asked me to ask you," I said.

'Okay, I'll set it up,' came his bemused reply. "I'm sure there's nothing for her to worry about." He was right. When I had the test a few weeks later, the results were negative.

The weekend we celebrated my son's barmitzvah stretched my reserves. I had such difficulty breathing I was afraid I would collapse during the ceremony. It was his special day, though, and I hoped nothing would mar the occasion. Every second felt like an hour. I took long, slow breaths. Now and then, I held my breath in an effort to force air through my blood so I could enjoy this family moment. Finally, the service was over. In short, faltering steps, I managed to get to the car and drive home. I fell on my bed, exhausted.

We held his party the following evening. As I watched everyone eating, drinking, talking and laughing, I was strangely at peace. I felt sure that, despite all my efforts, this would be my last Christmas. I accepted it. Underneath the jollity of the night, my cancer was the unspoken subject. I looked around. Of all the people present, only a handful had maintained contact with me: Arthur and Patsy, Sally, and my dear friends, Michael and Roy who visited me almost every day and who kept me in touch with the world at large. And there was my ever-supportive friend, Julie. She and her husband, Simon, lived so far across town she visited only occasionally, but telephoned almost daily. The rest of our crowd of 'friends' had become strangers.

As I gazed out over the throng, it occurred to me – as it does today - that few people know how to talk to someone with cancer. They simply don't know what to say. For one thing, they're afraid to use the word 'cancer'. When they discuss the subject, they lower their voices. They are fearful that if they don't talk about the illness, the patient will think they don't care. If they do, they're uncertain whether their approach will be construed as too forward or too patronizing. Most cancer patients believe – correctly – that only other cancer patients can understand how they really feel. For many, their fear of death is surpassed only by the fear that others will see that they are afraid. They withdraw into themselves. They know their time is limited. They create a distance between themselves and others. It's the easiest way to lessen the pain of eventual loss.

As I came to appreciate, most cancer patients, myself included, welcome greater closeness from their family and friends. The greatest difficulty is in coping with insensitive comments like, 'don't worry you'll be fine. The doctors know what they're doing.' Or, 'I'm sure everything will be okay.' 'Be positive. Don't give up.' 'Everything happens for the best.' Worst of all, I believe, is for the atheist to be told 'It's all in God's hands'.

These statements are insensitive, at worst patronizing. Cancer patients know how they feel. Instinctively, they know whether they are going to live or die. They want respect for their privacy and silence. They also need the opportunity to make contact on their own terms, in their own time. They do expect to be treated with consideration. Most of all, they do want to be listened to without passing judgment. Dying people seldom get a listening ear. For family and friends it's a crucial time to hone their listening skills.

Cancer is the ultimate test of the maturity of a family and the ability of the individuals in it to care for each other. Faced by a threat from the outside, a family will often act like a single organism to defend itself. Where someone within it threatens its security or its survival by getting cancer, a destabilizing effect takes place. Confusion reigns. Relationships take a battering, many falter, some come to an end.

I had been the breadwinner and father figure. I had been the entertainer and Mr Fixit. I had been the strong arm of defense. Losing me would weaken the system. As time went by, I would come to appreciate even more how each family faced with cancer has to deal with the dynamics of its own particular dilemma. Roles need to be re-examined and, if possible, re-assigned. When the patient perceives that the family is actively absorbing what they have learned from him or her and endeavoring to fill their previous roles, he or she is usually granted relief from mental pain. The need for sensitivity is paramount. Open and honest communication has to be maintained. And families who commit their loved one to an institution to avoid all this suffer even greater loss; they lose the opportunity for everyone to rediscover the wealth of love heard only in silent communication and through touch.

It occurred to me that the best approach when someone is facing a life-threatening situation is to allow him or her to set the agenda. The degree to which they are prepared to discuss their illness, and how they feel about it, will depend as much on their confidence and trust in you as on your openness and the degree to which you are prepared to embrace their pain and their suffering. Instead of making assumptions about how you think we feel or what you think we want, it is better and kinder to be attuned to the moment, to talk less and listen more, and to be appropriately responsive. I suggest that pity is the worst emotion to express, as this reveals your fear. On the other hand, your compassion will reveal the extent of your love.

I remembered how my friends had listened to me as I told them what I was doing. They told me the latest news. They related the current jokes. They smiled. That was something I appreciated. Long, mournful faces made me feel sadder than I was. I realized much later that by not confiding in them, I had unwittingly alienated many friends and acquaintances. It was the only way I could explain the disappearance of so many people I had considered friends.

My illness identified my genuine friends. Their visits made an appreciable difference. They helped steer my thoughts in other directions. Their presence offset my sense of alienation.

I looked at the crowd around me. It was hard to believe I

was going to leave them. That night I sat and meditated. I felt I had reached a turning point of sorts. I wasn't sure in which direction I was going. I prayed. I remembered Sally's words. 'Have faith. Give yourself over. Don't fight it.'

Christmas came and went. My father had nothing in his duffel bag to help, but his companionship was a source of unbelievable comfort. He talked about his adventures as a young man. His stories were witty and anecdotal, filled with tales of heroism. In Dad's tales, you were either a winner or a loser. In his own way, he was making a point: don't give up. Never say die. He didn't want to talk about death. He was determined to talk me into a winning frame of mind just as he had when he timed me for athletics at high school:

'Keep going. You can do better.'

Two days after Christmas, I had another blood test. I told Dr Sullivan how ill I felt.

"We'd better check you out."

My platelet count had fallen to 22,000. My white cell count was 0.8. The reason I felt so terrible was now quite clear: my hemoglobin had dropped to 4.8. On 28 December, I had my first full blood transfusion. I returned the following day for another 250ml unit of blood. Overnight, my hemoglobin moved to 5.2, my platelets to 29,000, my white cells to 0.9. I was now hooked on transfusions.

My eldest son had made plans a long time ago to celebrate his end-of-school vacation by following the West Indies cricket team who were touring the country. He was now reluctant to leave me. He had been my gardener and my right arm and was concerned that my health would falter if I stopped drinking wheat-grass juice. The blood transfusions had given me a respite. I said he should go, and he was relieved.

The effect of the transfusions had alleviated my symptoms. The anger was gone. Instead of being in a state of heightened alert, I felt curiously at peace. I felt it was now all right to die rather than go through an interminable period of treatment. For the first time in my life, I felt there was another dimension to my recovery – and it lay outside my sphere of influence. That very day, as I lay reading the Bible, I came across the following in John 5: 'I can of mine own self do nothing.'

I tried to discuss this with my wife.

"You can't give up," she said. "You can't stop now."

"I'm not giving up. I now accept what is happening to me."

"That means you're giving up."

"No it doesn't."

It was clear that she did not understand the difference.

"It means I've decided to surrender myself to forces beyond my control." My innate optimism had brought me thus far. I was now more hopeful than I had been in ages. Dying didn't matter any more.

"Transfusions aren't forever," I said.

At my next healing from Sally, I discussed what had happened and how hard I was finding it to explain my position to my wife. For Sally it was simple: "Your fate is in the hands of God. Relax and accept it," she said. She lent me yet another book written by Joel Goldsmith. He had been a prolific author. It was hard keeping up.

Goldsmith's message echoed that of Meares. They had known each other, but I only found that out years later. Goldsmith said that stilling the mind and the activity of the senses makes us consciously aware of the presence of God. 'In the Silence we find Allness.' I had heard the essence of that message before. It was the story of survival. 'To be clever is to be still,' John Ndmande had taught me as a child. His words travelled through time. Through them now, I perceived the timelessness of my existence. For the first time I saw myself within a larger context. There are no edges to existence. There are no borders. Death does not mark the end. I had first glimpsed the Allness in reverie. In meditation, I became aware of its vast and embracing expanse. I was enveloped in it. I was part of it. According to Goldsmith, whatever we perceive is an extension of God. To find him, he says, we have to look no further 'than our hands and our feet.' Meares had indicated to me that we cannot separate the dancer from the dance – and so our existence, and that of all things, cannot be separated from that which created everything. It occurred to me that it makes no difference whether we call it God, Universality, a Force or a Power. The ultimate truth is the same.

By accepting what was happening to me, I gained confidence. By not being cowed, the blood transfusions – and there were many more to come – became easier to bear. I no longer resisted what I first felt was an intrusion. I came to terms with my condition. I became my own witness.

In my childhood, I had been told that heaven was far away. I now knew it wasn't. The Allness was everywhere, it was at once the past, the present and the future – and I was part of its all-embracing magnificence.

CHAPTER NINETEEN

January 1985:
Platelet count 23,000; haemoglobin level 5.4; White blood cell count
1.0

I went back to the hospital. I stayed overnight for a slow, 3-unit, full blood transfusion. When I returned home the following day, the house was almost deserted. My father was asleep. Our younger sons had gone to town. Our eldest son was following the cricket tour. My wife was at work. I meditated. It occurred to me that the two younger boys would get bored unless they had a break. Summer vacations are long.

I decided to take them away on a short holiday. My wife stayed home with my father. We checked into a motel at Lakes Entrance, a picturesque seaside fishing and resort town a few hours' drive away. The coffee-enema equipment and vegetable juicer came with me. The blood transfusion had given me a boost of energy. I had no trouble driving, but walking to the beach was hard. My legs felt like lead. I was still breathless but I didn't want to spoil the holiday for the boys, and I wasn't sure what to do. They solved the problem.

"We'll go to the beach on our own," they said. "It'll be quiet here. You can meditate without us and you can watch television." On the days they walked to the beach, I rested, meditated, took coffee enemas and made juices. In between, I read or lazed at the pool. It was peaceful. On other days, I took them to ice-cream shops, restaurants and the fun fair. There were times when I simply sat on a sand dune and watched them as they tried to wind surf. For seven days, we had a wonderful time.

The fun fair was on every night. For the first few nights, I drove them to the fairground and fetched them later. Eventually, we agreed it was safe enough for them to go on their own. The sideshows and amusement rides were great attractions. It was a good decision giving them that holiday. They enjoyed the light relief. I booked a table for us one evening at a Chinese restaurant and they were shocked to see me eating vegetable spring rolls. I even shared a lemon chicken and boiled rice with them. We did the same a few evenings later, much to their added delight.

"Come on, Pop," my youngest said. It was the day before we were due to leave. "Please come to the beach with us."

I felt a little uncertain. He sensed my reluctance and said, "You can lean on us." Crossing the jetty – it was over a hundred meters long - was a major excursion. To me it felt like a ten-kilometer hike! Sitting on the beach on the opposite side of the lagoon – March flies notwithstanding – was worth the effort. I reveled as the boys frolicked in the water. I felt rejuvenated. It had nothing to do with the unpolluted air I was breathing so far away from the city.

Even so, the past two nights had been three-towel night sweat affairs. I had excruciating boils. My gum bleeds had not abated. As we repacked the car for our return trip, I was aware of how my breathing had changed. I was feeling down. I was out of air again. When we returned home, I telephoned Dr Sullivan.

"I think you should have another transfusion," he said. "I also want you to start a new course of antibiotics."

A few days later after the next transfusion I had a little breathing space. My hemoglobin went up to 6.1. My platelets were still only 23,000. My white cell count remained at only 1.0. It was obvious that transfusions weren't going to sustain me forever. The Gerson diet didn't appear to be working. I wrote to the Gerson Therapy Center in the United Sates. As I described my regimen to them, I couldn't believe how many tablets I had been swallowing – about sixty per day! I detailed how I had followed their diet, including the potassium mixture and Lugol's. I told them I had been unable to obtain crude liver injections but was taking the same in tablet form. I added that my doctor had dissuaded me from taking thyroid tablets. I explained that I had had a platelet transfusion to prevent further retinal bleeding. I repeated what I had told my doctor, namely that I would not be able to determine if my program was working if they kept propping up my blood levels with transfusions. I told them I had reduced the number of coffee enemas. 'What more could I do?' I asked.

Their reply was disappointing. They suggested that unless I entered their institution, they could make no more suggestions other than those prescribed in Gerson's book. They advised me that a new medical team had been formed in 1977. Since then, several new supportive treatments had been added to their program. Depending on the case, they used ozone, hydrogen peroxide, intravenous GKI drip (glucose/-potassium/insulin), live cell therapy, Laetrile and castor oil/clay packs. I was curious. I was also becoming more skeptical. I asked Dr Sullivan what he thought. His reply was judicious.

"No one in here will give you this treatment – in fact, some of it could be extremely dangerous. In any event, I don't have to remind you that you're not well enough to travel."

Mention of the word Laetrile in the Gerson program rang a bell. I was still munching apricot kernels. Dr Ernesto

Contreras in Mexico had, apparently, achieved great success with it. I thought, why bother with second-hand opinions? Go straight to the source. I made dozens of enquiries. Eventually I found an address in Tijuana and I wrote to it. I received a reply from Dr Contreras himself.

'It is obvious that in your case, since August 1984, you have started to tolerate it [my leukemia] poorly in spite of the excellent program you have been taking. With figures as low as those you have shown in December and January, your life is in real danger either by uncontrollable infections or hemorrhaging. If you were to come, I would use a combination of mild conventional treatments with a different non-toxic program. Splenectomy might help temporarily, but obviously not for a long time. I don't think you should stick to the very strict regime you have been taking which is not helping and is making you weaker and weaker every time. This is all I can tell you now. May God guide you to take decisions in this very critical moment."

Sincerely yours,

Dr Ernesto Contreras.'

What non-toxic treatment? I wondered. His words had struck a responsive chord. I replied, asking him for more details. His reply, in turn, held me riveted - not what he said, but the tone.

'By mild treatment, I mean mild conventional therapy. I would use Laetrile, mixed Proteolytic Enzymes, mega-doses of vitamins and minerals, and a 'special transfer factor' prepared from healthy lymphocytes called LEUKIN-5*. Unfortunately, I can't make any definite promises as far as a long-term complete remission is concerned. That is God's privilege. I understand your position and I want to help you as much as possible; but we have to be realistic. Your counts would have to improve by 50 per cent before you would be well enough to travel.

Praying honestly that you get better, I remain,

Sincerely yours,

Dr Ernesto Contreras.'

[*Note: Interleukin had just begun to make the odd headline. It was still in the embryonic stage in cancer research. Dr Contreras was clearly at the cutting edge of medical advances.]

I sat in silence for a long time after I read his letter. I had been a little despondent after his first reply. Now I felt more peaceful, more reassured. I had already made my choices. I was not going to succumb. I was also not going to fight. There was a reason for my continuing search. Dr Contreras understood.

A week later, I had a further blood transfusion. My counts went up a little: hemoglobin to 7.2, white cells stayed at 1.0, platelets dropped to 21,000. Breathing had become a little easier although the gum bleeds did not stop and the swollen lymph glands in my groin, under my arms and in my neck were still extremely painful. My ankles remained puffy. My spleen was now 23 centimeters long.

I took Contreras's advice. I reduced the number of Gerson juices I was drinking and stopped the liver and carrot juices completely. I was used to its taste by now, but they weren't working. I stopped drinking wheat-grass. It was becoming harsher and more difficult to swallow. In any event, my son and his juicing arm were still following the West Indian cricket tour. I also decided to reduce the number of tablets I was taking. A terrifying episode a few days later convinced me I had made the right decision.

I had just had lunch, and no sooner had I taken my pills

than a large Vitamin C tablet lodged in my throat. I could hardly breathe. Everyone panicked. No one knew what to do. My son whacked me between the shoulder blades in an attempt to dislodge the pill. I tried drinking water. It wouldn't go down. I tried chewing a little bread. It also wouldn't go down. I felt faint.

"Phone Denise," I gasped. Denise was the widow of my friend, Alan, and she lived close by. She drove me to the hospital. The doctor asked me questions but I couldn't reply, I couldn't breathe. My son told him what had happened.

"Dad also has Hairy Cell Leukemia," he added.

"I'll be back in a moment," the doctor replied. He didn't return but his registrar did.

"I suggest you sit there until the tablet dissolves," he said. "With your condition there's not much more I can do. At least you can breathe a little."

I was struggling for air. Some air was getting in. I sat gasping like a fish for about an hour. Vitamin C tablets take a long time to dissolve. From then on, I made sure I drank lots of water to swallow large pills safely.

CHAPTER TWENTY

February 1985:
Platelet count 24,000; haemoglobin level 6.0; White blood cell count 1.0

At the beginning of February, I decided to re-read Gerson's book. I thought I knew it backwards. Instead, I found a list of factors that would prevent his program from succeeding. Of the nine points listed, four applied to me.

(1) Extensive cortisone treatments. Mine had not been extensive, but I had two injections to relieve the pain in my shoulder. I had also taken half a bottle of Prednisone to raise my platelet level for intended surgery. (2) More than two recent transfusions. I had now received four. (3) A lymphocyte count of less than 10.0. My lymphocyte counts had not been above 7.0. (4) Extensive liver damage (Dr Gerson considered liver scans seriously added to liver damage). I had undergone one scan already.

I sat back. It was obvious that there was no point in continuing with the Gerson program as I had decided to reduce even further the number of juices I was drinking. To two of these I added the potassium mixture. I stopped the Lugol's solutions and took only two coffee enemas a day.

"Maybe you're allergic to some of the foods you're eating." My friend Mike said. He had come to visit me.

"What do you mean?"

"My partner's daughter had the most awful asthma. Nothing helped. They took her to a naturopath who found she was allergic to wheat. My son Jon, as you know, also has severe asthma. I took him to see the same woman a while ago. She found he was allergic to gluten. Ever since he's been off it, he's been much better. Why don't you visit this clinic?"

"How do they test you for allergies?"

"They use a computer," Mike replied.

I was intrigued, so I phoned them to make an appointment.

Once again, I suspended my critical judgment. Intelligence had nothing to do with my actions. As I would later come to appreciate, I had all the convictions of the uninformed.

Three days later, I drove out to the clinic, which was some considerable distance from where we lived. The waiting room was crowded. I was desperate to rest but I'd come so far, I couldn't back out now. After a lengthy wait, I was ushered into the doctor's room. He was a tall, grey-haired man in his sixties. He shook my hand, sat down behind his desk and explained how he used various herbs and vitamins to cure many different ailments.

"I can't offer you a cure for cancer or leukemia," he said. "However, I do believe that if we can detect any allergies, avoiding them may help improve your overall condition." He led me through to another room where I met his assistant, a down-to-earth woman in her late forties.

"Please take a seat," she said, "and take off your shoes and socks and place your feet on the metal plate."

I looked down. A circular metal plate with protruding wires lay on the floor. Gingerly, I rested my feet on it. I wondered if this was how someone felt when he or she was about to be electrocuted. She sensed my trepidation.

"Don't worry. It's attached to this computer," she explained pointing to the machine next to her. "I'm going to ask you to hold some vials. These contain different elements like zinc, iron, potassium and sodium. Other vials contain grains or juices. This machine is programed to show which ones you have a negative response to." One after another, she handed me dozens of different containers. She flicked switches. She turned dials. If modern science could do anything for me, I was prepared to suppress my cynicism. Eventually, the test was over.

She read the printout. "According to this, you have a strong yeast intolerance. Also gluten. Also sugars. I'd like you to come back in two weeks' time. We'll run another test." As I left, she handed me a list of dietary recommendations.

As skeptical as I felt, I bought gluten-free bread. I swallowed brewer's yeast, a dessertspoon of cold-pressed safflower oil and powdered kelp every day. I stopped eating most of the foods they suggested I avoid. It was not a difficult diet to adapt to. She also handed me a paper on Candida. "I'd like you to follow these recommendations, as well. You should do everything you can to boost your immune system."

I read the article. It pointed out that the most common symptom of the fungus Candida is thrush. This occurs as whitish raised blisters in the esophagus or vagina (not my problem!). It starts in the digestive tract and then enters the bloodstream where it greatly weakens the immune system. This allows immune-deficiency diseases – including cancer – to invade the body. Candida infections often arise from taking antibiotics that destroy the natural flora in the intestine, but this natural flora can be replaced by drinking a rich source of Vitamin B, such as yoghurt. Candida often resulted, the article stated, from food and yeast allergies. I was surprised to learn that certain fungi found in household dust and damp could cause Candida. I was sure there was nothing in our house that caused it.

"I don't agree," my father said when I told him. "I think there's water under the house: a stream perhaps. Whenever I go into your bedroom, it feels damp."

I wondered if he was right. There was a green strip running across the lawn. It did run towards the bedroom. There was no way I could remedy that problem! Then I remembered that I had suffered from thrush many years earlier when I had been on intense antibiotic treatment following back surgery. It had cleared up after eating copious amounts of yoghurt and taking Nystatin, an anti-fungicidal mixture. I telephoned Dr Sullivan for his advice.

"What would happen if I started taking Nystatin? Can it do me any harm?"

"No. And it's not a bad idea. You've been on antibiotics for quite some time."

For the next week, I took Nystatin every day after meals. Two weeks later, I returned for another test.

"The results are no better," she said, after examining the printout. "Stay on the diet." Then she asked: "Are you depressed? It shows, you know." She appeared genuinely concerned. I pointed out that it was highly improbable that anyone diagnosed with cancer would not be depressed.

I didn't return to the clinic. By now, my preparedness to try anything no matter how bizarre and unscientific was beginning to wear thin. I finished the course of pills I had bought. Many of them had been similar to the ones I had taken before. For a while, I continued to follow their dietary recommendations: lots of grains, nuts, pulses and a mix of cooked and raw vegetables. They did not advocate detoxification, feeling it was potentially dangerous and could cause infection.

To their credit, they had promised me no cure. They had given me no cure.

In time I would come to realize that depression in cancer patients is a constant – sometimes manageable, at other times less so.

CHAPTER TWENTY ONE

March 1985:
Platelet count 21,000; haemoglobin level 7.2; White blood cell count 0.8

My mind and body were at odds. Mentally I felt confident, strong and at peace. Physically, for the past two and a half months, only blood transfusions had kept me going. However, from the Gerson Institute's reply and my rereading of the doctor's book – as well as Dr Contreras' letters – it was apparent that my body was sliding downhill.

I telephoned Dr Sullivan the following day.

"When I was having an overnight transfusion," I told him, "a psychiatrist at the hospital came to see me. I told her all about my program. I think I'd like to talk to her. Can you please arrange a referral to her?"

He thought it would be a good idea, "Her name is Dr Diamond. I'll get my secretary to set it up." He did, but I had to wait two weeks for an appointment.

I used the intervening period to try something else. I decided to go on another fast. I had noticed that whenever my father didn't feel well, he didn't eat. He would go for days without food.

"I'm like an old dog," he said. "A sick dog never eats. It always gets better. When you're not well, your body can't digest food properly. Anyway, it helps to lose a little weight."

Fasting is quite distinct from simply eating less. Experiments on rats conducted at the University of Texas have shown that if their food intake is halved, the ageing process – measured on metabolic and genetic parameters – is slowed by a third. Of course, not eating enough can also impair the body's immune system. This concerned me. My blood levels were still falling. I agonized over the decision: do I fast or not? Eventually I repeated the eight-day juices-only fast I had tried several months previously. As before, I was so euphoric I was reluctant to come off it.

I wondered what other directions I could take through the maze. I took my sons with me to the library. It was a warm, sunny Saturday afternoon. They scanned the music section. I searched the medical section. I picked out Dr Issel's book, *'Cancer, A Second Opinion'*. It was written in English! David Perth had told me it had never been translated from German. I borrowed the book.

Unlike Dr Gerson, who maintained a uniform diet was suitable for all illnesses, Dr Issels believed variations were needed. He concurred with Dr Gerson that the diet for a cancer patient should be free from cancer-promoting substances. Issels believed that a diet should be low in animal fats but rich in vegetable fats. It must have as little fermentable carbohydrates as possible. These included glucose or glucose-forming carbohydrates. Protein was an essential component of all cells. As such, it was vital that the protein be properly synthesized. This, he claimed, could be achieved through the intake of all 27 amino acids. Twelve of these cannot be formed in the body. They have to be eaten daily with meals. Whole meal bread, soya beans, nuts, yeast, eggs, milk, fish and meat are the best source of these amino acids. Protein from sour milk products was the most easily digestible. Protein derived from meat resulted in a build-up of putrefying toxins. Issels recommended cottage cheese. He regarded fresh milk as unwholesome, sour milk better than yoghurt. A little meat, preferably from inner organs, was in order as long as it was not smoked. Lean fish was better than any type of meat. Saturated fats were out. Issels regarded all animal fats as 'dead solid fats'. He encouraged the use of Vitamin F, found especially in cold-pressed oils. He considered whole meal muesli excellent. He proposed that an inadequate intake of water caused metabolic and organic dysfunction. According to Issels, the average person suffers from dehydration. He believed that to maintain normal body functions, a person needed 40 – 50 ml of water per kg of body weight a day. The ideal, he claimed, was chlorine-free spring water. I came close. I had my water purifier.

Apart from diet, Dr Issels treated patients by artificially inducing fevers. According to his theory, elevated blood temperature stimulated the body's immune system. I was still suffering from night sweats and, at times, ran raging temperatures. The idea of introducing more fever held no appeal to me.

It was Dr Issels' concept of low-grade infection that most intrigued me. He maintained that tonsillectomies were one of the worst evils perpetrated by the medical profession on an unsuspecting public. Tonsils, he claimed, were hardly ever properly removed. The result was a source of continuing low-grade infection. As David Perth had told me, he also claimed that when teeth were drilled, they were not properly cleansed. Fillings plastered over these bacteria created a source of infection in the roots and the jaw. I had already discussed this problem with my dentist and the results of the x-rays had been negative. As for my tonsils, I'd had these removed three times: when I was four, eight and twenty-eight. Somehow, they had never been completely removed. I wondered if I still had any left.

"Even if you still had your tonsils," Dr Sullivan said when I asked him a few days later, "you couldn't have an operation now. Your platelet count is far too low." He looked down my throat. "Anyway, your tonsils look fine to me. I don't think they're life-threatening."

The Gerson diet had been of little use to me. I wondered if the Issels diet was worth trying? It didn't seem as drastic. I decided to finish reading his book before deciding. It was just as well I did. As I read on, I came across the name of Rudolf Breuss, an Austrian herbalist. Dr Issels regarded his work among leukemic patients as brilliant. Best of all, Breuss himself had written a book on the treatment of leukemia. I decided to find out more.

No one seemed to have heard of him. I was about to give up when I found what I was looking for: a footnote in Issels' book, giving the address of a health-food shop in England to which to write for more information. I had to wait a few weeks for a reply, but eventually the book arrived. I speed-read it. I was amazed. Breuss recommended what I had just done: fasting. A closer read of this book revealed his regimen for leukemia was not as severe as those advocated by Gerson and Issels.

According to Breuss, the body eliminates everything it does not need during a fast. It does so naturally. It only retains that which is vital for its continued existence. He held that the body would even consume cancerous growth and eliminate it. I had no hard cancerous growths and so appreciated why his treatment for leukemia was different.

As with Gerson and Wigmore, Breuss claimed we all have a divine source of healing within ourselves. It was essential, he maintained, to have a strong belief in this power. Breuss shared another belief with Gerson: he did not believe that his methods would work with people who had undergone chemotherapy or radiotherapy. Both these treatments destroy the body's natural defense systems. I decided to follow the methods of Breuss. It seemed easier to follow than Gerson's.

I tried to obtain some of the teas recommended for the diet but I could not find them anywhere. I wrote to the shop from which I obtained the book. In response, I received an order form listing all their products. I had to wait almost three weeks for them to arrive from England. Meanwhile, it was time to keep my appointment with Dr Diamond.

Long blonde hair framed her freckled cheeks and kind eyes. Dr Diamond was in her early forties and extremely vivacious, with a ready smile. I was disarmed and wasn't sure where to begin. I knew that many of her patients were faced with life-threatening diseases. She quickly put me at ease by discussing my leukemia. She wanted to know why I was doing what I was.

"Tell me everything," she said. "I think what you're doing is fascinating."

I told her about the Gerson diet, meditation (she knew Ainslie Meares), Dr Elisabeth Kübler-Ross and all the diets and fasts I had been on. She listened attentively and after about half an hour, and said, "you know, Dr Sullivan is probably the best cancer specialist in the country. He thinks what you're doing is amazing. I agree. Now tell me why you won't have a splenectomy?"

"If my blood counts were good enough to have my spleen out and the symptoms returned as they undoubtedly will, there won't be another spleen to remove. The risk of infection will be greater. In any event, why go through all that pain to gain just a few more months? It's not a cure. I still have a number of options available." I explained that I was waiting for the parcel of teas to arrive so I could start my new diet.

"I hope you keep John Sullivan informed of what you're doing?"

"Of course I do. I tell him everything."

I skirted around my emotional problems. She was wise enough not to press me. It took several sessions before I eventually felt comfortable enough to talk to her without reserve. I felt so lonely and so isolated. Apart from her, there was no one I could talk to about how I truly felt. There was no need for her to try to read between the lines.

Then the teas arrived from England.

The Complete Cancer Treatment advocated by Breuss does not allow any food to be eaten for 42 days. Fortunately, his treatment for leukemia was different. I could eat anything I liked except meat. I kept to the program for 36 days. The vegetable juice recommended was different from any other I had tried. It consisted of carrot, beetroot, celery, radish and potato. I drank three to four glasses a day. I also drank sage, kidney and cranesbill tea. I ate a little fish. I still avoided all those substances I had previously eliminated from my diet.

It was what Breuss claimed was the cause of leukemia that interested me most: depression. His cure was simple: "Relax and try not think too much."

I thought a better and less expensive solution might be to stop breathing altogether!

CHAPTER TWENTY TWO

April 1985:
Platelet count 21,000; haemoglobin level 7.8; White blood cell count 0.9

Try as I might to remain upbeat, I could not help feeling time was running out. A further blood test revealed my counts had fallen even more. Dr Sullivan had told me I could have any number of blood transfusions, but he had also told me platelet transfusions became ineffectual after the sixth. I had had one in December. It was now mid-April. A sudden nosebleed convinced him I needed more. Two days later, I received another full blood transfusion of four units. Depending on the amount, a transfusion given over a short period can be extremely painful. I knew that four units in one day would be painful so I stayed overnight at the hospital.

At my next visit to Dr Diamond, I explained more of the difficulties I was having.

"I think I should have another AIDS test."

"But you don't have AIDS," she said.

"My wife keeps insisting."

"Then do it," Dr Diamond said. "But trying all these different things must be tiring. I wouldn't have thought you'd have any energy for anything else."

I had the AIDS test that week. The result was unsurprisingly negative.

Every second week Dr Diamond offered me her non-judgmental and sympathetic ear.

Her medical advice was also extremely useful. I felt more

comfortable in her presence with each subsequent visit.

"Your father and sons surely keep you going. They're obviously very special to you," she said to me, one day.

She was right. My fear of losing my family was more of a spur to me that the diets. Yet I was not quite ready to abandon the diets: there were so many common threads to them, I felt there had to be an element of truth behind them. A few days later, while my wife and I were having tea with Mike and his wife Julie, she reminded us of mutual friends we had known in London.

"Sonny Brenner went back to his ranch in Africa. He and his wife couldn't stand the weather in London any more."

"Wait a moment," my wife said. "As I recall, I think his brother is a professor of oncology in Israel?"

"That's right!" Julie exclaimed. "You should phone him."

"I'll do it now," I said.

Israel has the highest incidence of leukemia in the world. I figured that if anyone had the answers, the doctors there should. Professor Brenner's reply was not what I expected.

"For your leukemia, the preferred method of treatment is a splenectomy."

"But is it a cure?" I asked.

"There is no cure. Your doctor would have told you that. You can only treat the symptoms." That was that. He was polite and friendly. He gave me the standard medical approach.

"If there is anything else I can do to help, let me know," he added.

"Yes. Please could you find the telephone number and address for me of Dr David Rubin? I believe he's a medical researcher in Israel." I had come across his name a few months earlier. He had conducted several trials using

Laetrile. He had also done several tests using selenium. I wondered if he could help. Right now, any path was worth pursuing.

"What do you want to know?" Professor Brenner asked. "I am familiar with David's work."

"I've been taking massive doses of Vitamin C. Forty grams a day, in fact. I've also been taking sodium selenate, selenium. Recently someone told me that the two ingredients are not compatible. Is this true?"

"Most definitely," he replied. "The only selenium you should take is yeast-bound selenium. You still shouldn't take it with Vitamin C. The combination is poisonous."

I had been taking Vitamin C and selenium for several months. It hadn't done anything to me. It hadn't done anything for me. Yeast-bound selenium is available only on prescription. It is also very expensive. I stopped taking selenium. Patsy had been taking it for a few years and it hadn't helped her, either. Another pathway closed.

I telephoned the naturopath, James Vaughan, who had provided me with the original set of place names on my map of discovery seventeen months earlier.

"Any more suggestions?" I asked. I told him what my most recent blood test had revealed, following my recent transfusion: hemoglobin was at 7.8, white cells were at 0.9, platelets were at 19,000. My spleen was a massive 26cm long. My ankles were puffier than ever. My gums would not stop bleeding; I carried a handkerchief at all times to mop up the blood.

"Something must be working," Vaughan said. "Your blood counts are so low, it's amazing you're still driving your car and getting around."

"Well?" I asked.

"Have you tried divination? It's used to determine which foods you're allergic to." I wondered if the allergy-testing machine at the clinic had missed something. Another attempt could do no harm.

Divination is an age-old method of determining the flow of positive and negative energy sources. It is still used today, water diviners being called up in times of drought. Did I have to walk around with a forked stick? I was curious.

"Alex Schmidt knows more about this method than anyone else I know. Why not give him a call?"

Amazing! David Perth had recommended Alex Schmidt to me some months before.

Schmidt was a man of medium height with greying, bushy hair and wide eyes. I explained Hairy Cell Leukemia to him, and I told him about the diets I had tried.

"Do you believe divination could be of some help to me?" I asked.

"Yes. I cured my mother's cancer with it. Not on its own, though," he added. "She took several herbs I gave her as well."

He took a fine thread out of his drawer, attached to an egg-sized crystal. He leaned forward and said, "If you hold this above any food, it will rotate clockwise or anti-clockwise. Like this, you can tell if you're allergic to that food or not."

"How does it work?" I asked.

"Suspend it above a food to which you know you're allergic. Whichever direction it turns means it will turn the same way above all foods you're allergic to. If it rotates the other way, it means you're not allergic to that food."

My skepticism must have shown. He spent the next several minutes assuring me it had helped his mother. He pointed to a large machine beside me. "I'd use that on my mother, only I'm waiting for a new part from overseas for the computer. Until that's fixed, I can't prescribe anything specific."

Frankly, I didn't believe him. My suspicions increased when he advised me that he would contact me as soon as the computer was operational. I decided that finding a cure for my disease was more important than my prejudices. I took the crystal and left. I suspended my judgment as I suspended the crystal above those foods I knew I had disliked or been allergic to from childhood: cabbage, cauliflower and marzipan. It turned the same way in almost every test I made. My family thought I was crazy. I tested every item of food in the pantry. I took my crystal with me whenever I went shopping.

"You can even test whether you're allergic to the food in a can," Schmidt had told me. I doubted him, but I tried it nevertheless.

"You're twirling the cotton," my middle son said.

"I'm not doing it on purpose." "Here, you try it." He did. It seemed to go one way on some foods, the other way on others. Even he seemed less skeptical.

I tried divination for a few weeks. I didn't follow all its suggestions. The crystal often turned in a favorable direction when I held it above foods I was determined to avoid: meat, peanut butter and coffee. After a while, I decided I was not benefiting from divination. Another path closed.

In time, I would come to reflect on how absurd the various methods of recovery I was trying were – and how others might have viewed my activities in the same light. But I was desperate to find my way out of the maze.

CHAPTER TWENTY THREE

May 1985:
Platelet count 17,000; haemoglobin level 5.6; White blood cell count 0.9

Despite all my setbacks, I was still committed to a dietary and detoxification regimen. I was taking one to two coffee enemas a day and I still meditated for up to three hours. I knew they weren't working as well as I hoped they would. They also took up so much of my time – and time was something I felt was in short supply.

"I think you should go and see Zoria," Patsy said.

"Who's Zoria?"

"She's a clairvoyant."

"I don't feel up to going. It's my birthday in three days' time. I'll think about it afterwards." I took the telephone number Patsy had given me and put it aside.

I was about to celebrate my forty-fifth birthday. I had chalked up another small victory. My plans for a small party at home were short-lived. I was awake most of the night with a raging fever and excruciating pain. My headache was so painful I felt as if my skull was going to explode into a thousand pieces. The following day I went to visit Dr Sullivan. He steered me in the direction of the hospital where I had another blood test. The results confirmed the worst. I spent my birthday in the Day Centre at the Royal Melbourne Hospital having another platelet transfusion.

The following day I had a full blood transfusion of five units, over a liter of new blood. It didn't make any difference.

My symptoms persisted. There was no relief.

I decided to visit Zoria, the clairvoyant, and I saw her the following day.

I entered the door of a small Victorian house. The hallway was the front office. Posters of Tutankhamen adorned the walls; Isis and Osiris were also prominent. There were posters of the constellations and the planets. The walls were lined with books on cosmology, Egyptology, astrology and numerology.

There was a faint scent of incense. I was intrigued. Then I was ushered into Zoria's sanctum. She sat behind a baize-covered card table. She was a plump, middle-aged woman, with a round face and her black hair was cut in a fringe. She gave me a warm, welcoming smile. Her dress was overflowing. She wore large, looped earrings. I was face to face with 'Madame Sosotris, famous clairvoyant'. She picked up a deck of tarot cards.

I was about to speak when she raised a finger to her lips. "Don't say anything. The cards will tell me all."

One by one, she turned them over and laid them out. My tarot card reading ability was poor but I recognized the Lady of the Rocks. I tried to remember what each one stood for. In a flash, she swept the cards aside and laid the deck down. She took out a sheet of paper, asked me for my birth date. I remembered how Reverend Bishop had done the same thing several months earlier. I wondered if their results would tally. She scanned the list, put the sheet aside and looked at me.

"You'll live to eighty-eight," she said. I was amazed. That was what John Bishop had told me, but then numbers can be manipulated. "You were a fashion designer in New York. I'm talking about your previous life now. You were very successful. You knew all the famous couturiers. But you contracted pneumonia. Antibiotics weren't around. You died in your early thirties." I was about to ask her so many questions. She shook her head and continued: "In this life, you will change your career. You will become a well-known impresario. You will be well-known again."

"Now," she said, "you can ask me any questions you like."

"What about my health?"

"Don't worry about it."

"Is there anything I should be concerned about?"

"You're not going to catch some terrible disease, if that's what you're worried about."

"I have a lot of stress," I said. I wanted to know if she knew what was wrong with me.

"Everyone has stress," she replied. I had drawn the joker from the card dealer. I paid her and, without thinking, thanked her.

As I stood on the sidewalk outside her house, I realized her cards had not uncovered my leukemia. I could not vouchsafe her story about my previous life. I could not verify whether her predictions were accurate. I decided to continue with what I felt most comfortable. I returned to my diet, my meditation and my comforting healings from Sally.

A chance occurrence at my next visit to Dr Sullivan took me down another path.

"Have you tried macrobiotics?" his secretary, Rhonda asked. I was sitting in the reception area waiting to see John. I looked up. I didn't think she knew anything about such things. She told me she knew of someone who had visited a Chinese herbalist. He had prescribed a macrobiotic diet and her friend was recovering.

In my visits to health-food shops, I had often come across books on macrobiotics and I had borrowed several from the library. I had also bought a couple of books on the subject and had spoken to several people about macrobiotic cooking. Most of the responses were lukewarm. I had been reluctant to change my diet while I was still on the Gerson program, but now this seemed like an exciting new direction to take.

"I know you've tried just about everything," Rhonda said. "Why don't you give this a go?"

"Do you have the man's name and telephone number?"

"No. But I'll get the information for you. I'll call you tomorrow." The following day she gave me Professor Chen's telephone number and I made an appointment to see him.

Professor Chen was in his seventies but he looked as if he was only forty. His unlined face glowed with health. He speech was animated. His figure was trim. He listened attentively as I told him all about me.

"You must change your diet," he said. "Your food must be cooked. To restore your energies, you must stop drinking raw vegetable juices. You must not eat meat, but you must eat a little fish." His advice amounted to a complete reversal of what I had been doing - but then what I had done had not worked. His advice confirmed what I had read about macrobiotic cooking. He suggested that half my food intake consist of whole cereal grains such as brown rice, whole wheat (including noodles) and rye. The rest of my diet should consist of vegetables, half of them cooked, beans and cooked fruit.

"You must cook everything with ginger," he added. "You should even put it in your morning bowl of cooked oats. And you must chew your food well. Saliva is the most important part of the digestive process. People eat too quickly. That's why they have so many problems."

For the next few weeks, I visited his clinic twice a week. He treated me with acupuncture, placing needles into my hands and feet and connecting them to batteries to increase their efficacy. He placed suction cups on my back to draw out bad vapors. He held burning moxie stocks close to the areas around my liver and spleen. Moxie sticks are made of a variety of mixed herbs, rolled together and compressed into cigar-shaped cylinders. These are ignited as one does an incense stick.

The suction-cup treatment concerned me. My platelet count was extremely low. The slightest bump resulted in a bruise. Coming out of the shower one evening, my middle son noticed several large bruises on my back. It was the result of the cups. I mentioned this to Professor Chen and he stopped using them on me. Instead of the vitamin pills I had been taking, I now took herbs.

Ginger is an essential herb in macrobiotic healing. The treatment suggested for leukemia was to apply a hot poultice to the *hara* (energy field) area below my navel. This is intended to stimulate the villi in the intestine to aid digestion. To do this, I grated a knuckle of green ginger, which I was supposed to wrap in muslin. I went from store to store but could not locate any. In the end, I settled on a pair of Janet's pantyhose. I wrapped the grated ginger in a piece of the fabric then heated it in boiling water. It was so hot I almost scalded my hands so I wore rubber gloves to overcome the problem. It was excruciatingly painful to apply it to my abdomen. The poultice cooled down very quickly and it required constant re-heating. I had to lie on the kitchen floor to be close to the stove.

"What are you doing?" my middle son asked when he saw me lying flat on my back. He had been doing his homework and come into the kitchen for something to drink. "That's a strange place to meditate."

I told him what I was doing. "I'll do it for you," he said. "I can handle hot things, as you know. It'll also save you getting up from the floor every few seconds."

For the next few weeks, he helped me every evening. Then I gave up. The poultices were too hot and far too painful. They weren't doing anything to arrest my falling blood counts. If Professor Chen's methods were going to work, they should have done so already. It was too late now. The blood test I had in the middle of the month, after the transfusion, showed my blood counts were falling faster. My hemoglobin was 6.8, my white cell count 0.9, my platelets only 16,000. I was sliding away. I had spent so much time chasing dietary programs I had cut back on meditating time. I had cut down on living.

A week later, I had my fourth platelet transfusion. As optimistic as I tried to be, it was clear that only someone else's blood was now keeping me alive. The transfusions were only palliatives.

In desperation I started meditating for up to six hours a day. The result was incredible. I felt a sense of peace such as I had not known since Dr Gloom had given me my fateful diagnosis. I still could not accept that I was so close to the finish line. As bleak as my prospects seemed, I still kept my hope. I was also realistic. At the rate my counts were falling, I wasn't going to last even another three months.

We will all die. I knew that. No one knows the moment of his final breath unless he is about to be executed. Even then, I suspect, there is always the hope that there will be a last-minute reprieve and, if not, that death will be painless.

"You can never tell if you are going to be hit by a bus," Dr Gloom had once told me.

I had heard this cliché so many times it irritated me.

Talking about death when you're under no imminent threat of it is of academic interest only. It is an abstraction. I knew there was now a real and measurable time limit to my life. It had altered my perceptions. I couldn't do anything to dismiss the thought of death. I couldn't avoid the issue. It was too real. I was dying. Death was in my face.

The path I had chosen was all or nothing. I had been galloping in one direction with blinkers on: die or be cured. The idea of being in physical limbo did not appeal to me. No one seemed to understand this. Everyone assumed I wanted to live longer. For the sake of my children alone, I was prepared to review the option of a splenectomy even if there was only a slim chance it could buy me a little time. The medical books I read - and the doctors I talked to - persuaded me that the chances of the operation itself being a success were less than slim. In any event, this was all speculation as my spleen was now so large and my platelet level far too low for me to undergo surgery.

CHAPTER TWENTY FOUR

June 1985:
Platelet count 13,000; haemoglobin level 5.6; White blood cell count 0.8

Eighteen months had passed since my leukemia had been diagnosed. I had exceeded the predictions of the doctors. Everyone had seen my efforts. My father believed I would win through. My sons believed this too. Their reality did not extend beyond what they could see. Years later they told me they never truly understood the gravity of the situation. I was living from transfusion to transfusion. My blood was getting thinner and thinner. I was getting more and more skin infections. My ankles were so swollen I felt sure the skin would burst. My spleen was sore. My breathing was becoming progressively labored. My heart beat like an engine straining under a severe load. Whenever I lay down, I could hear its heavy thump-thump as it strained to push my blood around. I couldn't walk more than a few paces at a time.

I needed a little more breathing space and I telephoned Dr Sullivan and described how I felt. And so it was that in the first week of June, I spent an entire day and night receiving a long slow transfusion. I needed five units of full blood to prop me up. It was my seventh transfusion. Lying in hospital that night, I reflected on how meditation and prayer had given me great comfort. I felt more at ease with the notion of a power determining my fate. How else could I explain the sense of peace I felt? Was I in a state of acceptance? I'd come a long way over the past months. I had tried everything available in an attempt to stave off death. I had even borrowed Arthur's exercise bicycle in an attempt to regain my stamina but found it too exhausting. I decided to conserve what energy I had left.

I was ready to die. It really was that simple. I wasn't afraid. And I was not in control. The concept of free will asserts that we have a choice in deciding what we do. Was my ego so large I would not accept that something I call God was controlling my destiny? Intuitively, I felt that if I stopped trying to influence events, everything would turn out all right – not only for me, but also for everyone around me. I had come around to the notion of having the serenity to accept the things I could not change. I was reminded of the promise of Kahlil Gibran in his book *'The Prophet'*, when he wrote, *"Come to bless the darkness as we have blessed the light."*

I was reluctant to leave my children. Their presence and their love made me want to cling to this life a little longer. There was so much to look forward to. My eldest son was in his first year at medical school. My middle son was in his final year of high school, planning to study engineering. My youngest son had two more years of high school. He talked about studying medicine. I wondered again about visiting the Gerson Institute in America.

I re-read the letter I had received from Dr Contreras. He had advised me not to stick to a severe dietary regimen. My strength was waning. I decided to start eating most of the foods I had long avoided: chicken, veal, and a lot more fish. My new menu dispelled the boredom of the bland diet I had been on but did nothing to restore my strength,

I remembered Meares' words: 'Fighting robs you of strength.' he said. 'The way to overcome a problem is not to accept defeat.' I needed a spiritual change of diet. I went to

Sally for another healing.

"Let it go," Sally said. "You weren't meant to go to the States." I listened to her and realized I was still clinging to what little control of my life I still had. I was disinclined to give up the certainty of what I thought I knew. I felt as if I was lying on a road. I could see a large steamroller coming towards me. I had two choices: I could lie there and be crushed or I could roll out of harm's way. I felt too tired to make the effort. I was bone weary. I considered a third choice: I could do neither. I decided to lie back and wait. 'To be still.' Perhaps the driver would stop in time. The answer was a short time coming.

When I attended Evanston's cancer support group, he told how he and his wife had travelled to India. He said it was at a time when he had exhausted almost all other possibilities and believed her was dying. At an ashram he met a holy man, Sai Baba, who told him he would be all right. Peter believed Sai Baba had cured him. Shortly afterwards, his health began to improve. I was about to take another pathway through the maze.

Over the past several months, I had come across the name of Sai Baba in various books and articles. I attached no more than a passing interest to the name. One evening I was resting after my most recent transfusion, reading the Bible. The television set was switched on. I glanced up. I noticed the program about to start was entitled *'The Lost Years of Christ'*. I stayed up to watch. I was enthralled. The program dealt with a generally unknown story of a time in Christ's life not accounted for in the Bible. From the age of twenty-nine until he returned to Jerusalem there is no information about him, although there has been much speculation. Sanskrit writers seemed to confirm that a man who was probably Christ had travelled to Asia. The program noted that it was only after this unaccounted-for period in Christ's life that his healings of the sick began. The question posed was whether he had learned the art of healing in the East. I was intrigued. As I watched, Sai Baba appeared on the program. I found the link between the healing powers of these men fascinating. Was Sai Baba another guru who had become fashionable? Could he really perform miracles as Christ had done 2000 years earlier? I was determined to find out more.

It seems that around 1872, an itinerant fakir settled in Shirdi in the state of Bombay. He became known as Sai Baba, a term of respect. According to legend, he performed many miracles. He gave spiritual lessons to all those who flocked to see him. Before he passed away, some time between 1910 and 1918, he told one of his devotees, an eminent politician, that he would return as a boy in eight years. Eight years after the death of Shirdi Sai Baba, a boy was born in the village of Puttaparti in the state of Andhra Pradesh in southern India. His name was Satyanarayana.

As a child Satya, as he was called, displayed some remarkable talents. To entertain his friends, he would materialize objects out of the air. After a basic education, he was sent to the high school where his older brother was a teacher. His parents hoped Satya would graduate to a post in the civil service. At thirteen, he had strange illness, marked by periods of intense pain and unconsciousness. When he recovered, his strange powers seemed to have been enhanced. He had never learned Sanskrit, but he was now able to quote long passages and he gave learned talks on Vedanta, the spiritual philosophy of the ancient scriptures of the Hindu religion. His father was concerned by his behavior. When he questioned him on what had happened, the boy told him he was Sai Baba. He soon gathered a large following around him. He began performing miracles, and gave spiritual instruction to his devotees. Over the years, Sai Baba expanded his ashram. He continued to guide and provide spiritual upliftment to those who thronged to see him. He healed the sick. At some point, the Greater London Council embraced his Moral Upliftment program and included it in their school curriculum. I wondered how I could make contact with this remarkable man.

Since setting out on my quest, I had met so many people who claimed to have the cure for this and that. They did so as teachers of meditation and visualization, as guides to mystical knowledge, as experts in the use of foods, herbs and spices, as possessors of healing crystals and as masters of numerology. I had met them all. As skeptical I had been I had still tried their offerings. Nothing had worked. I had met many other people who did not claim to have a cure. Some told me that only I could cure myself; others advised me that the answer lay elsewhere. One person had even told me that unless I learned to speak in tongues, I would never be cured. I rejected these notions. How could I prove or disprove an assertion based on the premise that if I failed to be cured it was because I did not have enough faith? How could I prove or disprove the assertion that if the cure worked, it was because I believed in that particular treatment, belief or whatever? Even as I considered that one did not have to believe in the efficacy of antibiotics for them to work, I realized I needed a miracle if I was to survive.

The answer came in the form of a postcard from one of Janet's cousins who lived in California. We were surprised, as we had not heard from her for several years. What was more surprising was what she wrote. She said she had heard how ill

I was although she did not know what treatment I was receiving. Her husband's cousin, Boris, was living in Sydney. He was a follower of Sai Baba.

I was so intrigued I telephoned him. It turned out I had known Boris thirty years earlier when we were at school in Africa. I asked him about Sai Baba.

"My late mother had cancer," Boris said. "She suffered the most terrible agony. She had been a follower of Sai Baba and she chanted his name and that of God all the time. Her faith in him and his message of eternal bliss helped her through her pain. It made her last days bearable. I felt helpless in the face of her dying but I was so impressed at the peaceful way she died, I decided to learn more about the man my mother had so devoutly believed in. I've been a Sai Baba devotee ever since." Then he asked me why I was so interested. I explained my desperate situation to him.

"I'll post some tapes and books to you," he said. "Let me know if there's anything else I can do to help."

I was dubious. I was also highly curious. When the parcel arrived a few days later, I opened it with trepidation. I found a tape recording, a letter and three books. The tape consisted of chanting I did not understand. The letter was a note of encouragement from Boris. The books were enthralling. I was drawn to many of the messages in them. I pondered on the ways I could put his sayings into practice. I discovered there were many groups of Sai Baba followers around the country, who held regular meetings at which his teachings were discussed.

There were two such groups in Melbourne, but they were some distance away. There was no one I felt I could ask to take me to these meetings. I was too tired to drive and Arthur and Patsy had left the week before to visit their son living in

Malaysia. As Patsy later told me, I looked so ill she and Arthur were convinced they would not find me alive upon their return.

I telephoned Sally. I discussed my dilemma with her. "I feel as if I've run out of time."

"What do you want to do?" she asked.

"I'd love to go to Puttaparti to see Sai Baba."

"What about your diet and meditation?" she asked.

"They appear to have kept me going thus far. They haven't helped to cure me. Now that Patsy's gone on holiday, I don't even feel inclined to go back to the church for healing."

"Shrug off those things for which you no longer have any use. I think your discovery of Sai Baba is another step in your spiritual development."

I telephoned Boris and asked him to send me more books on Sai Baba. He told me that if I was not well enough to travel to India to see Baba, I should write to him.

"One way or the other," Boris said, "you'll get an answer."

I asked him for an address to which to write. He made a cryptic comment when he gave it to me: "Sai Baba's presence is everywhere. Even to think of writing to him is enough to elicit a response. He awareness transcends time and space. He'll know if you've written."

I thought about the absurdity of his remark, suspended my judgment, and wrote to Sai Baba. I had nothing to lose except the cost of a postage stamp.

The letter I wrote was tantamount to my jumping off a cliff. It was letting go of everything I had once believed in. In one leap, I put all my life into the hands of an invisible force I could not see. I was either going to land in a heap on the rocks below or I was going to be rescued by a Superman wearing an orange robe. I put all my value judgments aside in an attempt to find a non-physical answer to a very real physical problem. If what Boris said was true, Sai Baba would not allow me to end up in a tangled heap at the foot of the cliff. My blood test that week had been the final shove. My hemoglobin was down to 4.5, white blood count 0.7, platelets 17,000. Two days later, I received another five-unit full-blood transfusion, my eighth.

I was not thinking clearly and wondered if this was because of lack of oxygen to my brain or because I was at a dead end. I had no idea what the outcome of my letter to Sai Baba would be. It was clear that after threading my way through an endless maze of unrequited promises and unfulfilled expectations, I had taken the road less travelled.

So this was what it had all come down to! I was so very, very tired. My blood counts had plummeted. Until a few months ago, the only thing that had kept me going was my doggedness. Since then the only thing that had sustained me were the transfusions and my abiding belief that, somehow, I would get through. I had, at best, two more platelet transfusions up my sleeve. After these had been used up, it was anyone's guess what would happen. Despite my assertion that I understood the difference between fighting and non-submission, my various efforts had undoubtedly weakened me. I had finally done what Sally had always told me to do: I had placed my destiny in the hands of the Unseen, the Allness, that something I call God. Had my decision been a grand illusion? Had I ever been in control? It was now up to that something I call God. It was its decision. I guessed it always had been so but I had stubbornly refused to accept this. Meditation had not cured me. In time I would learn it had not cured anyone else. What it did, though, was to give me the peace and calm to manage whatever I found on the road ahead. It had provided me with an insight into myself.

Doctors may stitch wounds and re-set broken bones but the actual healing process occurs beyond one's control. It takes place within the cells of the body. It does so without help from any human agent or endeavor – something more and more doctors are now admitting. I had started eating regular foods. I still avoided preservatives, additives and foods regarded as carcinogenic. I didn't want to weaken my immune system any further. I tried to balance the needs of my body with the needs of my soul. Over the next few days, I meditated more. Putting my thoughts onto paper also helped bring me down to earth, less up in the air. Writing helped me to affirm that I was still alive to life. I decided that I would accept that something I called God as the all knowing and all-powerful arbiter of my life play in which I was the principal actor. I waited for a cue that would show me my faith had not been misplaced. Had my prayers been heard? Could Sai Baba perform a miracle for me?

I contracted influenza and was confined to bed with severe chills and a raging fever. My powers of resistance were at rock bottom. I had been given a second course of antibiotics but I was not responding well. My low hemoglobin level prevented me from getting enough oxygen. My chest infection made it even harder to breathe. I had hoped to attend a Sai Baba meeting but I felt too weak to go. I did the only things I could: I meditated. I slept. I prayed. I couldn't get out of bed, so I stopped the coffee enemas. My father made three or four glasses of juice every day for me.

"Drink it," Dad said. "You have to eat something to keep up your strength. I've started drinking these juices as well.

Some of the combinations are quite delicious."

"I've put your name on our prayer list," Sally told me.

And then it all happened. The sign I had been waiting for. Two weeks after I had written my letter to Sai Baba, the answer came to me.

In time, I would realize that the events that unfolded then would change everything. Reason would return. Time would be measured by the second in the here and the now. The past, the present and the future were all one. I found there seems to be no limit to what we can endure with perseverance, patience, and the knack to make our own luck.

CHAPTER TWENTY FIVE

July 1985:
Platelet count 17,000; haemoglobin level 7.3; White blood cell count 0.8

As a regular subscriber to *Time magazine*, I received my copy every Tuesday. I awaited its arrival every week with anticipation. It was my window onto the world. I was a creature of habit with that paper. Invariably I would turn to the People section. Then I would read the Science section, then the cover story. The lead story in the issue of July 1, 1985 was all about the awful events surrounding the hijacking of a TWA flight at Beirut airport. Even so, for the first time ever, I turned to the section on Medicine. I had never done this before.

I could not believe my eyes. Underneath a photograph of a man receiving an injection, the caption read: 'Dr Queseda and a hairy-cell patient, now in remission, demonstrates how to inject the drug.' The headline read, *'What's become of interferon?'*

Interferon was discovered in 1957. It is a natural protein that exists within the cells of every living person. Interferons form an essential part of the body's immune system. They stimulate our macrophage white blood cells. They slow down the replication of viruses. When a virus invades a cell, our bodies produce interferon in minute quantities that stop a second virus from entering the cell. In this way, we are protected from getting two infections at once. Interferons prevent us from getting, say, chicken pox and measles at the same time. In the 1970s, interferon was touted as the Wonder Drug, a drug that would cure all cancers and other viral illnesses. There was only one problem: only human interferon can be used for testing on humans. Interferons are found in minute quantities in the body and are therefore extremely difficult and costly to extract. The cost of trialing interferon was prohibitive. At around several million dollars an ounce, this wasn't surprising. In the 1980s, genetic engineering changed the picture.

Scientists took the human gene that carries the specifications for interferon and implanted it into the common bacterium E. coli that had already been successfully grown industrially. The bacterium then produced interferon that could safely be used on people in meaningful numbers. Researchers found that while interferon slowed down the growth of some tumors, it had absolutely no effect on others. In most instances, it produced extremely unpleasant side effects. To make matters worse, even though it could now be mass-produced, it still cost upward of $5000 to treat one patient per year. Undaunted, a team of doctors in the United States of America persisted in testing the drug on several different types of cancers. The results on patients suffering from Hairy Cell Leukemia were dramatic.

I read that HCL is so rare it attacks fewer than 400 people a year in the USA. With so many thousands of people in need of new and effective treatments, no one was going to waste valuable research funds to find a treatment for such a rare disease. Trials of Interferon on other cancers had been erratic. Where the results were good, they were remarkable. In a few cases of advanced melanoma, those who recovered showed no sign of cancer within four months. It had produced complete remissions in some advanced cases of kidney cancer and Kaposi's sarcoma, a deadly skin cancer that often affects AIDS patients. The article I read continued to describe how interferon was trialed in the USA. There was no indication whether the drug was a cure or a palliative. The odds of finding a drug to treat so rare a disease were extremely long.

Was the story of interferon's success with HCL the reply from Sai Baba for which I had been waiting? I grabbed the telephone beside the bed. I dialed Dr Sullivan's number. I knew it off by heart by now. As I waited for him to answer my call, I remembered how we had talked about the possible use of interferon a few months earlier. John had mentioned that he had read about it being trialed overseas.

"From what I've heard," he had said, "it's only been trialed on patients who have had their spleens removed and who have exhausted all other possibilities. It may become available here one day. There is still no firm evidence that it works as an anti-cancer drug."

I heard his voice on the phone. "Are you okay?" he asked. What a question. I was euphoric!

"John," I said, "I've come across an article in *Time* about interferon. I want to be a trial patient. I am prepared to be a guinea pig. I feel this is it."

I read the article to him. He was so quiet I thought we had been cut off.

"Leave this with me," he said when I had finished talking. "I'll make a few enquiries."

Two days later he telephoned. "We can do the trial on you. The company that manufactures the drug has agreed to fly it over from Switzerland for you. You'll have to undergo a whole lot of tests before we start treatment and you'll have to sign a protocol. Can you check into hospital on Tuesday?"

I couldn't believe it. I had to wait a whole week. I didn't know what I had let myself in for.

The following Tuesday was the Fourth of July, 1985. The fireworks were about to begin. My friend Mike drove me to the Royal Melbourne Hospital. There, Dr Sullivan introduced us to Dr Rob Harris, a registrar at the hospital who had been assigned as resident program director to me. Slimly built, with close-cropped ginger hair and gentle eyes, Rob was in his early thirties. He was friendly. The laughter wrinkles around his eyes suggested he had a sense of humor, which I later found he surely did. He discussed everything with me, answered all my questions, and readily conceded what he didn't know. I liked his concern - especially when he apologized for all the tests he was about to put me through.

They were mind-boggling. For three days I was subjected to blood tests and blood pressure tests; urine tests; so many thermometers were pushed into my mouth to take my temperature I wondered whether they would ever get an accurate reading. I underwent another painful and bone-crunching bone-marrow biopsy. I was given a liver-spleen scan, a cardiograph, and several chest x-rays. I rationalized the dangers of radiation by telling myself that I already had leukemia. I was injected with radioactive dyes and scrutinized on monitor screens in the Nuclear Medical department, located in the bowels of the hospital. In case of radiation leaks, I supposed. I wondered about the effects on the people who worked there. I was x-rayed after swallowing barium porridge. I was x-rayed after swallowing acids and alkalis so I would fizz. I was x-rayed standing up, lying down and upside down. I was wired up and jellied up for several cardiographs. I had another CAT scan, another ultrasound scan of my liver. They took my temperature, again. They drew more blood.

What I couldn't see were all the tests they made on my blood in the laboratory downstairs.

"Well," said Rob Harris, after all the tests had been completed, "there's no doubt you have Hairy Cell Leukemia."

"Was there any doubt?"

"You know what red tape is like. The company supplying the drug wants every baseline test they can think of. They always want to cover themselves, in case …"

"Could there be a problem?" I asked.

"It's a new drug. No one has ever had it before in this country. You have the dubious honor of being the first."

"Thanks for nothing."

"You want to sign this?" Dr Harris asked. He handed me the dug protocol. There were about fifty pages of closely typed notes. They covered everything from an outline of the disease to every test I had to undergo. Rob handed me a Consent Form. I read the reasons that would enable me to withdraw from the program if I so wished: toxicity; allergic reactions; progression of the disease; major surgery; severe metabolic disturbances; severe infection such as septicemia and pneumonia; death. Then I read all the side effects, the first one listed was 'death'. The wording further down the page also stated that I could use my own death to withdraw. I laughed at the possibility of being able to make this decision post mortem.

I took the final plunge. I signed. My spleen was 28 centimeters long.

The next day I was given my first injection. I felt nothing. Six hours later, I felt the full impact of the drug.

The side effects of high doses of interferon are cruel. Now I knew why so many trial patients overseas had given up after only a few days. At first, I began to shiver. I felt cold. My hands felt numb. It was as if I had flu a hundred times over. I ached everywhere – my head, my joints, my limbs and even my fingers. I shook so hard my bed became the epicenter of an earthquake. My temperature began to rise. It shot up to 40°C. For the next few weeks it hovered around 41°C. The doctors were concerned. I was so feverish I had become delirious. I didn't know where I was. I didn't care. It was the middle of winter. All the windows were closed. The heating had been turned up. I begged for some relief. Eventually, one of the nurses found two large electric fans. She placed them facing me – one at the side of my bed, the other at the foot of my bed. To say that I was hot would be an understatement. Then I was freezing cold again. I shivered so hard and so long, my teeth hurt. They gave me several blankets and two hot water bottles to keep me warm. They made no difference. I felt like an abandoned Eskimo in the middle of an Arctic blizzard. I couldn't believe it was possible to feel so cold - or so hot. I begged them to open the windows for me.

"It's freezing outside" the nurses said.

"I'm not outside," I replied. Eventually they relented.

There was no respite. Each day I was given an injection. Each day I would wait for the response. Each day I reacted in exactly the same way. I was on a rollercoaster. No sooner up than down. I snatched sleep with the help of a sleeping pill.

The second or third night in hospital proved to be a testing time. I was lying in bed; the ward lights had been switched off. I heard the shuffling of feet. The curtains round the bed of the patient to my left and round my bed were drawn. I heard sobbing. I listened to the sounds of oxygen being turned on and off, instruments clinking in metal dishes, people whispering in hushed tones. I had no idea what was happening to or with the person in the bed. A while later, a face appeared between my curtains. "It will be all right soon. I hope we haven't disturbed you," a man said. "The priest is coming." A short time later, I heard the priest intoning the Last Rites. The sobbing continued. One of the nurses poked her head through the curtains.

"This was all very sudden. I hope you haven't been too unnerved? I'll try to move you to another bed if you wish."

As I wondered when they would move the body, the sleeping tablet I had taken earlier took effect and I fell asleep. When I awoke the following morning, I saw the curtains had been opened. I looked across at the bed next to mine. The man was still there. He was later moved to another ward. I heard from the nursing staff that he was discharged from hospital a week later. You can never tell.

For the next two weeks, I was subjected to one procedure or another. Test followed test. I was in a time capsule. I was unaware of the outside world. I floated from one injection to the next. I drifted from one bout of perspiration to another. I was either freezing to death at the Poles or boiling away to nothing at the Equator.

"It could be a few months before we know whether this has all been worth it," Rob said. I felt ghastly. I didn't care. There were moments when I felt that if I had died it would have been a blessed relief. When I didn't feel quite so desperate, I reflected on everything that had led up to my deciding to undergo this terrifying ordeal. I felt as if I was having a nightmare in which I was a middleweight boxer up against a super weight opponent. Every time I was knocked down, I was forced to get up. The endless rounds continued. I couldn't climb through the ropes. I was soaking wet from the effort. For the first time ever, I appreciated the meaning of the phrase 'to throw in the towel'. The first fourteen injections floored me. As welcoming as the thought of giving up was, I wasn't prepared to be counted out yet. I was fighting for my life.

Interferon suppresses the growth of leukemic cells. It also inhibits the production of blood. My counts began to drop. The day after the treatment began, I had a four-unit full blood transfusion. Four days later, I had a three-unit transfusion. The day after that, I was given a further two units of blood. My blood counts were bouncing up and down like a yo-yo. Ten days after the treatment began, my platelet level dropped alarmingly to only 9000. The doctors were in two minds about giving me another platelet transfusion. They did, anyway. We were all in uncharted territory. I was in danger of a sudden and fatal hemorrhage.

I had not yet received a direct reply to my letter to Sai Baba. Before I wrote my letter to him, Boris had quoted a well-known aphorism attributed to Sai Baba: 'take one step towards me, I'll take ninety-nine steps towards you.'

If I believed the article on interferon in *Time* would be Sai Baba's only response, I was in for a surprise. Carl Jung, the famous psychiatrist, talks of the synchronicity of events. I was never more aware of this than now. Events were moving at a pace I could scarcely match. I was lying in bed, at the end of my first week in hospital. I expected the nurse to walk into the ward with the syringe and other paraphernalia for my next injection. A figure approached and I looked up. It was not the nurse. Dark brown eyes smiled at me from a pleasant, light brown face. His black hair shone with a brilliant luster. He was dressed in a white caftan. He stepped forward.

"Sai Baba sent me," he said.

Before I could recover, he added, "I had a message from a

friend of mine who knows Boris, to contact you. My name is Ganesh." Sai Baba had indeed sent a messenger!

Ganesh sat beside me for over an hour. He related endless anecdotes of how Sai Baba had healed the sick. His devotees around the world followed his message of love.

As he talked, I became increasingly impressed at his deep faith and total belief. When Ganesh came through the door, I was feeling weak. Now I felt elated.

"Have you read any of Sai Baba's books?" he asked.

"Boris sent me two," I replied. "Are there more?"

What a question! Over the next several months, Ganesh lent me numerous books written by Sai Baba. He gave me tapes of speeches Baba had made. As our friendship grew, so we spent more time together. I listened to his seemingly endless stories about Sai Baba and his miracles. I attended bhajans (prayer meetings) at his home. He showed me several films from his extensive video library. From all this I came to understand the message of Sai Baba. His lessons helped me through a most critical time in my life. They validated the decisions I had made. They confirmed the direction I had taken. I don't believe I would have made it through that time without the support, albeit vicariously, of Sai Baba. There was so much to learn.

Moses, Krishna. The Buddha. Jesus. Sai Baba. It seemed to me that the spiritual message was the same. We are part of that something I call God. We are His children. We are His images on this level of existence. We have mistaken our bodies and our minds – those temporary projections of ourselves into the world of matter – for our real selves. We live our lives quite unaware of our true nature, which is not limited by time or space. We all possess an eternal spirit. Our real identity lies in that eternal and inanimate state of bliss and love. We can only realize this when we rise above ignorant selfishness. The cause of our dissatisfaction lay in forming attachments to the material of the transient body, in never being satisfied with what we have. Our immortal identity has been taught in every age. Sai Baba claimed that if we can remain detached from the results of our actions, if we can leave all to God's will, then the actions themselves become a spiritual pathway helping us towards liberation. As long as our motives are self-centered – seeking gain or fame for ourselves – we are bound to this level of existence. God is not concerned with punishment or rewards. We decide our fate. If we do good deeds we receive goodness in return. If we are bad and do bad deeds, we reap bad results. Sai Baba teaches us that our actions are for the good of mankind and for the glory of God.

When I first started reading Sai Baba's lessons, I marveled at the coincidence between what he said and what I had read in the Bible. Synchronicity seemed to occur at every level. 'Those who worship and meditate on me with unswerving devotion I straightway deliver from the ocean of death-bound existence.' (Lord Krishna). 'I can of mine own self do nothing.' (John 5:30). I found the nexus repeated almost endlessly. As someone who eschewed traditional religious beliefs, I found great comfort in the words of this swami.

Through his teachings, Sai Baba had attempted to raise human consciousness to a new level, devoting this life to it. His lessons touched my soul, not my checkbook. 'My life is a commentary on my message,' Sai Baba said. Like those before me, I found Sai Baba living proof of his own teachings. In my search to learn more, I re-read the Bible.

When I was child, John Ndmande had taught me, *'To be clever is to be still.'* Sai Baba often said, *'Only keep quiet and I will do the rest.' Jesus said, 'This voice came not because of me, but for your sakes.'* Meares taught me to sit in stillness. As someone who was always doing one thing or another, my inner voice called to me that I would do better to heed the lessons I had learned.

Around the end of the second week, one of the nurses sat down beside me. She held an orange in her hand.

"I can't give you your injections after you've been discharged from the hospital," Sue said. "You can come here every day or we can arrange for a district nurse to call on you. Or you can learn to inject yourself." The idea of travelling 25 km to and from the hospital every day to have an injection was too tiring to consider. The thought of waiting around for a nurse to visit me held no appeal.

"I can't inject myself," I said. "The thought of it is enough to make my toes curl."

"That's why I brought you this orange," Sue smiled. A needle materialized in her hand. "You can practice on the orange. It'll give you some idea of what it'll be like. The orange won't feel a thing."

"In your own time," Sue said, handing me the orange and the syringe. "In the meantime, I'll give you your injection for today."

For two days, I practised on the orange. I injected it with whichever liquid was at hand. Water, orange juice, coffee, tea…

"Can I have a go?" my youngest son asked. "Can I see what it feels like to give an injection?" Every day, without fail, my sons visited me after school and university. On that day, my youngest son was bored. He injected the orange with cold tea until I was sure it would burst. When he left me some time later, he put the orange on the table next to my bed. I had intended throwing it away but the following morning noticed it was missing.

"Have you seen the orange that was on the table?" I asked one of the nursing aides.

"I gave it to my friend," she replied. "I'm sorry, but I didn't think you wanted it. They bring you fresh fruit every day."

"That orange is full of tea," I said.

"You are having me on" she replied.

It took me a minute to two to impress on her what had happened and that I was being serious.

"I'd better find her!" she shrieked. She dropped her tray on my bed and raced off to find her friend returning a short while later. "Whew! That was close."

"So you got to her in time?"

"Well, she gave the orange to another one of her friends." I burst out laughing. I could picture some innocent person sinking their teeth into it ......there was so much tea in that orange, she would have been showered.

I practised on oranges until I became quite adept. Then Sue handed me a kidney tray. In it were a syringe, swabs, needles, water ampoule and a vial of interferon.

"Prepared to try now?" she asked. She showed me how to snap off the end of a sterile water ampoule, how to swab my skin and how to withdraw the water and re-inject it into the vial of interferon. Interferon is freeze-dried when it is prepared so it has to be reconstituted with water to make it injectable. When the interferon had dissolved, she showed me how to draw it out of the vial and then substitute a smaller needle for the large one she had used. She tapped the syringe.

"You have to make sure there are no air bubbles," she explained. The procedure took about five minutes. I then tried to inject myself. I tried about ten times. I flinched every time I tried to push the needle deeper into my skin.

"I'll do it for you," Sue said. "Maybe you'll do it tomorrow." I forced myself to push the needle into me and it took me some time before I worked out how to stab myself without pain.

"I think you can go home in a few days," Rob Harris said to me. It was Day Fifteen. "Your counts are still down but you should be stable enough. Can you manage giving yourself the injections?"

"I'll certainly do my best."

"It'll take three to four months before we can tell whether the drug has worked or not. In the meantime, I'd like you to come to the hospital every Friday so we can check you out. There are still more tests to do.'

I had, in the words of a well-known song, well and truly 'sold my soul to the company store'. In return for my life-saving treatment, I had to suffer the tests they asked for. No one knew yet whether it had been worth the price.

Seventeen days after I entered hospital, it was time to leave. It was a Saturday morning. Rob Harris came into the ward as I packed my pajamas, slippers and dressing gown into a bag. I was still so weak I could hardly stand. My bag and its contents seemed to weigh a ton. The blood test I had had that morning showed my hemoglobin was up to 10.4, white blood count was still only 0.9 and platelets were 13,000.

"When do you think, the side-effects will slow down or stop?" I asked him.

"Your guess is as good as mine. Hopefully it'll improve. See you in a week's time. Good luck." We shook hands.

I saw Dr Harris almost every week for nearly two years. I interspersed my visits to him with consultations with John Sullivan, who had moved his consulting rooms to another hospital. Between them, they provided me with the best medical advice available. The weekly blood tests provided me with an ongoing baseline with which to monitor my status.

The short time I had spent in hospital brought me into close and intense relationships with some of the other patients, in particular, Andrew. He had acute myeloid leukemia. When his illness was first diagnosed, he tried meditation and the Kelley diet, which is similar to the Gerson diet. Almonds were essential to the regimen as well as plenty of raw yoghurt and lima beans. He was at death's door when he received a concentrated course of chemotherapy. His leukemia went into remission for several months. Then his condition deteriorated and he came back for further treatment. He was extremely positive about his prognosis.

"I'm going to follow the medical approach," Andrew told me. "I think all that other stuff is good, but it's not for me. Anyway, I've tried meditation and diet." A week later, he was discharged. I saw him often when I went to the hospital for my weekly check-ups. His hair grew back. He looked a picture of health. I didn't see him for several months, and heard he was in remission. I forgot about him until some time later when I was in the Day Centre having a blood test. The postcards on the walls reminded me how many patients kept the nursing staff informed of their whereabouts and how they were keeping.

"Have you heard from Andy?" I asked Cynthia.

"Didn't you know?" she replied. "He died about three months ago."

Does one ever truly become inured to hearing that someone you knew well had died? I knew Andrew only briefly yet I was shocked to hear the news.

I had come to know several other patients. Over the

months, they dropped out of sight. Whenever I enquired about them from the nurses, I did so with trepidation. I always feared the worst. Mostly I was right. With few exceptions, all the people I met during my period of hospitalization had died. The unanswered question was how long I could keep going.

I had come to realize that relationships are made up of such fragile strands. The threads which bind a husband to a wife, a mother to a son, are as tenuous as gossamer. Suddenly, the fabric parts. One or the other becomes diseased. Why? It seemed to me that most people with cancer suppressed their feelings. They defer examining them. They put up with their problems in the hope that they, not unlike a skin condition, will eventually clear up. 'Time heals all', they say. 'Let bygones be bygones'. It doesn't always work like that. Time only heals wounds that have been repaired. At the time, I wondered whether my leukemia was a side effect of starved affections and unfulfilled desires.

What I have no doubt about is that we all need to be loved. We all need someone to love. It's an integral part of our human condition. It helps us grow. It helps to keep us alive. Without love, we wither within and die. To be authentic, such love has to be unconditional. It cannot depend on a reward system. Unconditional love is rewarded with love or kindness from the most unexpected directions, in the most unusual forms.

'Why?' I asked, 'are cancer patients so nice and likeable?' Every cancer patient I ever met was always eager to please, so eager to suppress his or her own wishes. The truth, as I came to discover, lay in an intense desire to be liked. People will do almost anything to achieve this, even if it means doing the opposite of what they really want to do. By acting contrary to their basic nature, they hardly ever do what is right for them and so are continually disappointed when other people do not treat them as they would wish to be treated. These behavior patterns are programed into us in childhood.

When we were children, we wanted to be liked by our parents. We wanted to be loved. We wanted attention. We submitted ourselves (how could we do otherwise?) to whatever behavior was necessary in order to be liked, or rewarded. We did whatever we had to do in order to avoid punishment, deserved or not.

If the state of our physical health is predicated by the state of our emotional health, so this in turn is predicated by the degree to which we were truly loved and nurtured in our childhood. By truly loved, I do not mean smothered, indulged or patronized. If we are truly loved, we are loved for who we are and valued for our presence rather than our achievements or our compliance with our parents' dictates and unfulfilled hopes. If that rare gift of a sense of worth is bequeathed to us in our childhood, we will have more resources upon which to draw in our adulthood. I have no doubt that my sense of self-worth and why I felt I was worth saving was largely due to my father's unconditional love for me.

Most of our parents were unskilled in parenting. I think that most still are. Why else do the patterns repeat themselves from generation to generation! We never seem to get it right collectively. By the time we have acquired a reasonable amount of wisdom our children have flown the nest or passed the point where they could benefit from our experiences. Sadly, we seem to have forgotten the advantages of an extended family. Once upon a time, the grandparents within the group resolved all major decisions. The elders of the tribe fulfilled a similar role. Their wisdom was always there for those coming after to draw on.

I have discussed this with many cancer patients and people who do not have an illness. Almost all agree with me that we seem to have lost the ability to say 'No'. If we did so as children, we were punished. We failed to make a stand for our own independence. We failed to assert our rights. Ordered by our parents to do their bidding, we never dared say 'No!' The fear of rejection and abandonment is a very powerful weapon. And if we did refuse, the consequences were stenciled indelibly on our bottoms and our psyches. Over time, we come to accept this pattern as normal. We don't realize we have been conditioned to please in order to avoid rejection. We haven't accepted that whatever doesn't feel right, isn't right. Feeling is something we are taught to avoid. We never give expression to what we really feel which is why we find ourselves in situations over which we have no control. Slowly but surely, we become trapped by our frustrations. Instead of correcting the problems or confronting their causes, we find excuses.

This is perhaps contentious, but I have to believe that most cancer patients seem to fulfill two criteria: they are afraid to confront their problems and they don't know how to handle them. They 'eat themselves up' by taking on the very disease that expresses their deepest fears, their direst frustrations, and their longest-simmering resentments. They end up making statements like, 'You make me sick', or, 'I can't stand this any more', or 'I've had enough!' It occurred to me that if the Unconscious were as non-discriminating as we believe it is, it would take what we tell it literally. The words would become self-fulfilling. The anguished body reflects the anguished mind. The snake consumes itself. We destroy ourselves.

Dr Sandra Levy, a former head of the behavioral medicine branch of the National Cancer institute in the United States of America, found that women with breast cancer who were 'passive, stoic and helpless' fared less well than others. There also appears to be a definite link between prostate cancer and reduced sexual activity. I wondered whether someone simply not having enough 'breathing space' in his or her relationships caused lung cancer. How else, I asked, can you explain why some people who smoke like chimneys never get lung cancer? There is no doubt that the effects of smoking cigarettes, breathing noxious fumes and pollutants do weaken the body's immune system. They do facilitate the advancement of lung cancer and other respiratory problems. Sunbathing does stimulate melanomas. Pesticides and herbicides do cause liver damage. Radiation can cause leukemia. But cause and effect aren't always so clear-cut. Perhaps the answer lay at a deeper level. It is said that a defective gene causes the 'trigger' that fires off a genetic change. It seems odd that so many billions of dollars are spent unsuccessfully each year to find the oncogene or virus that causes cancer when the 'trigger' may not be a defective gene per se.

The firing mechanism may well be the brake put on our natural flow by the imperatives of our parents or some traumatic childhood experience. When our basic nature, the path of our innocence is upset, our bliss is disturbed. Child abuse is more common than we dare to acknowledge, although the damage is often more psychological than physical. If we can unearth and recognize the landmines we've carried with us all our lives we can try to defuse them. We can move to a safe distance from them. When they are no longer a threat to us, we can recapture our freedom, our essence. When we can reorganize our priorities we can deal with our problems rather than defer them. Seeking and admitting the truth can give us the strength to cope with disease.

I have discussed this with so many people. So many agreed with me. I wondered whether I was steering their thinking to agree with mine. Carl Jung found parallels in the wisdom of primitive healers who recognized that unresolved issues in our lives somatise in our bodies. They can make us mortally ill. Elisabeth Kübler-Ross shared this view. It was reassuring to realize I was not alone in my thinking.

As I described earlier, my childhood was a time of almost total insecurity. This uncertainty was exacerbated by the fact that until I chose to leave home, we moved house six times. Until my leukemia was diagnosed, I moved a further thirteen times. They say a rolling stone gathers no moss. It also cannot settle long enough to acquire stability. In time, I would come to understand that I could trace my almost compulsive self-reliance to these childhood experiences.

But, I wondered how does anyone ever know when a seismic change produces a life-threatening aftershock? If the firing pin was cocked in our childhood, when was it activated? How do we deal with it? It's hard enough to recall what happened when you were a child; it's even harder to lift the lid on emotions and emotional pain we have suppressed as adults. In time, I would come to appreciate the damage I had suffered as a child unable to reveal my nightmare experiences. Of course, stress in later life can also provide a similar 'trigger' even if there was nothing in our childhood to disturb the flow. The body is readied for fight-or-flight behavior in response to stress. It is how we have survived for millions of years. Times have changed. We have not had time to adapt. It isn't always acceptable now to respond with an instinctive response. We can't beat up everyone who upsets us. We don't vent our anger. We don't cry when we're upset. We don't open our hearts easily. The stress that builds up is not released. Chronic unrelieved stress weakens the immune system. The result is a heart attack, cancer - or leukemia.

My view is confirmed by recent studies in a still relatively new field called *epigenetics*. Until recently, most of us were taught that our DNA is hard-coded and that nothing an individual does in their lifetime will be biologically passed to their children. Research over the past decade, has provided evidence that genes have a 'memory'; that the lives of your grandparents – the air they breathed, the food they ate, even the things they saw – can directly affect you, decades later, despite your never experiencing these things yourself. And that what you do in your lifetime could in turn affect your grandchildren.

Studies of animal behavior, for example, have shown that the offspring of a mother with good nurturing skills are more likely to be good parents themselves. Importantly, well-nurtured animals show long-term brain changes, especially in an area called the hippocampus, where genes that respond to stress are silenced in the presence of good mothering. This epigenetic effect is passed on to the next generation and continues until the cycle of good mothering is broken.

Epigenetics adds a whole new layer to genes beyond the DNA. It proposes a control system of 'switches' that turn genes on or off – and suggests that things people experience, including nutrition and stress, can control these switches and cause heritable effects in humans.

In a remote town in northern Sweden there is convincing evidence for this radical idea. Lying in Överkalix's parish registries of births and deaths and its detailed harvest records from the mid 1800s is a secret that confounded traditional scientific thinking. Marcus Pembrey, a Professor of Clinical Genetics at the Institute of Child Health in London, in collaboration with Swedish researcher Lars Olov Bygren, found evidence in these records of an environmental effect being passed down the generations. They have shown that a famine at critical times in the lives of the grandparents can affect the life expectancy of the grandchildren. This was the first evidence that an environmental effect can be inherited in humans.

Equally compelling evidence has also been found in meticulous Dutch medical records. During WWII, the Nazis blockaded towns across the Netherlands for more than six months. With each person allowed a mere 580 calories of food, over 22,000 people died from malnutrition and thousands of babies were born underweight. When scientists examined this data they found that not only were the infants who survived more susceptible to health problems but also their children born years later and well fed were also significantly underweight.

The idea that inheritance is not just about which genes you inherit but whether these are switched on or off, the 'triggers' I referred to, raises questions with huge implications. The search to find what else can affect these switches took a recent and dramatic turn.

After the tragic events of September 11th 2001, Rachel Yehuda, a psychologist at the Mount Sinai School of Medicine in New York, studied the effects of stress on a group of women who were inside or near the World Trade Center and were pregnant at the time. Produced in conjunction with Jonathan Seckl, an Edinburgh doctor, her results suggest that stress effects can pass down generations. Meanwhile research at Washington State University points to toxic effects – like exposure to fungicides or pesticides – causing biological changes in rats that persist for at least four generations. This work is at the forefront of a paradigm shift in scientific thinking. It will change the way the causes of disease are viewed, as well as the importance of lifestyle choices and family relationships. What people do no longer just affects them, but can determine the health of their children and grandchildren in decades to come. Nurture rather than nature may determine who we are far more then we previously thought. As Marcus Pembrey has said, 'We are all guardians of our genome.'

While there is no way of discovering what stressors in my grandparents' lives had been passed on to me, I was keenly aware there had been many triggers in my own life. There were so many feelings I had suppressed, so many affronts I had encountered, so many choices I had avoided making. These were as nothing compared to the realization that I had to look forward and so could no longer put the resolution of all my varied problems on 'hold'. I could not defer making hard choices. I could not mark time. I could no longer pretend that by ignoring my current difficulties they would solve themselves. My disease showed me that death could be an easy way out. Coping with life was proving to be much harder.

Which brought me to another question: If the meditative techniques of Meares and Goldsmith could reduce stress levels, isn't prevention better than cure? One of the more significant answers seemed to lie in a growing body of evidence that psychologically depressed people have depressed levels of white blood cells, a major part of the body's immune system. Significantly, these depressed levels have also been found in people in unhappy marriages or who simply live with an unempathic partner. In a group of thirty-eight married women, those whose marriages were poor were found to be psychologically depressed and these same women showed lowered levels of white blood cells. Their herpes antibodies were also raised indicating increased viral activity.

Janice Kiecolt-Glaser, a psychologist at Ohio State University, and her husband, an immunologist, conducted a study on medical students. They found those students who felt stressed by examinations showed a fall in the activity of their specific white blood cells called natural kill (NK) cells. The function of NK cells is to destroy infectious organisms. Students who were stressed and lonely fared even worse; their NK activity reduced even further. The Kiecolt-Glasers also found that recently bereaved men were more likely to die than married men of a similar age. Every piece of research I found seemed to reflect, from one angle or the other, what I was facing.

At this moment, though, I wanted to go home.

"Welcome home, Pop," my eldest son said, as he wrapped his arms around me. His brothers echoed his words. It was good to be back with the boys.

CHAPTER TWENTY SIX

August 1985:
Platelet count 48,000; haemoglobin level 9.2; White blood cell count 0.8

It was almost two weeks since my return from hospital. I felt as if I was on my way to recovery. I was becoming more confident about giving myself injections. I felt buoyed, but my body spoke a different language: the bouts of fever continued as before, the night sweats continued unabated. I was wrung out. I couldn't sleep. One minute I was hot, the next cold. I ached in every joint and every limb, and deep within my bones. The air-conditioner was set on HOT. I had six blankets and two feather quilts on the bed. I wore socks, a tracksuit, a sweater and winter-weight pajamas. I couldn't believe it was possible for anyone to feel so cold.

"I have no idea when the side-effects will ease up," Dr Sullivan said to me when I asked him what I could do. "I'm sure it's dose-related. But you have to keep to the drug company's protocol for the next six months. Are your gums still bleeding?" On that score at least, there was some good news: I was still getting sudden bleeds, but less often. No matter how bad I felt, the words in Sai Baba's books offered me great solace: *'His extraordinary Grace, saving us from death, is given so that we use the extra lease of life for the unfoldment of our Self into the Wisdom that reveals our identity with Sai.'*

Three weeks after I returned from hospital, I woke one morning to what I can only describe as a revelation. I don't know if this was the result of studying Sai Baba's books or because the side effects of the interferon had heightened my awareness, but the result was the same. My realization was that total health depends upon being truly loved. I was awed at the simplicity of the concept. The feeling that accompanied this notion was that I was bathed in the love that emanated from that something I called God. I lay in bed and felt this strange sensation sweep over me. I felt light. I felt euphoric. Was this what Sai Baba and Jesus had meant when they said that we are all a part of God's love; that in such a state of harmony, there can be no dis-ease. Was this the truth for which I had been seeking? I had never recognized the potential effect of that something I called God. I had rejected the notion of a Supreme Being or universal force as incomprehensible. I still reject the notion of a personal god. This new feeling was so strong I was awed. Was it so simple? Love is ease. Lack of love is dis-ease. Was this the truth behind every successful recovery?

'To be clever is to be still,' came the echo from my childhood. I was listening now. I realized that love, as a concept meant little. Love as an emotion suffuses the body with a feeling of life and energy that acts as an antidote to distress and disease. It had taken me a killer disease to realize it.

One Friday it was time to head for the Royal Melbourne Hospital for my weekly check-up. I was preparing to leave when suddenly I started to shiver. My teeth rattled in my head. My body shook with convulsions. The pain in my side continued. In less than five minutes, the quake was over. For a moment, I thought I should rest and cancel my appointment. I decided to go. The blood test results were encouraging. My hemoglobin was up to 10.3, white cell count was 0.9, and platelets were, incredibly, at 70,000. My spleen had returned to the midline of my abdomen but was still well over 20 cm long. I was elated.

My joy was short-lived. No sooner had I stepped into my car to return home than the shivering started again. I was freezing cold. I sat in my car in the parking garage under the hospital for over an hour not feeling confident enough to drive. I switched on the engine, turned on the heating, and waited. Eventually I warmed up. I drove home, very slowly. There was no doubt that the interferon was working but it was using my body as the battlefield in its war against my leukemia. The battle raged on and so did my fever. That night I prayed to Sai Baba. I, who had been a devout atheist, was now a devotee. For the next few days, I meditated longer and longer. Slowly but surely, I gained a little strength, though every little task was still so hard to do.

For the first few weeks after my return from hospital, Arthur and Patsy did my shopping, bought my vegetables and whatever else I needed – organically grown rice, grape juice, bread. I lowered my Vitamin C intake to 10g a day. I continued taking folic acid and Vitamin B complex in the belief that they would boost my immune system. As my hemoglobin level began to rise and my breath returned I started shopping on my own again. I re-read Gerson's book and decided to follow part of his maintenance diet by drinking two to three glasses of vegetable juice and one of raw calf's liver and carrot juice every day. I also started taking two coffee enemas a day. (I had stopped these shortly before going into hospital). To buy the liver, I recommenced my visits to Jim, the butcher. His brusqueness had not waned.

"So, you're still with us, are you?" he shouted, as I walked in. "We thought you were a goner."

I told him what had happened during my stay in hospital.

He grew quieter and quieter.

"Come to the office at the back. Let's sit down and have a cup of tea," he said.

For several months, I visited Jim twice a week. We drank tea. We talked for what seemed like ages but was, in fact, never more than half an hour or so. Then one day he gave me bad news.

"I'll have to sell the shop. I've borrowed too much. The bank wants its money back."

"Isn't this a good business?" I asked.

"It certainly is. But they want me to pay back quicker than I am paying, and I can't afford it. Times are tough."

"What are you going to do?" I asked. Jim and his shop seemed inseparable.

"I'm going fishing," he said. "Jean has cancer. Can you believe it? My second wife. First one and then the other. At least the fish won't get away."

By the time Jim sold the shop, I had stopped drinking raw calf's liver and carrot juice. It was just as well. It wouldn't have been the same if I had bought it from someone else.

Just how effectively the interferon was working was revealed a week later. The drug company's protocol demanded that I have a monthly bone-marrow aspiration to check the levels of leukemia cells in my marrow. Different doctors carried out these tests at different times. The doctor that day was John Scarlet, who had performed two previous aspirations on me.

"I think it's getting easier to do these," he said, as he sucked the marrow through a syringe out of my hipbone. "It used to be harder before. Your blood was so clogged up with leukemic cells it was almost impossible to extract any marrow. It must have hurt you."

It still did, but the blood tests confirmed his feeling that my counts were still very low. Three days later, I received a four-unit full blood transfusion. I felt so much better. I could breathe more easily. I took things one day at a time, single-minded about getting better. I still didn't know how to offset the effects produced by the injections. Raging fever. The hot and cold periods of shivering and sweating continued. Aching everywhere. Headaches. My lymph glands were still swollen though they didn't hurt as much as before. My gums had stopped bleeding. My spleen was slowly shrinking but was still large and a cause of discomfort. Weariness was still my constant companion.

CHAPTER TWENTY SEVEN

Spring 1985:
Platelet count 90,000; haemoglobin level 10.9; white blood cell count 1.2.

"We have to increase the dosage," Dr Harris said at my next visit.

"What for?"

"It says so on the protocol," he replied.

Originally, each injection consisted of one three-million-unit vial a day. The drug company wanted this increased to six million units. The effect on me was dramatic. My blood counts dropped sharply.

"I don't like this," Rob said when the results of my blood test landed on his desk. "The interferon is suppressing your leukemia. It's also suppressing your blood counts."

"What are we going to do?"

"Let's wait a while and see what happens."

For three weeks, he kept a close watch on my counts. They continued to fall. He made a hard decision. "I think you should go back to three million units a day," Rob said. "I'm going to phone the drug company and tell them I've changed their rules."

"Won't they object?"

"Probably. But I don't think they'll do much about it. You're the only person they have trialing their drug in Australia. If you stop, their program will go out the window."

He was right. They didn't object. Slowly but surely, my blood counts began to rise. The odds looked better and better.

Several people commented on how much healthier I looked. The yellowness was fading from my skin. The trial in the United States of America had already indicated that more interferon didn't necessarily imply a better result. My case confirmed this.

I was still getting severe stabbing pains in my side. I was concerned about my rate of progress.

"Your spleen was so large," John Sullivan explained. "The sac containing it grew to enormous proportions. Now it's shrinking. That's probably what is causing you so much pain."

Despite the fact that none of the alternative treatments had worked and had cost me a small fortune, I was demanding in my expectations that the interferon would produce a more dramatic result. I was so tired it was as if my blood counts had hardly improved. It was spring. The weather did little to raise my spirits. I seeded the lawn in front of the house. Its barrenness had always been an eyesore. I planted bulbs for the next season somehow confident I would be around to see them bloom. I read voraciously. As soon as my sons returned from school, they plunged into their homework and study for the end-of year exams. My middle son was two months away from his school-leaving certificate. My eldest was due to take his first-year medical exams. The scholarship my youngest son had won demanded he maintain good results, which he did, year in, year out. They were so occupied I had to wait until mealtimes to talk to them. My father slept late on most days as well as in the afternoons. He seemed to be out of sorts. I meditated. I took coffee enemas. I made juices. Patsy visited me often and always with a dish of some health food or delicacy. The night sweats were occurring less frequently so my sleep pattern improved. My blood counts had evened out.

One afternoon, driving home from the hospital where I had been for my blood test, I heard a talk on the radio about, of all things, interferon.

"Everybody thought interferon would be the miracle drug that would cure all diseases," the interviewee said, "but it has failed to live up to expectations with the exception of one particularly rare form of leukemia." I was clearly the exception.

Uppermost in my thoughts at the time was a reluctance to pursue the same objectives I had in the past. My priorities had changed. What had once seemed so important now seemed trivial. I knew that nothing would ever be the same again. My concept of my place in space and time had changed. I felt that I had to continue along the path I had taken no matter where it would lead. I was filled with some trepidation and not a little excitement at the prospect. I felt sure that if I kept sight of the signposts and remained mindful of the words of Sai Baba I would win through. His words were a constant beacon: *'One's anger is one's greatest enemy and one's calmness is one's own protection. One's joy is one's heaven and one's sorrow is one's hell.'*

In time, I would come to understand that recovery from a deemed terminal illness is not unlike the process of bereavement, of the sadness, the profound sense of loss and the mourning that follows the death of a loved one. The person I was before my diagnosis was, to all intents and purposes, dead. Much as I may have wished for things to be back to where they were B.C. (before cancer), my time would now be counted in A.D. (after diagnosis) years. I was in a new land where I had already started to learn a new language and meet new people while still staying true to myself.

My innate optimism kept me going through a seemingly endless cycle of sameness. Through that spring I went to the hospital every Friday for a check-up, another blood test. Every Friday I collected enough interferon, syringes and swabs to see me through the week. The drug company's protocol was exhaustive and exhausting. I had more x-rays, more CAT scans, more radioactive injections for more liver and spleen scans, more ECGs. Hovering in the background was the specter of AIDS. I knew a positive result could not be excluded because of the number of transfusions I had received. So far, I had undergone two tests. Both had been negative. Moreover, when I had had my first test, AIDS testing was still in its infancy. No one yet knew what the incubation period was. No one knew yet about the link between HIV-positive and full-blown AIDS. Each time I had a transfusion I became an player in a game of Russian roulette with a needle for a gun aimed at me. It was a scary time.

On one particular occasion, I was scheduled to have yet another CAT scan. To make certain organs more visible, a radioactive dye is injected into the body. My response to a similar test some years earlier had been most unpleasant.

"Can I have the test without the injection?" I asked the nurse.

"No." She was emphatic.

"I'd like to discuss this with the doctor, if I may."

"He'll never agree," she said, peremptorily. She returned with the doctor a few minutes later. They took up positions on either side of me.

"Now what seems to be the problem?" the doctor asked. He was clearly not impressed by my request.

"I had a rather severe reaction once. Please can you do this test without the dye?"

"I've never been asked this before by a patient. This is most unusual."

"It is my body," I replied. "I presume I do have some say in what you do with it."

"I suppose you do." He left the room, telephoned Dr Sullivan and returned a few minutes later. "We'll do the test without the dye," he said drily.

The test was to measure the size of my spleen and liver. I was aware that it was not essential to the test to be injected with a dye, although it would have made it easier for them. Three weeks later, I returned for yet another CAT scan.

"A-ha!" said the same doctor. "The man who would say no."

I ignored the sarcasm in his voice. I was not amused. I knew my body. I knew more about my disease than he. I also knew more about the procedures and tests required by the protocol than he did. I was not going to be bludgeoned into submission.

"You gave old so-and-so a hard time," John Sullivan said to me a few days later.

"Was I wrong?"

"Not at all. It is your body. You can always refuse. He should have handled it differently. I suspect he's learned a lesson."

The interferon was clearly working. I was not. Whenever I thought the effects of the drug were lessening, they struck me even more severely.

"I've discussed the problem with Dr Sullivan," Rob Harris told me at my next visit to the hospital. "We think you should stop the interferon for a while."

"Do you think the effects I'm having are from the drug?"

"It could be worse," Dr Harris replied. "You could be

developing a sensitivity to the treatment. The only way we can find out is for you to stop for a week or two."

I found out later that such sensitivity could be fatal. They were wise to make me stop.

The result of stopping the treatment was dramatic. Within days, my blood levels stabilized. Then they shot up. My platelet level went over 100,000. For two weeks, my counts remained high. Then they plummeted. Within six weeks, they fell by almost half. It was time to start the interferon again. For a few glorious weeks, we believed I could forsake the drug. It now seemed I would have to remain on it forever. At first, I was extremely angry. Then I was disappointed. Slowly I calmed down. I was back on track. At last, I was downwind from my foe.

CHAPTER TWENTY EIGHT

Summer 1985:
Platelet count 93,000; haemoglobin level 13.2; White blood cell count 2.1

It was December. My middle son had finished his school-leaving certificate. My other two sons had completed their exams. The pattern of activities in the house had returned to normal. I regained my composure. Every day was a bonus. I found time to make vegetable juices when my wife was at work. Despite my belief that I would survive and my assurances that that our insurance policies would protect her and the children financially if I died, she believed her psychologist who told her I was going to die and so took what she considered a pragmatic longer view and found a job. I read, meditated, reflected. I listened to music. I contemplated on how close I had come to dying. I considered that my death sentence had been commuted to a life sentence. I now had to serve time. I came to appreciate this immeasurably.

At the end of January 1986, my eldest son developed rubella. At the same time, I developed several sores on my body and severe pains in my muscles. These symptoms did not appear to be drug-related. The doctors were concerned that I had also contracted rubella, as I had never had this childhood illness. Dr Sullivan put me on an intense course of antibiotics. The symptoms cleared up. Someone suggested that interferon might have warded off rubella's worst effects. No one was sure.

I was still so weary. No one could tell me whether this was

the effect of my leukemia or the interferon. Some doctors suggested it was a combination of both. It was a strange tiredness, not the sleepy, yawning tiredness that comes at the end of a workday or the lack-of-puff tiredness that comes after strenuous exercise. It was a feeling of being completely drained of energy; as if someone had pulled out the plug connecting me to my power source. Suddenly I had no more current, no more life force. Words cannot describe this tiredness. It was something I had never experienced before. Mega-doses of Vitamin C did not help even though many naturopaths prescribe it for tiredness. Resting didn't help. Sleeping didn't help. In fact, whenever I felt so tired, I could not sleep. I discussed this with Patsy.

"I know the feeling well," Patsy said. "Only a cancer patient can appreciate what you are talking" about." I have spoken to many patients about this problem since. Everyone has had had the same experience, but no one has a remedy. Was this was nature's way of slowing us down so we can heal and recover? Probably.

As time went by I would come to appreciate this level of fatigue is a common side and after-effect of cancer and its treatment. No one really knows why.

The months passed. My blood counts improved. Whenever I could, I attended Sai Baba devotional meetings. My routine of giving myself an injection every day continued. I meditated more. I slept more. I was disquieted by my continuing need for so much sleep. I had hoped that my improving hemoglobin count would take care of my weariness. It was not to be. I was caught between the tiredness and my desire to be rid of it. I felt that I had to do something, anything, to correct the situation, to take control and not leave the course of my recovery solely to a daily vial of interferon. Everything was in a state of flux, a state of transition. As such, it was up to me to adjust to these changes. The thought helped me clear my mind. It helped me establish a new dimension to my treatment. The words of Sai Baba gave me strength: 'Initially we seek a cure for physical disease; but we receive the more important cure for our mental illness and we are prompted towards spiritual awakening.'

A pair of retired couples occupied two of the houses across the road from where we lived. Each of the men spent hours each day working in their gardens. The results reflected the years they had spent tending them. I had often watched them from a distance, amazed at how absorbed they were in their endless pursuit of weeds and worms. I marveled at the results. They were prize-winning showpieces of color and neatness. I had never been an enthusiastic gardener, only infrequently pruning a few roses and fruit trees. I had, on a few occasions, mowed the lawn. I had found gardening boring and time-consuming.

I decided it was time to try something I had become adept at farming out to others. I decided to take up gardening. I discovered it had the same effect on me as meditation. I lost all sense of time and space. The feeling was one of complete relaxation. When I meditate, I am aware of my surroundings at the periphery of my senses. I attach no significance or attempt to interpret anything I hear or see. I have no sense of self.

I found gardening produced the same effect with the same long-lasting tranquility and with much less effort. And I didn't have to adopt a formal posture to achieve this. I felt 'earthed'. I felt less 'charged up'. My garden soon reflected my efforts of spending so much time on my knees.

I would come to appreciate that the stress of trying to

meditate was an added and unnecessary burden to bear when there was more than enough stress to go around. Meditation is not the cure for cancer. It had taken me some considerable time to understand this.

Now was a time to be still. To believe that I only had a few months to live would have been to comply with the predictions of Dr Gloom and all the tracts I had read about my disease. Some doctors still try to set the time of their patients' deaths by pointing the bone. Thankfully, most doctors are now less inclined to make these predictions since so many patients are proving them wrong. None of the patients I have spoken to had any idea of trying to prove their doctor wrong when they were first diagnosed. Their first reaction to being told they had cancer or leukemia was one of panic and disbelief; panic at the thought that they had so much to do and so little time in which to do it – and disbelief that this should have happened to them. I believe that the only way to overcome this awful sense of dread it to listen to the inner voice of intuition we know we all have but seldom give ear to: the voice that forbids us to quit before the end. The will to live is our most powerful ally.

"What have you been doing?" Don asked. His garden was one of those I admired. "I've been watching you for some time. I had a word with Stan; he is the chap with the beaut garden who lives next door to me. We've decided we'll mow your lawn for you. You can do the rest. Your mower's no good anyway. It's tearing up the new lawn you've put down." Don knew I had leukemia. He knew I suffered extreme tiredness. He had offered his hand in friendship. I accepted. Later, I persuaded my sons to take on this chore. Ron was over seventy, and although he was in great physical shape, it didn't seem right he should do what my own sons were equally capable of doing.

Don and Stan provided me with good advice and I welcomed their help. Our garden looked better and better. I installed a drip-watering system. I planted kiwi fruit vines. My youngest son provided the muscle to help me build a trellis to support the vines that would bear fruit some day. Someday? Yes, I was making long-term plans. I was contemplating a future. In a most curious way, gardening helped me come to a better understanding of how to manage my leukemia. It stabilized me at a time when I felt the previous Joel had been uprooted and replanted. I was still trying to find the patch on which I felt most comfortable. My garden helped me realize that the only way I could overcome my difficulties was to create an environment in which life flourishes. The way to do this was to keep my thoughts in a 'garden mode'.

Leukemia, as with all other cancers, is like no other problem. It cannot be shelved. It cannot be put aside to be tackled at some future date. The symptoms won't let you ignore it. You can't hang around waiting for a miracle. Its progression is relentless. The results of my efforts in the garden heightened my awareness that as I had sowed, so would I reap. This realization was vital to my recovery. It helped me appreciate that although my journey was a lonely one, I was not on my own. My newfound spiritual strength gave me the courage to face the adventure of my lifetime.

CHAPTER TWENTY NINE

Autumn-Winter 1986:
Platelet count 90,000; haemoglobin level 13.7; white blood cell count 1.7.

My recovery progressed slowly. I felt more at ease when I was completely alone, when I was able to concentrate totally on getting better. I had discussed some very personal issues with Dr Diamond over the past several months. She understood what I was going though. She understood my need to find my own space. To be on my own. She made enquiries on my behalf.

"I have some very dear friends who have a weekend retreat," she said. "Their house is empty all week. I'll ask them if they would be willing to let you use it. I imagine you would have to supply your own food and provide your own linen."

Shortly afterwards, I met Ed and Lillian at their home in the hills outside Melbourne. It was a warm, sunny afternoon in April. Ed had close-cropped, wavy grey hair and gentle, pale blue eyes. His handshake was as warm as his smile. Lillian was slightly shorter than Ed and slim. She gave me a broad but guarded smile. Her brown eyes sparkled as she spoke.

"Would you like a cup of tea?" she asked. "I've thrown together a very light lunch. I hope you like it."

We talked and talked. I told them about my diagnosis, and the transfusions that followed. I went into detail about how I had found interferon and how I had responded to it. They also understood why some personal aspects of my life had become untenable.

"If you're looking for somewhere quiet to stay during the week," Lillian said, "you're most welcome to use our house. We don't come up during the week. We have a business to run."

I couldn't believe my luck. This was just the place I needed to spend quiet hours on my own. They gave me the keys to their house and for the next several months, their mountain home became my retreat and my salvation. The house was set in a rambling garden under towering mountain ash, eucalyptus and spreading elm trees. Rhododendron bushes and azaleas lined the footpaths. The flowerbeds were a riot of color. As winter advanced, the rains came. When the snow began to fall, I dashed out of doors to gather wood for the solitary wood-fired stove set in a corner of the spacious pine kitchen. The heat from it radiated for only a few feet. Despite the natural beauty of the place, winter became a test of endurance. The outside temperature hovered around zero Celsius. It was so cold I slept on a blanket in front of the stove. I ate in front of the stove. I read and wrote my journal in front of the stove. Ed had chopped enough wood to last several winters so I was spared that chore. I also ate in the kitchen. I rekindled my dormant cooking skills. I had taken my juicer with me so I kept up the regimen of vegetable juices. I decided that the carrot and liver combination served no further purpose so I stopped drinking the brew. I stopped taking coffee enemas. It was too hard to take all the paraphernalia with me. It was also too cold to lie on the floor in the bathroom.

For two to three days each week for the next several

months, I was a monk in my own monastery. I injected myself daily with interferon. I found time to think, time to be on my own, time for solitary, undisturbed peace. I started writing this book. I am sure I would have walked the hills if the weather had been warmer but the only walking I did was to the local shops to replenish my stores. I regained a little of the weight I had lost. My retreat gave me a respite. I don't know how I would have managed through the rest of the year without it.

I still had to attend the Hematology clinic every Friday at the hospital. Because of this timetable and the need to see my family, I could never stay in the hills later than Thursday. I looked forward to seeing my father and my sons who understood why I stayed away. Janet and I had separated but at this stage neither of us was willing to be apart from our children or my father.

"Peter and Jane are coming to town," Patsy told me. "Do you want to come with us?"

"Yes," I replied. The thought of receiving more healing at this time from Jane Smith seemed like a good idea. The day before my appointment Patsy phoned to tell me she could not attend. I went on my own.

The hall in which the Smith's were to conduct their healing was on the far side of town. It was a wet, rainy and bitingly cold day. I didn't feel like going out but Patsy had made the arrangements. I felt obliged to go. It took me some time to find the address. The hall was deserted. I sat in my car with the heater on and waited for over an hour. No one arrived. I drove home. I felt sure this was an omen that the healings I received from Sally were sufficient. In any event, Jane had told me what she believed was the answer to my problems. Patsy's explanation convinced me I wasn't meant to see the Smiths again.

"But I told you they had changed the venue."

"No, you didn't.'

I showed her the note she had given me.

"I was so sure I had," she replied, embarrassed. Realizing her error she added, "Anyway, you can always see them when they come back again."

I dreamt up countless excuses to deflect Patsy whenever she asked me to join her in receiving healings from David and Jane on their subsequent visits.

Patsy was a lonely woman. She confided in me that Arthur treated her as a possession and although he was extremely wealthy gave her only a meager allowance, chose her clothes for her despite the fact that their tastes differed, and insisted on being served his dinner at six o'clock sharp. With her desire to please and her desperate need for attention, the healings provided her with much-needed physical contact that helped to fill the void in her life.

CHAPTER THIRTY

Spring 1986:
Platelet count 98,000; haemoglobin level 14.3; white blood cell count 2.3.

I was torn between the expectation of another full season and the reality of an extremely bleak winter. I wanted so much to enjoy the sunny days that lay ahead. Driving up and down the mountain was draining me of the little energy I had. I was still so tired. I went through the motions of planting new flowers and raking up the fallen leaves. I would have gone crazy without this distraction. There were vague stirrings in my mind. As with the summer before, I felt that if I could link my being to the growth of my plants there was a chance I would actually survive to see them bloom. It wasn't a logical plan but rather a feeling that the earth itself was my only guarantee of stability.

The Sai Baba devotional meetings I attended once a week helped bolster my spirits. The answer to our problems, Sai Baba said, lies in the realization that, like the tree for which there is an eventual ripening of the fruit, for each of us there is a 'right time' that requires 'austere patience'. It was sage advice. It also reminded me that in order to stay downwind of my foe, I needed to tread carefully and slowly – and to be patient.

My next bone-marrow aspiration was a turning point. As I steeled myself for the insertion of the needle, Dr Harris paused. He had not performed a biopsy on me for some time. "You look like a pincushion," he said. "I think you've had enough. The drug company has enough results to persuade them that their product works. I'm going to tell them we're stopping." I was so relieved. My blood counts indicated that the number of circulating hairy cells had greatly diminished. It was September. My physical condition appeared to be improving. But, I asked, was I out of danger? Dr Harris and Dr Sullivan adopted a wait-and-see approach. There were few guidelines for them in this case.

A few days later, I was sitting in the day center waiting for a new supply of interferon I started talking to Mary Hopkins, a grey-haired sixty-year-old I had seen on many occasions. We had swapped yarns whenever we met. She had acute lymphoproliferative leukemia. A chemotherapy drip ran into her arm.

"I feel so awful today," she said. "My blood counts are so bad."

"What are they?"

She told me. Her white blood cell count was 5.0. Her hemoglobin was 12.0. From my point of view, they were excellent. Her state of mind was not.

"How do you manage to be so positive all the time?" she asked me. I was surprised at her question. She had always seemed so sure of herself.

"I'm not sure what being positive means. There are many times when I feel so tired I'd really like to pack it all in. I sometimes think it would be so much easier to die than to live."

"My doctor doesn't seem to be positive about my outcome," she said, glumly. Her doctor's words had distressed her.

"Do you believe everything your doctor tells you?"

"Yes. Don't you?"

"Not everything," I replied.

My reply surprised her. Her attitude confounded me. Is what the doctor says what the patient thinks? In her case, it seemed so. She died a few months later.

I refuse to accept that anyone except your executioner knows when you are going to die. Sai Baba's words concerning the 'right time' were true. I had tried many alternative treatments. None of them had worked. I had been engaged in wishful thinking. The answer lay outside my vision but I knew it was there, hoped it was there, prayed it was there. I was totally convinced there was an answer to my problem. And I found it. My determination had kept me going long enough to become the right patient at the right time for the right treatment.

Three weeks later, I reached another milestone when I was at the Royal Melbourne.

"Still so tired?" Dr Harris asked me.

"Are you kidding? I don't know if the treatment is worth it. I feel like a zombie."

"I think we must buck the system. The dosage you're on is far too high."

Until now, I had been on three million units every day. With every injection, I gave myself a tenfold dose of all the symptoms of the flu. There didn't seem to be anything I could do to counter the side effects. "I think we should cut it back to three times a week," Rob said.

"I won't argue with you. What are the chances of my blood counts improving?"

"I don't know," Rob replied. "I doubt if it will make any difference except that you won't have to inject yourself every day."

I was thrilled. His next bit of news was equally pleasing.

"I don't think you need to come to the hospital every week for a check up. Once a month will do."

My joy was diluted by what Dr Harris then said. "I've resigned from the hospital. I'm taking up a position as the head of a pathology laboratory. It's an offer I can't refuse."

Dr Harris had been my program controller for almost fifteen months. Together with Dr Sullivan, he had been a constant source of encouragement and enlightenment. I was going to miss his quiet humor, gentle manner and informed opinion. I told him so. I wished him good luck.

"I expect I'll hear about you from John. I'll be working at the same hospital." This news was reassuring. Dr Sullivan had moved to St Andrews Hospital, now the Peter McCallum Cancer Institute, a few months earlier. I alternated my visits to the Royal Melbourne with visits to St Andrews, attending the RMH for my interferon, and St Andrews for John's sage advice, easy manner and, not least of all, his friendship.

"You don't have to visit the Royal Melbourne any more," Dr Sullivan told me a few weeks later. "The drug company will supply you through the pharmacy here."

The staff at the Royal Melbourne had undergone several changes. Cynthia, Sue, Fiona, Julie and Kathy had all left, and now Rob Harris. The times they were a-changing.

"I can't carry on like this any more," I said to Dr Diamond a few days later. "I'm sure my extreme tiredness and desire to sleep all the time are because I also feel emotionally down."

"Have you spoken to John Sullivan about this?"

"Yes," I replied.

"What did he say?"

"He said he thought that if my tiredness was the price I had to pay for being alive, it was a small price to pay."

"I agree," said Dr Diamond. "John doesn't believe your tiredness is completely related to your personal issues. I don't either. You still have leukemia, and interferon does have some pretty nasty side-effects, but I'm sure you'd feel better if you had fewer other issues to contend with."

"I don't have a choice. I'm locked into an impossible situation at home."

"You always have choices," Dr Diamond said. "What would you say to you and Janet seeing a marriage guidance counselor?"

"Okay." There was no point in struggling any more. I had tried my best. I was bogged down. I felt like a fish suspended in a bowl of water that, in turn, was placed in another bowl of water. I was now totally out of my depth. Maybe somebody else had the solution.

"You're so upbeat in every other way," Dr Diamond said. "It would be a real pity if after everything you've been through your problems at home brought you down. There must be something we can do."

"I wish we could," I replied. "I've fought so hard to be there for my sons. I can't imagine what life would be like without them."

I was face to face with what I had felt for some time. The only way to 'take the bends out of my road' was to take another road.

A few days later, everything was put on 'hold'. My father took a turn for the worse. Returning from the shops, I saw him in the kitchen. He had a kettle in one hand, a tea bag in the other.

"Are you making tea?" I said, stating the obvious. "If you are, I'd like a cuppa, please."

He smiled. He made the tea. He started to talk. I didn't

understand a word.

"Can you repeat that?" He did.

It was gibberish. As he spoke, it was clear to me that he didn't know that his words were not coming out the way he intended. As suddenly as it started, it stopped.

"Here's you tea," my father said in normal speech. "Why are you looking at me like that?" he asked. I was lost for words. I was disconcerted. As we sat drinking tea, his next remark made me feel even stranger.

"Why don't you do something about all the ants?"

"What ants?"

"The ones crawling all over the walls and the ceilings." I didn't answer him. There were no ants. My father was hallucinating. I telephoned his doctor at the hospital. I knew her well as I took my father there every month for a check-up for his angina.

"You'd better bring him in," Dr Kouzman said.

Tests soon revealed that Dad's uric acid levels were sky high. His prostate was enlarged. His body was loaded with toxins. A trans-urethral section was the only solution. My father underwent surgery the following day to clear the obstruction. It was a most difficult time. My father had suffered a few heart attacks years before. He was on constant medication for his angina. The doctors were concerned that at eighty-four he was not strong enough to withstand the treatment. But my father was as tough as his old army boots. He smiled and joked his way through the operation performed with a spinal block.

"It was harder for me than for him," the surgeon later told me. "Your father told us so many jokes, I thought I'd injure him he made me laugh so much."

Apart from having to take a few more pills, my father

recovered completely. He had no recollection of going to hospital and he didn't remember anything about the ants. He didn't believe me when I told him his speech had been unintelligible.

It was good to have him home again. He was to be my anchor in the months ahead, which were to be times of great change.

On my next visit to Dr Sullivan, I said, "I want to stop the interferon; for a while, at least. Let's see what happens."

"Okay. But on one condition: you come here once a week for a blood test so I can keep a close check on you." I agreed. I stopped giving myself injections. My blood counts began to rise. My energy level improved.

My next blood test showed that I could not survive without interferon. My counts had started to fall again. Hemoglobin was at 12.0. Platelets were down to 70,000. White blood cells were down to 1.2. I went back to injecting myself three times a week. After the delay, it was as if I was back to square one. The side effects wiped me out. For days, I battled a raging fever. I was shivering cold and boiling hot within minutes. My temperature shot up to 40°. My body felt as if it was caught in a vice. My headaches tortured me.

In moments of quiet reflection between these violent earthquakes, I knew I couldn't carry on like this. I realized we all have an inner strength we can draw on in times of need. Our wants destroy us. Our needs energize us. I knew I had to stay downwind if I wanted to remain a survivor. I felt in tune with a story related by Sai Baba about the master of a house who is dying. His wife and children pestered him with their anxiety. 'What is to happen to us when you leave us?' they wailed. The dying man turned to them in equal despair. 'What is to happen to me when I leave you?' Then he died.

I had been given a respite, but for how long? I could not find peace in my living. I came to realize that people achieve a strange accommodation between their rational and emotional sides, burying their true feelings. We tend to put up barriers to make sure we don't get hurt and, in the process, shut ourselves off from new experiences. Even if we have some self-knowledge, most of us would rather suffer in silence than admit an error of judgment. All too often we discover that things and people we depend on to make us happy have the power to make us feel unhappy. Who would confess he or she chose the wrong life partner or made the wrong business decision? The security of what we know and what is familiar feels preferable to the insecurity of what we don't know. All too often people remain in a bad relationship rather than breaking it off and trying something new.

Just how much I had been deluding myself that things would change was brought home to me in a flash when, after telling my sons I would be moving out, they said, "What took you so long?"

In 1987, I moved out of the family home. I did not have the energy to sustain the marriage.

Shortly afterwards, by complete chance, I met René. She was separated with three sons of her own, close in age to mine. I had always believed that before I died I would meet someone I would love and who would love me in the fullest sense of the word. It had been my abiding hope. I had survived long enough to see it realized.

Like me, she is an optimist, sees life in every color, and is ever ready to explore untrodden paths, has been my constant companion, loyal wife, and support throughout the rest of this story.

CHAPTER THIRTY ONE

Autumn 1987:
Platelet count 94,000; haemoglobin level 14.9; white blood cell count 2.3.

It was May. I had been to visit Dr Sullivan. I was preparing to leave. He handed my prescription for interferon as well as my maintenance supply of antibiotics. I handed my prescription to Fred Doble, the pharmacist at St Andrews' Hospital. He was usually friendly, always smiling. Today his face was set. He shifted from foot to foot, greeting me distractedly. I had an awful premonition that something was wrong. I was right.

"The company supplying us with your interferon has sent me a bill. I'm sorry about this, but I'm afraid I shall have to pass the charges on to you."

"How much?" I asked. I knew that interferon had cost billions of dollars to research. Before genetic engineering reduced the cost of manufacture, it had cost several thousand dollars an ounce.

"It'll probably be more than $102 a vial ...' I didn't hear the rest of his sentence. A quick calculation in my head told me three injections a week times four weeks a month times twelve months a year equaled more than I could afford.

"What will you charge me?"

"I'll have to add a dispensing fee. I'm not sure. It could be around $125 each."

That would amount to more than $1600 a month! (Note: All these figures have been calibrated in 2013 values). When I first went onto interferon as a trial patient, the company had a stake in me. After all, if the treatment worked, it would be another arrow in their formidable quiver of drugs. When I signed the protocol, it stated that the availability of the drug would be assessed after one year. I had now been on interferon for over eighteen months. On several occasions, I had discussed the issue with Dr Harris.

"There's nothing to worry about," he had said. "I've spoken to them. They've assured me they'll keep supplying you free of charge. I guess you're their sentimental favorite. You were the first trial patient in Australia. Anyway, as a patient at this hospital you can always get it on the free list."

Dr Sullivan had mirrored the words of Dr Harris: "Don't worry about it," he had told me. "You've been on interferon for so long, they're not going to stop supplying you."

I left the pharmacy and raced back to Dr Sullivan's rooms. "Have you heard they want to charge me for the interferon?" I said.

"So Fred told you? He told me this morning. I'm sorry I didn't tell you. I didn't know what to say."

"What are we going to do?" At that moment, John's secretary signaled there was a call for him.

"That'll be my call to the drug company. Hold on, I'll be right back."

He emerged from his office a few minutes later, his eyes downcast. "They won't budge. I reminded them of their promises to Dr Harris and me. They said the trial was over and that the protocol stated quite clearly they would assess supply after a year. They say you've had an extra six months free of charge. They were pretty adamant."

I was shocked. I wasn't going to take this lying down. I wrote to them directly. I received a polite reply stating that I could hardly expect them to supply me with interferon forever. 'We are pleased you are making a good recovery,' the letter added. I had clearly outlived their expectations.

Dr Sullivan's letter of intercession also failed to move them. "I should have obtained their agreement in writing," John said, ruefully. "They're such a large company, you wouldn't expect them to worry about supply to one patient." He was most upset that he had not been more businesslike in his dealings with them.

I wrote a letter to the Minister for Health. My plea for funding for interferon was turned down.

The following day, I telephoned the Royal Melbourne Hospital. The professor of oncology, Professor Fox, came on the line. He was, as usual, friendly and enthusiastic.

"The original interferon trial is over, but we're now blind-testing interferon with another drug. How would you like to go on the trial? There is, however, no guarantee you will receive interferon. You may be given another drug. You've got a fifty-fifty chance?"

"What is the other drug?"

"We don't usually disclose such information to patients. Let's say it's probably a placebo."

I was caught in a headwind against which I could make little headway. After all this time, there was no point in going onto a program on which I might receive a shot of water. Unless I was on interferon I would soon be back to where I started. I wasn't sure what to do. I called Dr Sullivan.

"Leave it with me," he said. "You still have enough interferon for ten days. I'll see what I can do in the meantime."

He telephoned me a few days later. "I've been in touch with the head honcho of hematology at the Austin Hospital. If you give him a call, he said he'd see what he can do for you."

Two days later, I was seated across a desk from a tall, lean and grey-haired doctor.

"What seems to be the problem?"

I was taken aback. I thought Dr Sullivan had told the Austin the full story. "Don't you know? Didn't Dr Sullivan talk to you?"

"Yes," he said, casually. "He mentioned that you have Hairy Cell Leukemia and that you'd like to go onto interferon therapy. Is that correct?"

Something was amiss. I had a feeling we had cross lines. I was right.

"We'd have to admit you to the hospital as an in-patient," he said. "You'd have to have a bone-marrow biopsy and blood tests, as well as liver and spleen scans."

"But I know I have Hairy Cell Leukemia," I said. "Everybody knows I do."

"If this hospital were to agree (and I'm not saying they will) to supply you with this drug, we'd have to confirm your condition with a proper set of tests."

"You can get my records from the Royal Melbourne Hospital. Why would I have to undergo tests to prove what is already a proven fact? In any event, I've been on interferon for the past eighteen months."

"It's hospital policy," he replied. "I'm sorry, but I can't change the rules. Splenectomy is still the treatment of first choice here. It's more cost-effective."

I looked at him in amazement. He misinterpreted my look.

"If you'd like to undergo surgery, I can try to arrange this at short notice. It would depend on your blood counts and the size of your spleen."

He was polite and seemed genuinely concerned. I told him the operation was unnecessary. I also told him I thought it was a retrograde step to take simply because I could not afford the cost of the drug. His reply floored me.

"I'm sorry, but interferon is too costly. My hands are tied."

As politely as I could, I thanked him for his offer and left.

"A man called you," said Dad, when I returned home. "His name is Mr Doble. He wants you to call him back him. He says he has good news." It was past five o'clock. There was no reply. I had to wait anxiously until the next morning.

"I still have some interferon from my previous delivery," Fred said. "It's not much, but it'll keep you going for another few weeks. You won't have to pay for it. In the meantime who knows...?" I thanked him. He had granted me a reprieve.

It was all I needed. Two weeks later, I received a telephone call from Dr Sullivan.

"Joel," he said, "I've been talking to Professor Fox at the Royal Melbourne. Things have changed down there. I think you'll find your problem's been solved. They'd be happy to have you back. Why don't you go and have a chat to him?"

This time round things look much rosier. The drug company that had originally supplied my interferon had clearly had a rush of blood to the head. They wanted more money from everybody. The hospital was not prepared to pay the higher cost so they switched their purchasing order to a competitor who also made interferon. Fate had intervened. My problem had been solved!

I was at the Royal Melbourne for one of my monthly check-ups when Professor Fox approached me. A genuine, caring and astute man with a ready smile, he was open to new avenues of research.

"Just thought ... how would you like to enter a trial a new drug for your leukemia?"

"What's wrong with the interferon I'm on?" I asked. "It's working."

"I know, but there's a drug called 2-deoxycorformycin. It's an adenosine deaminase inhibitor. It's apparently been trialed on ten Hairy Cell Leukemia patients in the United States of America. I believe they've all gone into remission."

"Is it a cure?"

"Joel, you know there is no cure. But you won't have to be on interferon for the rest of your life. A few treatments could restore your blood levels and your spleen to normal. There should also be an absence of hairy cells in your blood."

"Sounds like an idea worth considering. I'd like to discuss it with Dr Sullivan."

"That's okay. In any event, it's still not available here."

A few days later, I discussed the new drug with Dr Sullivan. His answer shocked me. "I'd be a little nervous about using 2-deoxycorformycin. At one time, it was used on patients with lymphoblastic leukemia. The results were mostly fatal. Then they tried reducing the dosage and found that it seemed to work on some patients with HCL. The good thing about those cases was that it required only a relatively short treatment period. At least fifty per cent of the patients went into remission.'

Any thoughts I might still have entertained about being a guinea pig for deoxy- were destroyed a few weeks later at the Royal Melbourne pharmacy as I waited for my syringes and needles.

"The doctors would like me to trial deoxycorformycin," I said to the pharmacist. "Do you know anything about it?"

"I sat in on the meeting."

"Oh really? What meeting?"

"A representative of the drug company manufacturing it was here. He outlined its success, but also told us there had been disease progression in some patients. He was testing us out. When we told him we had only one patient with Hairy Cell Leukemia, so he lost interest."

I decided to find out more and checked out several medical journals. I learned that of the fifty per cent who failed to go into remission, a large number had died. I also found out that the drug was in the experimental stage, and the side effects were horrendous. It was just as well that nothing had come of the notion. If I had stopped using interferon and deoxy- had been ineffectual, the chances of obtaining interferon again would have been extremely poor. As I was to find out later, it was just as well I did not agree to join the trial.

CHAPTER THIRTY TWO

I was still treating myself with injections of interferon when a year later I read with an at-a-loss-for-words feeling an article in the authoritative *New England Journal of Medicine* about a new drug being trialed in California. Just as interferon had proved the breakthrough drug in treating Hairy Cell Leukemia, so this new drug had been found to be even more effective. Given that HCL is so rare and affects an almost insignificant number of people, it seemed as if the gods were on my side. Again.

The drug is called *2-chlorodeoxyadenosine or* 2-CDA. It had been on trial in America and Sweden only. The results seemed almost too good to be true. Treatment consisted of a continuous twenty-fours a day infusion for seven days only. There were no side effects. No lasting tiredness. Out of twelve cases reported, eleven had obtained total remissions. The remaining one was in partial remission. I decided to keep this new drug up my sleeve as long as interferon injections once a week were keeping my leukemia at bay. Then, without warning, my world turned upside down.

On a bright sunny morning in October 1989, my father died in peace, in bed, at home. Believing he was sleeping late, I had tried to rouse him. Dad had had his last heart attack while asleep. I sat beside him and told him over and over again how much I loved him. I would like to think he heard my voice through to eternity. Eventually, I called our family doctor who arrived shortly afterwards. The colors and scents of that morning comingle with the still felt pain of my loss. I vividly recall how the bright red and fragrant rose bushes outside my front door were in full bloom. My subsequent research into our family tree and a visit to the village of his birth, Karsakiskis, in Lithuania, has bound our roots even tighter. My heart aches at the absence of his physical presence. No day goes by when I do not think of him. No day goes go by when I do not talk to him. Dad is as much a pillar of strength for me today as he was when he was alive.

Even as I mourned my father, eight months later, I decided to return to the country of my birth after an absence of fourteen years. With a carton of interferon, enough to last for weeks, in my suitcase, I went back to South Africa in July 1990. Over the following few weeks, I visited many of my family and friends. Apart from the pleasure of re-uniting with them after so many years, I was staggered by two disconcerting discoveries about my family. One was that I have a half-brother as a result of an affair my father had with a black African woman when he was living in the Transkei; the other was that I had an uncle, one of my mother's brothers, living in the USA. Tracking my uncle down was easy, and I decided that if my tiredness allowed me, I would endeavor to meet him the following year and, as soon as I could, begin my preparations for the journey. Finding my half-brother remains as elusive today as it was then.

As enjoyable as it was to meet everyone I thought I might never see again, I was grateful I had decided to leave South Africa with its increasing crime, gated communities and just about everyone I knew cowering behind razor-topped garden walls and patrolling guard dogs.

The trip had been emotionally and physically draining, so I decided to rest, continue my writing, and to see my sons as often as possible. I also had a trip to the USA to organize.

Ahead of that journey, I decided to find out if I was

eligible for 2-CDA. I wrote to the Scripps Institute in California describing my symptoms even though by now my spleen was no longer palpable, and my blood counts were almost back to normal. I explained the flu-like symptoms the interferon injections produced and the uncomfortable eczema I was experiencing. They wrote back saying that to be eligible to take part in the trial I would need to discontinue interferon for approximately three months and that my blood counts would need to drop significantly to meet their baseline requirements. This would have meant rolling the clock back to where I started from: struggling to breathe, stopping every few steps to catch my breath and let my heartbeat return to normal, palpitations, painful boils, enlarged lymph glands, swollen spleen, distended liver, and bleeding nose and gums.

The months flew by. I travelled to the USA where the Institute told me that I was also ineligible for the trial as at that stage it was reserved for US-citizens only. Moving on, I flew to Daytona Beach to meet my uncle Henry and then to Chicago for the first time to meet the rest of my mother's close-knit family. I had no idea at the time just how fortunate I had been to complete the trip.

I had been experiencing chest pains for several months and what I read confirmed what Dr Sullivan told me at my next appointment.

"I think we will have to reduce the dose or take you off interferon completely. Your chest pains are the side effect of long-term usage of the drug. Your heart may well have been affected already."

For several years many people, who had heard about my miraculous survival, had approached me in the hope I could help them. The opportunity to help others going through what I had opened a new path out of the maze. Almost overnight, I had a full appointment book. I was working hard so my tiredness seemed a logical consequence – until I saw Dr Sullivan for my next visit. He suggested I have another bone marrow biopsy to find out if any leukemic cells were still circulating through my body.

The result was positive. My leukemia had re-emerged. I was surprised at how coolly I accepted the news of its recurrence. I wondered if I had come to view my body as something so separate from me I felt detached from it. My tiredness apart, my writing and counseling had given me something to look forward to every day. I went back to reviewing the literature on Hairy Cell Leukemia.

It was as well that I did.

As I had discovered earlier, the institute trialing 2-chlorodeoxyadenosine (2CDA) considered my blood counts too high to allow me to join the trial. I had also found out that only citizens of the USA could be on it. I discussed my options with Dr Sullivan.

When he had obtained interferon for me, he had dealt directly with the drug company that was testing it as it was still a trial drug and the government had not approved it. We were faced with the same situation concerning 2-CDA. At his behest, I contacted Professor Fox and gave him all the information I had gathered. He told me had heard of the drug but that as it was not on trial in Australia and so the government would not allow it to be imported. It could take years before they approved it.

"However, I'll do what I can," he said.

I did not feel confident when I left his office with René.

Two days later, at 1 o'clock in the morning, he called to tell me excitedly that the National Cancer Institute in Washington had agreed to include me in its trial and would send 2-CDA to us by express mail.

"It's not what you know. It's whom you know," he said delightedly.

I don't know who was more excited - he or me!

Ten days later, he called me again to tell me to check into the Freemason's hospital. He arrived later that afternoon holding an 8in. x 10in. postal pack containing a black, plastic bag.

"It's to keep out the light," he said, as he instructed the nursing staff what to do.

No one knew what to expect. No one had any experience administering the drug. He inserted a needle into my arm, taped it up and connected me to the drip. For seven days in that December of '91, I received a continuous infusion of 2-CDA. There were no side effects except for a craving for Lobster Mornay. Professor Fox visited me every day, as did Dr Sullivan. Between us, we succeeded in lowering the levels of my bottles of Scotch whisky. My sons as well as René and her sons also came to visit me every day – the boys parking their bicycles and dumping their satchels in the ward, cluttering up the place. The oncology nurses were confounded. They have never observed these side effects of chemotherapy before.

I was confident about the outcome. Within a few months, my blood counts had stabilized. It seemed I had won the battle, but had I won the war? I would have to wait and see. In the meantime, I devoted all my working time to writing and counseling.

With a sense of having gained a more secure lease on life, I married a second time. I watched my sons and a stepson graduate. I decided to collate the notes I had made for the writing of my first book and to get it published, ever mindful of the words of Sai Baba:

> *Life is a challenge – meet it,*
> *Life is a dream – realize it,*
> *Life is a game – play it,*
> *Life is love – enjoy it.*

CHAPTER THIRTY THREE

It was clear my heart problems brought about by the side effect of the interferon had become worse. Without warning, one day my heartbeat went from a normal 72 beats per minute to almost 300. I had suffered my first attack of SVT – supraventricular tachycardia – that usually results from serious heart disease and often requires prompt or emergency treatment. It can be life threatening especially if arteries are blocked and blood flow obstructed, as they were. I was also suffering from ischemia, a lack of blood and hence a lack of oxygen supply to my heart. The chest pains I had been experiencing were, in fact, angina.

Over the next several months I had several attacks of SVT mostly accompanied by angina pain felt in my chest and along the right side of my jaw. On each occasion, I was rushed to hospital by ambulance. On each occasion, an injection of a calcium channel blocker called *verapamil* brought my heartbeat under control.

At one of my scheduled visits to Dr Sullivan and after reviewing my blood test results, he said, "I'm going to refer you to a top rate young heart specialist by the name of Dr Manny Manolas. I am sure you will get on well together." With that, he made an appointment for me to meet Dr Manolas the following week.

Dr Manolas greeted me with twinkling eyes and a ready smile. He made me feel at ease at once, but I quickly discovered there was a serious side to him. In order to measure and diagnose the abnormal rhythms of my heart, he attached an electrocardiograph or ECG machine to me.

Looking at the results, he suggested that I should have a coronary angiogram to check my heart and blood flow. A few days later I checked into hospital where he punctured the femoral artery in my right groin and inserted a catheter that he guided to the area of my heart he wanted to study. He next injected an iodine dye into my artery to highlight the area more clearly on the X-ray pictures he watched in real-time on a screen above my head. I asked him if I could watch. He agreed. It was a strange feeling to see my heart pulsating. It was alarming to see how narrow some of the arteries in it were.

"I'm going to have to open those narrowings for you," he said. "They're very constricted."

Angioplasty is a procedure used to dilate an area of arterial blockage with the help of a catheter that has an inflatable small sausage-shaped balloon at its tip. He found three narrowings he was able to open up. Apart from a slightly sore groin, the most uncomfortable aspect of this procedure was that I had to lie motionless with a pressure pad on my groin until the following morning so the puncture he had made would not pop open.

As successful as his procedure was, the rapid heartbeats continued. I wondered if my hemoglobin had fallen again which might indicate that my leukemia had returned. My next blood test indicated, thankfully, that this had not happened.

My heart suddenly started racing again a few weeks' later. I could hardly breathe. I called Dr Sullivan. He wasted no time and called an ambulance. The paramedic who was with me kept telling me to try and breathe more slowly, but I had no control over what was happening. I was hardly conscious when a doctor in the emergency department of the hospital to which I had been taken gave me an injection. My heartbeat became normal almost as quickly as it had started.

"Verapamil is quite an amazing drug", he said.

Fortune smiled on me again a few months later when I visited Dr Sullivan. Apart from his infectious laughter, ready wit, and eagerness to share stimulating and interesting books he was sure I would love to read, Dr Sullivan was interested in all aspects of medicine. In time, I would learn that his colleagues also regarded him as the compleat doctor. On this occasion, he truly surprised me.

"I've been listening to an amazing audio tape in my car," he said. "Here, listen to it."

He handed me the tape.

"It might be the answer to your SVT problems."

The tape was marked *'Audio Digest Foundation, 1993. Internal Medicine. Atrial Irregularities. Vol. 40. No. 07'*. I still have it.

As I drove home, I listened in fascination to Dr Melvin M. Scheinman, MD, who was the first person to perform radio frequency ablation in humans. He described how, instead of using verapamil or introducing a pacemaker to slow down heart rate, he had used radio frequency energy to ablate, or seal off, one of the electrical pathways in the heart. The technique, called RF ablation, was still so new he had performed it on only seven patients at the time.

I called Dr Sullivan as soon as I had parked my car. He told me he had expected me to call and had already made enquiries to find out if there was anyone in Australia who could perform this procedure.

"His name is Dr Jitu Vohra and I've made an appointment for you to meet him."

I met Dr Vohra a few days later. By now I had learned to ask questions, so I asked him how many procedures he had performed. "I've done a few of these operations – and I worked with Dr Scheinman." Once again, I was on the frontline of medical discovery.

To perform this operation, I was given a light anesthetic. Even though I knew what he was going to do, I watched in fascination and with some degree of alarm as he inserted small catheters into a vein in my left arm and, using live x-ray images, guided them into different areas of my heart These were connected to monitors that allowed him to check which area of my heart had been causing problems. In order to find the exact spot he asked me to stop breathing - and immediately induced an attack of SVT. With my heart now racing at breakneck speed and still holding my breath, I tried to stay calm by telling myself everything was under control. I didn't feel a thing as he located the spot and vaporized the electrical pathway he was looking for. Talk about finding the smoking gun. I took a deep breath. At once, my heart rhythm returned to normal. It has remained so ever since.

Around this time, I found that a number of people I was counseling were facing unusual and rare cancers. As I was a survivor of one of the rarest of leukemias, I came to be regarded as one of them and so they were open to my helping them to explore new ways of coping. It was clear that their doctors were either ignorant of their conditions as they had never had to deal with them before or because they did not know how to talk to them. The Internet was in its infancy and Google as yet unknown, so easy access to relevant information was difficult to find. Against this background, I set up a company called *Medisearch* and over the following couple of years uncovered data that proved invaluable to my patients. For me, it confirmed my view that fear of the unknown is far greater than the fear generated by even the worst news. As I had come to appreciate, knowing the facts gives you choices and with them a sense of control over your destiny. On the other hand, overestimating how much control we have over our lives can present its own set of problems as when I called my cardiologist during a painful attack of angina confident that my action would lead to him performing another successful procedure to clear any blockages.

Angiograms and angioplasty procedures are routinely carried out in a catherization laboratory or cath lab, an examination room containing all the equipment needed to visualize and treat arterial blockages. Confident that I was about to undergo a routine procedure, I settled down as Dr Manolas once again punctured my femoral artery and began inserting a catheter. Suddenly I felt as if the entire hospital had collapsed onto my chest. The weight was overwhelming. The pain was excruciating. Try as I might, I could not breathe. I felt hopelessly trapped.

"Hold tight," he said. "You'll be fine in a moment."

I can relate, with absolute confidence, that if you are going to suffer cardiac arrest the best place for this to occur is in a cath lab with your cardiologist standing beside you so he can shock you back to life. This episode persuaded me that I would never again view any medical procedure with indifference or overconfidence.

I had by now come to the realization that most decisions are based on incomplete information, therefore the only way to tilt the odds in my favor was to learn as much about my leukemia and heart conditions as possible. I had also become aware that luck played an equally important role as when I had discovered interferon and 2-CDA. In the summer of 1996, chance intervened when I underwent further angioplasty.

For a few weeks I had been swimming in an attempt to build up my fitness. No matter how hard I tried, I could not increase the number of laps. I felt as if I was paddling in slow motion through a vat of treacle. I had once been a strong swimmer and had played water polo for many seasons. I knew that only a determined effort could help me break through to the next level. I persevered for a while, but it made no difference. I felt stuck. I contacted my cardiologist who suggested I have an angiogram to check on my heart. A week later, as I lay waiting for this procedure, a nurse came into the room to inform me that that Dr Manolas had injured his back while showering and that I would have to make another appointment for when he had recovered. At this point, Fate intervened. My cardiologist's assistant, Saibal Kar (sounded like Sai Baba), walked into the room. With his slightly chubby face and youthful smiling eyes, he reminded me of a naughty schoolboy. He was a man at ease with himself. He later told me he had earned his medical degree in India and was working in Melbourne as a fellow cardiologist before heading off to the USA. He casually asked me when I had last had a chest x-ray.

"Why?" I asked. I knew that a chest x-ray is not usually part of an angiogram routine.

"We've got the time, so let's check you out."

I later discovered he'd noticed a subtle sign on my hands that alerted this extraordinary insightful doctor to the diagnosis.

A few hours later after the x-ray, Dr Kar came to see me. He was direct but, as always, extremely polite.

"Joel. The x-ray tells me you have a tumor in your lung. I'd like you to have some more tests to find out about it. I hope you don't mind?"

For a moment I was stunned. I had a lost-for-words feeling as a kaleidoscope of jumbled thoughts tumbled around in my brain. I knew enough about lung cancer to know that it was a killer. I knew it was, and still is, the leading cause of death from cancer. After my ordeal with leukemia, I was dumbfounded to think I had another cancer. As soon as Dr Kar left the room, I regained control and telephoned Dr Sullivan, my sage and trusted oncologist who had guided me all along, to tell him the news. I told him they wanted me to have more tests. He was adamant that the cancer should not be 'perturbed' by a biopsy. He wanted it removed whole.

He was clear: "They can make a definitive diagnosis of the type and stage after the tumor is out of your body."

Over the following two days I had a PET scan, a bronchoscopy, a sputum test, a CT scan of my brain, a further x-ray, a bone scan.

"Joel," Saibal Kar said. "You appear to have non-small cell lung cancer. I think we found it early enough, but you will need to have surgery to remove it. Since you're in the hospital and I know there are some really good surgeons here, I am sure I can arrange to have it removed in the next couple of days."

I asked him what had prompted him to suggest I have an x-ray when I had come to the hospital for an angiogram. He said he had an uncle in London who had gone into hospital for an angiogram and, by chance, had been diagnosed with lung cancer. He recognized the same diagnostic signs in me.

I told him what Dr Sullivan had said and that I wanted a few days to research and then interview the best surgeons in town before anyone cut me open. I have no idea whether he found my request unusual, but he agreed to discharge me so I could pursue my plan.

Over the next few days, through family and friends, I compiled a list of surgeons. At the same time, René and I read up everything we could about the various types of lung cancer and found that small-cell lung cancer rarely, if ever, responds to either chemotherapy or radiotherapy, whereas early diagnosis and surgery was the only hope of long-term survival for non-small cell lung cancer. Two days later, I had five lists of surgeon's names. Two names appeared on all of them: John Goldblatt and Laurie Simmons.

I wondered whether I could get both of them to agree to operate on me. It seemed logical. Goldblatt was in his early forties and was generally considered to be the surgeon of choice with steady, golden hands. Simmons, somewhat older, had decades of experience in thoracic surgery. There was only one way to find out. I interviewed them. I found out that Laurie had lectured John who had been one of his top students. I asked them if they would be willing to work together. They readily agreed.

By now, Dr Manolas had recovered from his fall and between them arranged for me to be operated on a week later on the 1st of March 1996. In addition to a general anesthetic, I was given an epidural block to ensure I felt no pain for several days after the operation. This major surgical procedure, called a thoracotomy, involved sawing through my ribs and cracking open my chest (thorax) to gain access to my heart, which they stopped, and a heart-lung machine used to keep the blood flowing and the lungs breathing.

A few days after the operation, Dr Simmons walked into my room to tell me that the tumor he had removed was, indeed, non-small lung cancer. They had removed the middle lobe of my right lung as well as a mediastinal mass they found in the space behind the breastbone. With a huge smile on his face, he added that it was the best result I could have hoped for: T1.N0.M0. What this meant was that the tumor was less than 3cm in size, the lymph nodes had not been affected, and it had not spread to any other organ. I could not have been any luckier.

My jubilation and pain-free period did not last long. During the operation, they had cut the nerves and lining of my lung as well as a rib under my shoulder blade. While retracting my rib cage, another rib had broken. Every time I breathed, I felt as if someone was scraping the inside of my lung with broken glass. The epidural had worn off. Dr Goldblatt said to me later that he had a woman patient who told him her lung operation was more painful than giving birth. I now understood what women go through. I gritted my teeth. I meditated. I tried slow breathing. I prayed for relief from pain. Worse was to come.

They had inserted tubes into the side of my chest to drain my chest of fluid and blood, and to help my lungs refill with air. The tubes were connected to a machine that created a gentle suction to help the fluids drain out into a sealed container beside my bed. The plan was to remove the tubes when the drainage had stopped and no air was leaking from the incision. It was mid-morning a few days into recovery. I was lying in the hospital bed with my wife, René, reading beside me. The male nurse had just checked everything and left the room when I suddenly found it almost impossible to breathe.

"I can't breathe," I struggled to say.

"I'll call a nurse," she said, repeatedly pressing the call button and then dashed out to find help. A nurse soon appeared, looked at me, and in an irritated tone of voice said,

"There's nothing wrong. Everything's been checked."

"But he can't breathe!" my wife insisted, growing more agitated. Normally she is calm in these circumstances, now her instincts were shouting 'this is serious!'

At that moment my eldest son arrived and in a flash realized what had happened.

"I'm turning off the pump," he said.

"You can't," the nurse said. "Only a doctor can."

"I am a doctor," he responded. He leaned down and switched off the machine that was pumping air into me instead of sucking stuff out of me. It took some time before I could breathe fairly normally again. I had survived a tension pneumothorax that could have killed me within a few minutes had Greg not intervened.

There was a humorous sequel to this close call. I still had so much air in me that for days afterwards wherever I pressed the skin on my chest and shoulders I could hear a pop. I had become human bubble-wrap!

This incident had shaken me up. Once more, I was reminded that no matter how much in control I felt, there were some things I was powerless to effect. This was the first of two preventable medical errors that almost killed me. Down the line I would learn that this is not uncommon. Called *iatrogenesis*, adverse effects and complications caused by physicians or hospitals are the 3rd leading cause of death in the USA. I had almost become one of these statistics. It was not comforting to consider just how randomness rules our lives. As René admitted to me much later, my lung cancer diagnosis overturned her view that I was bullet proof and that for the first time she realized I might actually die.

Up to the time of surgery, I had been working on a manuscript for a second book to help people face the challenges of a cancer diagnosis. As soon as I came home from the hospital, I continued writing what was to become an internationally recognized resource: *'What to do when they say 'It's cancer.'* Research for the book took years and occupied much of my time in addition to my counseling practice that was growing rapidly in large part due to the publicity from ongoing sales of the first edition of this book. Writing *What to do when they say 'It's cancer.'* was informed through my own experiences and those of the people I counseled, so part of what I wanted to convey was that while you can't always change the situations in which you find yourself, you can always change your response to them. You can see them as a profound experience of living rather than a nightmare over which you have no control. My cancers forced me to rearrange my priorities, learn new coping skills, re-examine my relationships with people and, for want of a better word, with that something I call God.

It was just as well I had come to this wisdom. Two years later and after experiencing chest pains on and off for several weeks, Dr Manolas suggested it might be time to be admitted to the cath lab again. Once again, he punctured the femoral artery in order to insert a catheter into my heart. No sooner had he injected the dye into me and the picture of my heart appeared on the screen above my head, he stopped and said I had too many narrowings for him to proceed.

"I think it's time for you to have open-heart surgery."

Dr Manolas had talked about by-pass surgery in the past but I had always put him off even though stents had generally replaced angioplasty as a preferred way of opening - and keeping open - blocked arteries.

I reminded him that Dr Goldblatt had operated on my lung cancer and that I would prefer him as my surgeon.

"I was going to suggest him, anyway."

Two weeks later I woke up in intensive care and learned I had undergone 5-way coronary bypass surgery during which the doctor had, most ingeniously and in the most innovative way, detoured all five of the major vessels to the heart by joining a mammary artery with a single artery taken from my left arm. I was now a member of the 'zipper club', admission to which is open to anyone who has had an incision down the breastbone for coronary bypass surgery. Within a day, I was walking up and down stairs to regain my fitness. Ten days after surgery I went home to recuperate. To this day, Dr Manolas marvels at the way Dr Goldblatt had performed the procedure because the bypass he created continues to remain as unblocked as it was the day after surgery. Much later, I would also read that one of the long-term side effects of interferon was a second cancer, invariably in the lungs.

My counseling practice continued to grow as my second book progressed from manuscript to publication in three other languages and in six countries. It was reviewed and highly commended by Professor Paul Bunn in the USA, by Professor Richard Fox and Professor Michael Quinn in Australia and by the sage and brilliant Dr John Sullivan who wrote the foreword to this book. The book's publicity through rounds of national and international radio, television and press interviews brought me an appointment as a counselor on staff at the School of Public Health, LaTrobe University. I was busy with life. I visited Dr Sullivan every month. In between I had my regulation blood tests until one day, as I sat across the desk from Dr Sullivan, he picked up the pathology report his assistant, Rhonda, had slid under the door. His usual smile faded. Something had upset him.

"It looks as if you may need more jungle juice."

My leukemia had surfaced again. It seemed incredible. Seven years earlier, I had been successfully treated with 2-CDA now known under its trade name, *Cladribine*. The question I now faced was would the drug would be as effective as before.

"At least you won't have to go into hospital again," said Dr Sullivan. "They've changed the protocol. You can inject yourself under the skin just as you did with interferon."

And so I injected myself once a day every day for a week. If I failed to comprehend I had suffered another recurrence, it was because by now I had become steeled to reality. In much the same way as I easily handled my by-pass surgery, I carried on working even though I knew the outcome was unpredictable. I took the view 'Oh well, here we go again!' With each successive injection, I was reminded, very emphatically, that my life depended on the point of a needle. As optimistic as I was and no matter how much I felt in control of the events in my life, there was no doubt my survival intersected with the cutting edge of medicine. Two blood tests and several weeks later, the smile reappeared on Dr Sullivan's face as he told me that my counts were improving rapidly. My hemoglobin was 10.8, my platelets 149,000, and my white cell count 6.0. Every day, he wore a fresh rose from his garden on his lapel. With the scent of new promise in the air, that day I would swear I could smell it from three feet away.

Five months later everything turned upside down again when, without apparent reason, my hemoglobin level plummeted suddenly and dramatically. Hairy cell leukemia generally affects all blood counts, so only one of them falling was highly puzzling. Dr Sullivan was upset by this turn of events and suggested an urgent 4-unit blood transfusion

One of the most boring yet essential requirements prior to a blood transfusion was cross matching to ensure the blood I was getting was compatible with mine. There are eight different common blood types, which are determined by the presence or absence of certain antigens. These are substances that can trigger an immune response if they are foreign to the body. As some antigens can trigger the immune system to attack the transfused blood, safe blood transfusions depend on careful blood typing and cross matching.

I was unaware I had experienced a second medical misadventure until a day later when René and I went to visit friends who have a beach house down the Great Ocean Road. Although mid-summer, it was one of those warm overcast days when the sea was grey-green and the waves hardly more than knee high. As we sat looking at the sea at Urquart Bluff Beach, I suddenly felt utterly exhausted, out of breath, dizzy, chilly, nauseous and, worst of all, feeling as if I was falling over a cliff. I forced myself to remain conscious. It was the most wretched feeling. René saw how pale I had become, immediately took the wheel and drove us back to Melbourne.

I have little recollection of the trip other than thinking I was dying. I had never felt like this through any of my previous crises. René called Dr Sullivan to tell him what had happened. He told her to take me directly to the hospital and arranged for me to have a blood test. She was, as ever, cool under fire.

It may have been that because it was over the New Year holiday period staff was less than alert, but they had mismatched my blood, in particular the antigens. This became clear when, after Dr Sullivan had contacted the blood bank and ordered them to check the results of the previous cross match with the new one, they found several discrepancies. With a grim look, Dr Sullivan then told me I now had autoimmune hemolytic anemia, AIHA. The reason I felt so dreadful was because my body's immune system was fighting itself. In the process, it was destroying my red blood cells. In an attempt to counter this, he immediately started me on a course of prednisolone eventually increasing the dosage from 25mg to 40mg a day. One blood transfusion followed another. Between January and March I had five blood transfusions. No matter how many I had, my body was destroying my red blood cells faster than it could replace them. In an attempt to arrest the progress of the AIHA, and because the cortisone seemed to have no effect, Dr Sullivan put me on a course of high-dose intravenous gamma-globulin, itself an antibody he hoped would neutralize my body's attack on itself. I received five of these infusions over the following nine weeks as well as a further two blood transfusions. It was all to no avail. The ultimate irony was to follow.

Sixteen years earlier Dr Gloom had recommended a splenectomy in order to alleviate the progressive symptoms of my hairy cell leukemia. Sixteen years earlier I had refused, knowing it was not a cure. Interferon and 2-CDA had cured me – and I still had my spleen.

As Dr Sullivan explained, the spleen - together with bone marrow, the thymus and lymph nodes - is one of our body's organs that form part of our immune system.

"Removing it is your last resort."

I was stunned. I had survived leukemia, lung cancer, atrial fibrillation, five-way coronary bypass surgery, and a near fatal tension pneumothorax. On June 11, 1999 I underwent laparoscopic surgery to remove my spleen in an attempt to stop the breakdown of red blood cells. Within a day, my blood counts improved. Once again, I thanked my lucky stars that I had a guardian angel in the shape of Dr Sullivan with his seemingly inexhaustible medical knowledge, ability to think outside the square, courage to challenge the system, and passion to care for each patient as if they were his only patient. He never timed appointments so always ran over time, a fact no one ever complained about. I was going to need him more than ever over the following months.

The splenectomy was intended to arrest the progression of the autoimmune hemolytic anemia, but my continuing fatigue, despite a further 2-unit blood transfusion, puzzled Dr Sullivan. To determine what else might be wrong, he ordered up a review of all my blood tests over the past few years. He also asked me to have another blood test and a urine test. We knew my creatinine levels were high but more recently had become even more elevated. Creatinine is a by-product of the energy used by muscles that passes through the kidneys to be filtered and eliminated in urine. The range for normal creatinine levels is between 64-104. Mine had crept up to 203. Three months later it had reached 256. Dr Sullivan had requested the blood test to further check the glomerular filtration rate (GFR), which tells how well the kidneys are filtering the blood. The urine test was to check how well my kidneys were working and whether there were any elements in it that would confirm what my kidneys had failed to filter. It was time to have a kidney biopsy to find out what was wrong. It was also time again to find and interview the best kidney specialists.

As I had done when looking for the best surgeon to operate on my lung, I turned to my family and friends over the following days and compiled a list of nephrologists. At the same time, I read up everything I could about kidney diseases. I soon learned that the biopsy procedure was precise but that complications could arise. I soon had five lists again. I was spoiled for choices, as so many names were in common. By chance, one of my cousins and an internationally known nephrologist, Professor Geoff Boner, was visiting us from overseas. He cast his eyes down the list and said, "Gavin Becker is your man. I know him well." I phoned Dr Sullivan and asked him to refer me to Professor Gavin Becker, head of the Nephrology Unit at the Royal Melbourne Hospital.

With his sandy complexion, slightly chubby face and relaxed manner, Professor Becker immediately put me at ease. An avuncular man with a rather dry and keen sense of humor, his razor-sharp eyes reflected his encyclopedic knowledge of his subject. His explanation helped me better understand what was at stake and I appreciated his direct and disarming honesty. He told me he did not personally perform biopsies but one of his doctors did. He assured me he would monitor my progress and talk to me after the results came through.

Every one of the innumerable bone marrow biopsies I had undergone had left a harrowing memory; all of them flooded my brain as I lay face down and felt a sharp sting as the doctor injected a local anesthetic to minimize the pain of the biopsy to follow. I felt the pressure of his hands as he made a small incision in my back to insert the needle. I heard the loud click of the spring-loaded biopsy needle as he fired it into my kidney. He repeated this several times using real time imaging to ensure his penetrations were accurate. It took him about an hour to complete the procedure by which time I was bathed in perspiration. I was also extremely pleased it was all over. On my way home the following day, feeling a little sore, I wondered what the test would show. The results did not take long in coming. Professor Becker was meticulous in his explanation.

When the blood bank mismatched my blood causing the autoimmune hemolytic anemia that had almost killed me it had damaged my kidneys' ability to filter my blood. This had led to diabetic nephropathy, more as a result of deterioration of kidney function than of diabetes. It also destroyed the hormone in the kidney that stimulates the growth of red blood cells in bone marrow. He told me I now had less than 40% function in each kidney. The damaged nerve cells in my kidneys had also caused peripheral neuropathy that would, over time, lead to increasing lack of feeling in my legs, numbness in my feet, and pain. But there was good news.

To keep my blood pressure down and so reduce the burden on my kidneys, he prescribed a trial drug, *irbesartin* that also acted to delay progression of the diabetic nephropathy. To control the neuropathic pain he prescribed a recently discovered drug, *gabapentin*. He also prescribed a newly synthesized drug called *erythropoietin* to replace the hormone, hemopoietin, my kidneys no longer produced. Erythropoietin, commonly known as *EPO*, was to become increasingly infamous in the hands of athletes, particularly elite cyclists, to improve their performance by boosting their hemoglobin count. Over the following eleven years, I injected myself once a week with it. My wife wryly commented that the supply of EPO in our refrigerator had the black market value equivalent of several weekends away in luxury. I am glad to say, I no longer need it. My kidneys appear to have stabilized.

CHAPTER THIRTY FOUR

In 1971 President Nixon of the USA had signed the National Cancer Act in an attempt to find a cure for cancer. Incredible successes had been achieved – interferon for example - yet the change to overall mortality had not been great and the death rate for cancer in the U.S.A., for example, adjusted for population size and age, had dropped by only 5% from 1950 to 2005. Against this background, in February 2000, the Cancer Council of Victoria offered me an invitation to go to Paris to attend The World Summit against Cancer - a new initiative intended to re-invigorate the Nixon plan.

From the start, it was an auspicious event. No expense seemed to have been spared as we sat down to a sumptuous dinner with Louis XIV cutlery and glassware at the Hotel de Ville hosted by the mayor of Paris. The meetings and seminars were held in the grand and opulent Élysée Palace where I was one of a select group to sign the Charter of Paris. I also met with the conference host, President Jacque Chirac, and presented him with a copy of my second book, *'What to do when they say 'It's cancer'- A Survivor's Guide.'*

My awakening came at one of the meetings where I met some of the world's leading cancer experts and a Nobel prizewinner. The debate was between those who advocated prevention and those who favored cure. As I listened, I was struck by the fact that no one mentioned what people were supposed to do while they waited for a cure - and no one spoke about the effect of a cancer diagnosis and treatment on the family as a whole. No one used the world 'patient'. To me, there was an air of unreality in the room. Over the following few days, the impact of what I had witnessed convinced me I had to do something to redress this issue. By the time my plane landed back in Melbourne I had drafted an outline for an organization dedicated solely to meeting the spiritual and emotional needs of patients and families facing cancer.

For the next few months, my plan became clearer as I discussed my ideas with René, my family, friends and colleagues. I realized I would need to establish a not-for-profit organization so that no one would be excluded or economically disadvantaged from seeking help. I decided to model the organization around a telephone counseling service as this had the widest geographical reach, was easily accessible and also provided a low cost but effective model. I decided that the service had to be staffed by telephone counselors who would have to either survived cancer or some other life-threatening illness or cared for someone with a terminal illness in order to be admitted to the training program. By November, I had recruited six people. I searched the world but found there was no suitably adequate or robust training program to adapt or emulate, so I used my own highly researched book *'What to do when they say 'It's cancer'* as my guide. The model was and remains unique. The training program would eventually expand from thirty-eight to ninety hours. In December, our pro bono lawyer who had prepared our Constitution and applied to the Taxation Office for tax-free status called excitedly to say that our credentials had been approved. On January 11, 2001, *Can-Survive* with its *Hopeline* telephone counseling service was born. I put my counseling practice on hold and spent the following ten years as chief executive officer of the organization that helped many thousands of people around the country seeking comfort and guidance as they faced the challenges of a life threatening illness.

Nine years later I turned 71. My three sons had all married and had children of their own. Two of my stepsons had done likewise. My third stepson was in a settled relationship. René and I now had 9 grandchildren. Our life was full, and we had many other rewarding plans and projects to complete together. Two more grandchildren would later come along to form, what we call, "the United Nathans."

Everything has a season under the sun, as did I. Exhausted by the endless search for funding, I merged the organization with a home hospice service and stepped down from my role as founder, chairman and CEO in order to restart my counseling practice, to update my previously published books, and to keep writing.

Across time, I came to expect the unexpected. Ahead of our overseas holiday in October 2010, René accompanied me to see Dr Sullivan to get a letter detailing all my medications. He did not seem his usual self and on leaving his rooms, we shared our concern for his apparent vagueness. A few weeks after our return, I was helping René make the bed when, without warning, I lost all feeling down the left side of my body. I sat down and told René I could not move my arm or leg. She was about to call an ambulance when I asked her to wait a few minutes. Although she had coped well with all my crises and never told me what to do, I saw alarm in her eyes. We realized I had suffered a stroke but I was not convinced it was serious. I also did not want to miss an appointment I was scheduled to attend downtown. Mindful of that fact we would have to call an ambulance if the dead feeling continued, we kept talking. A few minutes later I could feel sensation returning to my arm and leg. Promising her I would call the doctor, I left the house and drove to the meeting. About two hours' later and after the meeting, I was about to head home when I called René. She was insistent I call my cardiologist on my cell phone to tell him what had happened.

"I'll send an ambulance to your house right away," he said.

"I'm not at home," I replied. "I'm downtown in my car."

"Drive straight to the hospital and park in the ambulance bay. I'll tell them to expect you."

Within minutes of my arrival I was wheeled into the emergency department where a doctor administered oxygen, inserted an intravenous drip into my arm, and popped an aspirin into my mouth. Shortly afterwards, I had a CT scan and MRI. By this time, René had joined me as we waited for Dr Manolas to arrive soon afterwards. He was astonished that I had ignored the gravity of the situation, had not called an ambulance or him, and had driven my car downtown to a meeting. He said he wanted me to stay under observation and that he had asked a neurologist to conduct tests to assess what, if any, brain damage I had suffered and what had caused the stroke. Over the following few days I had an array of tests all of which eventually confirmed I had a 'shower' of spots on the right side of my brain and that the mini stroke had been caused by blockages in my carotid arteries, the right one of which was ninety percent blocked. In order to clear it I would have to have an operation called a carotid endarterectomy. This involves making an incision along the side of my neck, opening the carotid artery, and removing the fatty deposits blocking it. I tried to call Dr Sullivan to tell him what had happened but could not get through.

Two days' later, following my meeting with the vascular

surgeon to discuss the operation, my cell phone rang. It was an oncologist I recalled had worked at the hospital where I was first treated with interferon. He asked me if I knew the names of any of Dr Sullivan's wife's friends, as he needed to call them.

I asked him why. He realized he had caught me unawares.

"He's in the Epworth hospital on the Neurology ward."

"What's he doing there?"

"It seems he may have breathed in a spore that attacked his brain."

I didn't know what to say. I felt choked. He guessed my reaction and said he'd call me back. I phoned the neurology ward, one floor below mine, and asked to speak to Dr Sullivan. I was told he wasn't taking any calls, so I called his personal assistant, Rhonda.

Between tears, she told me he had been aware something was wrong around the time I had last seen him and had tried to treat himself. She said he was now sliding in and out of a coma so it was futile for me to try and contact him. She promised to let me know his progress. The following day I had surgery to clear the blocked carotid artery. When the surgeon showed me the photograph he had taken, I was amazed that such an ugly, large, cigar-shaped chunk of fat had been growing in my neck.

Rhonda phoned a few days later to tell me Dr Sullivan had not come out of coma. It was the 28th November 2010. He died the day he turned 65. I cried. I still cry.

Dr Sullivan had been my guide, rescuer and friend for twenty-seven years. My own experience of him - as well as what many other patients and doctors told me - was that he was a man who was alive to the present and passionate about everything medical and otherwise. He was the **compleat** doctor. A sage. A man who demanded his allied health professionals lived up to the same high standard of caring he did. He embodied for me 'the good doctor' who cares more about the needs of his patients than following protocols or being politically correct. His thinking process was often astoundingly counter-intuitive. I have never missed his advice, his explosive laughter, his villainous chuckle and the fresh rose in his lapel so much as I have in the three and a half years since his death. In regard to every medical encounter since then, and I have had a few, I invariably ask myself 'What would Dr Sullivan do?'

Even if he were alive right now, there is nothing he could do to help me overcome the life-threatening condition I now face: age.

To recap: none of the alternative non-medical treatments I tried so desperately saved me. I also don't know anyone who has been cured by any of them, although countless books have been written by people who claim they have. I understand only too well just how desperation can compel you to ignore common sense and pay good money for false hope. We live or die by the choices we make.

Through all the challenges I have faced, the spirit of my Zulu mentor, John Ndmande, still hovers around me and whispers 'to be clever is to be still.' Through his wisdom, I have come to acknowledge that I may be the captain of my ship but not the sea upon which it sails; I can trim my sail but I cannot change the direction of the wind or the movement of the tides.

ABOUT THE AUTHOR

Joel Nathan was born and educated in South Africa where he became a successful creative director in advertising. Disgusted by the Apartheid system, he emigrated with his family to the UK where he continued his career. Seeking more sunshine, he moved his family to Australia where, after two years and at age 43, he was diagnosed with a rare and incurable type of leukemia.

Through and after his eventual recovery, he was, for several years, a Patient Advisor to the Cancer Council of Victoria and a facilitator in the Palliative Care Unit at La Trobe University. He was a member of the National Institute of Clinical Studies' Program into Pain Management.

In 2000 he was a signatory to the Charter of Paris at the World Summit Against Cancer where he realized that while medicine was focused on prevention and cure, no one discussed how patients and their families were supposed to cope in the meantime. Upon his return, Joel founded Can-Survive, the first volunteer suvivors-based telephone counseling service in the world dedicated to patients and families facing cancer or other life-threatening illness. In recognition for establishing the service and for his groundbreaking program in training and educating doctors and palliative care specialists, nurses, and allied health professionals to be more effective in dealing with their patients while attending to their own, emotional and spiritual needs, in 2008 Joel was honored with an Order of Australia Medal.

He has been guest speaker at a number of events such as the International Psycho-oncology Conferences in Australia and Canada, and at nursing conferences in Australia and New Zealand. He has presented papers on survival, carer burnout, grief and loss, and held inspirational workshops on how to make the most out of life.

Joel is the author of *Time of My Life* (Penguin Books, 1992), and *What to do when they say, "It's Cancer" – A Survivor's Guide* (Allen & Unwin, 1998) published in nine countries and four languages, and endorsed by leading medical specialists in Australia and the USA.

Joel is married to his second wife, René, and between them have 6 sons and 11 grandchildren (to date).

Joel holds degrees in Psychology and Philosophy and works as a specialist counselor with individuals and families living with cancer or other life-threatening illness.

For more information, go to www.joelnathan.com.au

www.ingramcontent.com/pod-product-compliance
Lightning Source LLC
Chambersburg PA
CBHW061630040426
42446CB00010B/1341